THE MAN OF
ALL TALENTS

THE MAN OF
ALL TALENTS

The Extraordinary Life
of Douglas Clark

Including contributions from 'Duggy' himself

STEVEN BELL

First published by Pitch Publishing, 2020

Pitch Publishing
A2 Yeoman Gate
Yeoman Way
Worthing
Sussex
BN13 3QZ
www.pitchpublishing.co.uk
info@pitchpublishing.co.uk

A CIP catalogue record is available for this book
from the British Library.

ISBN 978 1 78531 682 1

Typesetting and origination by Pitch Publishing
Printed and bound in India by Replika Press Pvt. Ltd.

CONTENTS

Dedicated to a whole, great generation. And to my baby son Bruno, who was born during the writing of this book.

With special thanks to:

Martin Bell
Nicola Bell
Matthew Isherwood
Elizabeth James
David Gronow
Chris Roberts
David Thorpe

INTRODUCTION

'As legends go, he was the genuine article.'

NOTHING MUCH happens in the sleepy towns of northern England. Sure, Leeds and Manchester are now wonderfully modern and cosmopolitan, but just a ten-minute car journey in the right (or wrong, as the case may be) direction from those big-city lights will take you to towns and villages set in the rolling countryside that time appears to have long forgotten.

The local farm shops are widely regarded as the beacon of hope for jobs and investment in the area, as well as the lucrative weekly treat of a bag of expensive shopping and a 'froffy coffee'.

The pubs and working men's clubs are dilapidated and the regulars like it that way, as modernisation would only hike the price of a John Smith's Extra Smooth further up towards the dreaded £3 mark.

I, the author, am from the small mining town of Featherstone, West Yorkshire, and a more tightly knit community you could never envisage. 'He's a character,' we tend to say of one another when names come up in conversation. It gets said a lot – they're all characters. It's a rugby league town where the local part-time club, Featherstone Rovers, sits at the epicentre – at least since Margaret Thatcher closed the local coal mines that supported the area and its families.

After my first book was set in Brazil, I wanted to bring a local and forgotten sporting story into literature

– something historic, from these lands that Father Time has left behind.

I discovered the story of Malcolm Kirk, a man from my very own Featherstone, who followed the stereotypical route of a local lad who was fit and strong. He got a job 'darn t'pit', and he was good and lucky enough to play 'for t'Rovers' as a young man in the 1950s. His rugby career also saw him play for Wakefield and Doncaster. A giant man with a big heart and strong as an ox, he realised that second-tier rugby league wasn't a sustainable long-term career. Conveniently, some of his team-mates at Doncaster had contacts in the relatively new and upcoming world of professional wrestling, and saw him and his mammoth physique as perfect for the sport.

By the time the flared trousers and the 1970s came around, Mal found himself on national TV on a weekly basis as ITV's *World of Sport* displayed him and his fellow behemoths sweatily grappling with one another every week to a transfixed audience of millions. His natural talent, huge physique and intimidating aura saw him become a hit not just in Britain but around the world under the guise of a bad-guy persona in 'King Kong' Kirk.

'Bye-eck, now he was a character,' is the sure-fire response you'll get when bringing up Kirk's name around Featherstone. It is said past tense due to the fact he tragically died prematurely in an accident that made national headlines. Everyone, it seems, has a Mal Kirk story; usually a hilarious one they tell with a beaming smile on their faces and a glint in their eye.

He wrestled the top stars from around the globe. He even appeared in a major motion movie – a comedy, of course.

There have been a couple of good and interesting long-read articles written about his life and untimely death, but, unfortunately, even with the help of his daughter Natasha, we weren't able to unearth enough information about his sporting or personal life to be confident enough to begin the ample task of writing his biography.

Travel 25 miles west on the M62 and south just below the town of Huddersfield, and you find yourself at an even more sleepy backwater than Featherstone, in the village of Netherton, where I now live with my wife and baby son. The closed-down mining industry of Featherstone is replaced here by the closed-down textile mill industry – but at least we still have a great farm shop.

Whilst researching Mal, I had begun to follow various rugby league and wrestling history social media pages, and continued to follow them even though I had pretty much given up on the project.

I was waiting for the kettle to boil one summer afternoon and scrolled through my Twitter feed. I saw a shared picture that caught my attention. It was of an exhibit from the Imperial War Museum that displayed the image of a large man in a black-and-white photograph; he was wearing rather odd attire – white vest and leggings, with velvety-looking black pants over the top and knee-high boots, all of which was delicately embroidered with flowery patterns. His image was surrounded by dozens of trophies, championship belts, sports apparel and medals from both the spheres of sport and war. The display was beneath the text: 'As legends go, he was the genuine article'. His name was Douglas Clark.

I never made that cup of tea as I spent the 30 minutes I had to kill in an internet wormhole, reading information on this man. During most of that time, I was attempting to work out if the man I was reading about on the plethora of different web pages could possibly be the same one – questioning how one individual could have achieved and done so much across so many differing fields in one lifetime.

I was left further astounded when I read that he had lived most of his life, and died, in a borough of Huddersfield just four miles away from the kitchen in which I stood. Eerily similar to Mal, 'Duggy' was a coal miner, a rugby league player and a professional wrestler.

Completely by accident, I had found my story. I had found Duggy's story.

More than an amazing and unique sporting story, my research quickly began to teach me more about the man behind the legend, too. A man who, despite leaving school at just 14 to embark on a lifetime of physicality, was a deep-thinking wordsmith; a teetotaller who would do anything for his community and his family; a gentleman who could – and would – quote Shakespeare both verbally and in his writing; an anti-alpha male who would take the young or shy under his ample wings; a skilled chess player; a devout Christian; a man of poetry; a leader of men; a *Man of All Talents*.

Douglas Clark kept diaries, journals and also handwrote some memoirs in later life. I am pleased to say that, for the very first time (with the exception of some of his war diaries), selected excerpts from all of these carefully preserved papers are published in this story of his *Extraordinary Life*.

PROLOGUE

By Douglas Clark
Extract from his memoirs

In the year 1891, second day of May, Douglas Clark was born in the village of Ellenborough, Cumberland. His father, John Clark, was in business as a coal merchant and carrier; a man about five foot eight and a half inches and weighing around 15-stones. He was first a man of muscle; no doubt developed by the hard occupation he followed lifting and carrying those one hundredweight (cwt) sacks of coal from house to house and filling the same with a tremendous shovel lifting one quarter cwt at a scoop.

Douglas' mother was Elizabeth Clark. Although only about five foot three inches she weighed close on 14-stones and came from a hard working family. She possessed great strength and endurance after bringing up a family of nine. She used to rise at 5am and never retire until 11.30pm.

Such were the stock that Douglas sprang from, it was rather surprising that when Douglas was born he was the least of the family and a poorly child suffering from a bowel complaint. It was lucky for him that his mother was one of the best nurses, although unqualified, in the district. After Douglas had been taught to walk – twice – his mother brought him up on sherry and white of eggs, this being the only food that would stay on his stomach.

At the age of six he was quite a normal-sized boy and was on the ordinary family menu – plenty of good, plain food.

It was soon evident that Douglas had no great liking for school but preferred the woods and fields in which Ellenborough abounded. He was never happier than with his school pals Joss Jackson, Palmer, Dan and Ted. They would roam the wood together bird-nesting or wasp-nesting; just as long as they were in the sun or climbing their favourite trees together they were as happy as sun-boys. This love of the open-air life got them many a good hiding for playing in the woods instead of going to school. But there is no doubt climbing the trees, at which they were all expert, developed muscle and broadened the shoulders and lungs and fitted Douglas for the strenuous life that was to follow.

At the age of 12 he used to help his dad at the coal yard on his free day, Saturday. When dinner time arrived he would deliver coal in half cwt bags to the customers that were without coal while his dad was on the collecting. But half hundredweights were not enough for Doug and we soon find him carrying the full one cwt – though unknown to his dad!

One day, Douglas was carrying a bag with so much ease that a well-known villager questioned the weight of the coal. Thereupon Douglas dropped the sack, took down the scales weighing two cwt, and proceeded to weigh the sack. But the gentleman in question said that he 'didn't mean anything by it', but Doug would not allow him to proceed until he had satisfied him that good weight was in the sack. He then lifted the sack of coal on to the wagon, then walked off with it as though it were a bag of 'chaff' – and that at 12 years old.

We now find Douglas in the local Northern Union Rugby Football team, playing in the forwards, and a very promising boy at so early an age. He was soon recognised as the best forward in school football and soon earned himself the nickname of 'Baby Elephant' because when he got hold of the ball you could see the track he left behind him in the rush towards the line.

Ellenborough was in those days proud of its local nine-and-a-half stones world champion Cumberland & Westmorland wrestler John Cunningham, one of the best and smartest 'buttockers' that ever stepped into the ring.

Douglas wanted to 'have a hold' and Cunningham, who was two and a half stone less, had great difficulty in felling the school boy and after a few nights practice Douglas so improved that Jack could not throw Doug however hard he tried. Douglas had been taught by his dad to pick up a 'buttocker' off his feet, but never to set him down unless you had clean thrown him.

Well, between the pair they had given Doug the right start in wrestling which was to land him in such good stead.

At the age of 14 he was in the coal mines as a pit pony driver taking empty wagons to the coal face and bringing away the full ones and it was while he was thus employed at the Robin Hood colliery that the roads in the pit had become so low that it was decided to withdraw the horses and that part of the pit would have been closed down but for someone suggesting that William Corrie of Broughton Moor, a tremendous big strong miner, might be able to carry to the top of the brow. Thompson and the boy Clark to do the lower places. Corrie was induced to come from the Bertha Colliery at ten shillings and sixpence per day, two shillings and sixpence above the average pay, while the boy received two shillings and ninepence. It was a successful undertaking. Clark grew leaps and bounds. His legs began to broaden out and he boasted a calf as big as any miner in the pit, nearing seventeen inches, and possessed tremendous strength. Several times he requested the manager Mr.

Fawcett to allow him to crack the top places and so earn a rise. The manager remarked, 'Tut-tut my lad, you are only a boy yet, you must never attempt to push an empty tub up that steep place of Canneson Brow.'

A little time after this, one day Corrie was at lunch and Tom Cameron was shouting for a tub when Corrie told Clark to go and bring the full tub weighing 12 cwt of coal away and he, Corrie, would take the empty tub after his snack. Clark saw his chance had come. He brought the full tub away as far as the low places, then proceeded to push the full tub back to the top of the brow, which he accomplished without one stop.

Cameron noticed the tub replaced and called out 'Thank you lad,' but when he saw the full tub had been returned he asked what the game was. Clark said, 'I wish you would tell Mr. Fawcett what I've done, he would allow me to track tub for tub with Corrie and I'd get a rise.'

Well, Clark got his rise, as did Thompson.

PART 1

*'It is excellent
To have a giant's strength;
But it is tyrannous
To use it like a giant.'*

— William Shakespeare

1

A COAL BOY, A LAKER, A CANDLESTICK MAKER

October 1906
Ellenborough, Maryport
Cumberland

IT WAS 5am and the first true cold snap of the impending winter had hit the Lake District. It was still the black of night and a low mist hung over the Irish Sea. A strong breeze blew easterly into the shore, causing waves to crash into Maryport Lighthouse as a light coastal drizzle blanketed the town and its tiny suburb of Ellenborough. Black smoke began to bellow from the chimneys of the small townhouses as the first adults to rise stoked the kitchen fires with coal to heat their homes before the rest of the family woke. No smoke, however, came from one chimney.

'Sorry mam. I completely forgot coal cellar was empty. Mr Clark will be 'ere on his rounds soon. We're getting a delivery this morning, I promise,' a middle-aged man said to his elderly mother in the tiny but freezing end terrace house just the two of them shared. As he talked, his breath was visible in the air. Only two lit candles cast any light into their kitchen: one on the mantlepiece, the other in the window. The old lady gripped the collar of her dressing gown tight up to her chin as the few teeth she had remaining chattered together.

A quiet and distant clip-clop of a horse's hooves on the cobbled road filled the moustachioed man with relief. John Clark had turned his stallion on to their street.

'That's him now!' said Mr Robson to his mother, frantically making his way to the back door in his slippers. He went down to the coal cellar entrance, which sat beneath the kitchen window – the candlelight from inside just making it visible enough for him to see what he was doing as he opened the heavy wooden doors, the glorious sound of the horse and cart getting louder all the while. The noise was soon joined by whistling and footsteps coming down the path the house shared with its neighbour.

'Morning Mr Robson!' a large set young man cheerily boomed as he appeared around the corner of the house carrying two hundredweight sacks of coal, one over each shoulder. It was 15-year-old Douglas Clark.

'Morning, young Doug. Thank God you're 'ere. We're empty. Mam's freezing in there. Thought it could have been death of 'er.'

'OK Mr Robson, I'll leave these here for you,' Duggy replied as he lowered both sacks down to the floor near the open cellar. 'I'll take some straight in and we'll get you lit.' He delved into one of the sacks, his giant, blackened hands reappearing with at least six large lumps of coal in each. He turned and casually walked through the back door, wearing a long fleece coat and a flat cap, his charcoal-covered face barely visible in the darkness. Mr Robson attempted to drag just one of the floored sacks closer to the cellar, but he could barely budge it, such was its weight.

'Morning Mrs Robson!' said Duggy as he knelt down in front of the fireplace and began to place the invaluable chunks of fuel into the fire bed. Mrs Robson began to smile.

'Thank you, Douglas. I saw your mam last week. She's so proud of you, she was all, "Our Duggy this, our Duggy that." How is she?'

'Oh, she's fine. I try not to get under her feet too much now I've left school. But between working with dad down pit and doing my rugby and wrestling training, I barely see her.'

'I heard you were doing well, Doug,' Mr Robson said quietly as he attempted to strike a matchstick.

'I'm playing with the older age groups now, sir. I can't wait until I can wrestle with the older lads too. I don't want to sound arrogant, but ...'

'You can throw them poor young boys like confetti?'

'I could. But I don't. Don't seem fair. But I've got the junior county championships tomorrow at Braithwaite, so that should be much more of a challenge.'

Mr Robson placed a flaming, rolled-up newspaper on to the perfect coal pyramid Duggy had built. Within seconds, the edges of each rock turned a violent, glowing red and began casting heat into the freezing temperature, so much so the air around the fireplace visibly shimmered. Mrs Robson allowed the tight grip she had on her dressing gown under her chin to loosen.

Three loud claps echoed from outside. They were the sound of a horse's shoe hitting the cobbles. It was Duggy's father, John, sending the signal through the stallion that he was waiting.

Mrs Robson and her son spoke over each other, both expressing their gratitude to the young man.

'My pleasure. Take care now.'

'Good luck tomorrow, son. And give your mam my love!' Mrs Robson yelled as Duggy closed their back door behind him and jogged back up the narrow path. As he effortlessly leapt on to the back of the wagon, the horse snorted as his dad cheerily sang an unidentifiable song under his breath. The cart began to move up the street as smoke finally began to rise out of Mr and Mrs Robson's chimney.

The following morning, Duggy slept in later than he had planned, after a week of hard graft. He was desperate to make it to the wrestling competition, so he jumped out of bed and got ready as quickly as possible. He packed his kit and ran downstairs, where his tiny mother, Elizabeth, was laying out breakfast for all of the family. Duggy gulped down a glass of orange juice and then grabbed a slice of toast. He bent down low, kissed his puzzled mother on the cheek and said, 'Wrestling. I'll be home for tea.' He shouted goodbye to the rest of the house and with that shut the door behind him.

His siblings began to appear from their various bedrooms and hiding places. Duggy was the middle one of the nine children John and Elizabeth had been blessed with. Sarah was the eldest, already 24, Lizzie was the youngest, still just a baby.

Duggy picked up his bike, which had fallen down on its side in the small front garden. Away he went, leaping aboard the bike as he ran with it, already building momentum to take on the 18-mile journey to Braithwaite as swiftly as his legs could pedal.

He knew the local land instinctively; he rode out of the village, up on to the hills and through the fields. Within 30 minutes, he was at the village of Cockermouth. He quickly passed through and was soon back on to rural terrain. He pedalled east, across to the northern tip of Bassenthwaite Lake, where he turned south. The mist hung heavy over the lake as Duggy rode the potentially treacherous journey down and across the hillside.

In little over one hour, he had made it to his destination. Just in the nick of time, he registered for his age group competition. The local style of wrestling, a hugely popular sport in the north of England, was known as 'Cumberland & Westmorland'. In this type of grappling – just one of countless regional wrestling styles worldwide that go back almost to the beginning of mankind – the two competitors would stand chest to chest, grasping one another around the upper body. The right arm of each would be under his or her opponent's left armpit, with a tight interlocking grip taken between the shoulder blades. Once the umpire is satisfied with the tie-up, he calls *'En Guard'*, followed by *'Wrestle'*. Using strength, technique and 'chips' or 'throws', they attempt to unbalance one another. The one who clearly hits the floor first loses, and a 'fall' is awarded to his opponent. If the umpire cannot decide who has crashed to the ground first, he will award a 'dog-fall', and both wrestlers will score a point. The first competitor to secure two falls is declared the winner, although some matches and tournaments are sudden-death, one-fall-to-a-finish contests. The matches take place in open fields, with spectators close by the perimeter of the circular ring, and the wrestlers wear traditional attire consisting of white vest and leggings with black, embroidered velvet pants over the top.

Of the many sports and pastimes the folk of England's northernmost counties took part in, wrestling held pride of place. Almost every village, town and county would have a local champion. But culminating the wrestling season every year (still to this day) is the world-famous Grasmere Festival – a full weekend each August Bank Holiday during which all the champions of each age group and weight division from across the counties and beyond battle for the ultimate champion to be crowned.

Below, in the words of Douglas Clark himself, is a summary of some of the terminologies used in the sport, the origins of which go so far back. Many believe it was introduced to these shores by the Vikings.

- *'HOD' – A hold. Placing right arm under opponent's left, and left arm over opponent's right. Each then gripping own hands. This is preparatory to the commencement of actual wrestling and before any of actual wrestling and before any of the various 'chips' are employed. The moment the holds are taken, wrestling commences.*

- *'FALL' – A 'count' or 'score'. Secured by throwing, from a standing position, an opponent to the ground. Should even the knee of either competitor touch the ground, this is sufficient to be counted a 'fall'.*
- *'CHIP' – A wrestling trick [such as:]*
- *'BACK HEEL' – Draw forward your opponent. Place right heel behind his left. Grip the lower part of his back and at the same time throw your weight on his chest.*
- *'BUTTOCK' – Generally used by men of small stature, particularly against bigger men. Place left leg across opponent's and left foot just in front of his left. At the same time, slip your hold to his neck. Then, pulling down his head, apply the hip to his middle. Your man should then come clean over the hip. A beautiful fall.*
- *'CROSS BUTTOCK' – Step quickly with the right foot extended towards opponent's right foot, placing right a few inches in front of opponent's right foot and pull him over-leg.*
- *'INSIDE CLICK' – Place right leg between those of opponent and hook the back part of knee round his left knee. Then jerk him forward onto his right knee.*
- *'CROSS CLICK' – Similar to 'Inside Click', except that with the right leg you take your opponent's right leg from under him.*
- *'HANK' – The moment an opponent comes forward, place leg between his legs, turning your leg round his right. Then place instep on the outside of opponent's ankle. Follow up by lifting and turning him and finally throwing. N.B. – a very effective 'chip' and one which is successfully used by lighter built men against much heavier opponents.*
- *'OUTSIDE STROKE' – Place inside of foot to nearest leg of opponent, and just above ankle on the outside.*

Simultaneously, twist him the opposite way and throw him off his balance and on to the ground.

- *'SWING AND HIPE' – Step a few inches (with right foot advanced) towards opponent. At the same time, lift and swing him in circular fashion once or twice towards the left. Steady yourself. Apply right knee to the inside of opponent's left. By this movement it should be possible to turn your man in the air and in the fall his shoulders come to the ground.*

- *'TWIST OFF THE BREAST' – Lift your opponent on your chest, swinging him in so doing. Quickly reverse the movement and throw him, when he will fall with neck and shoulders touching the ground.*

Many athletes who compete in the sport will train to perfect one or two of the above manoeuvres and attempt to execute their preferred 'chip' in almost every contest. The more chips that can be perfected, the more versatile and unpredictable the wrestler will be.

In less time than it took him to get there on his bicycle, using a full array of the above manoeuvres and without giving away a single fall himself, Duggy easily won his tournament. He described himself as 'feeling 6ft tall'. In truth, not yet 16 years old, he actually wasn't far off 6ft tall. His naturally thick frame, enhanced by the hours of hauling those sacks of coal, had made him an irrepressible physical force at his young age. After each victorious fall, he would help his stricken foe back to his feet and shake his hand. Occasionally, he would even apologise.

Into the late afternoon, the temperatures once again dropped towards zero and cloud gathered on the hilltops before beginning to climb down them, making for a dark and murky autumnal evening. But Duggy needed to wait right until the end of the trophy presentation to collect his prize.

When called forward for the award, the ripple of applause was all that was needed to warm young Duggy up. 'Well done, lad,' the patrons would say as he walked past them. Presenting Duggy with his trophy was a very tall, slender man wearing a black top hat, a long, black overcoat, a white shirt with a large, sharp collar and a cravat.

'Well done, young man,' the gentleman said to Duggy as he shook his hand and presented him with his prize.

'Thank you, sir,' replied Duggy, who couldn't hide his befuddlement at the modesty of the trophy he had travelled and battled so skilfully for. It was a long, slender copper candlestick – and quite an old one at that.

As what remained of the crowd dispersed and darkness began to fall, a rather disgruntled Duggy was now wrestling with another opponent: his bicycle. He was trying to figure out a way to securely fasten the candlestick to the bike frame for the long and bumpy ride home.

'You don't look too proud of your prize, sonny?'

Duggy looked around, his gaze starting at floor level. He saw a pair of polished, shiny black brogue shoes. As he lifted his gaze, he saw the top-hatted gentleman who had presented him with the trophy.

'Well, fancy coming all the way from Elbra' for that thing.' Duggy nodded towards the dangling candlestick.

Smiling almost to the point of laughing, the nobleman asked the youngster how much he felt his award might be worth.

''Bout ten bob,' Duggy answered, shrugging his shoulders.

'Then here you go,' said the man, delving into his pocket. 'I'll give you the ten shillings for it.'

'No thank you, sir,' came the instant response from Duggy. 'Mother would never believe I had won if I hadn't anything to show for it, and beside, this is my first win. I am surprised at what the prize is, but I am very proud of what it means.'

'That is the answer I wanted to hear, son,' the man told him. 'I enjoyed your wrestling. So here, take this ten shillings anyway and get yourself some tea on your way home.'

'Thank you, sir,' a smiling and grateful Duggy said before riding off.

A policeman who had been observing the discussion from a distance stopped Duggy. 'What did you say to that old toff to make him laugh so much?'

'Nothing much, sir. Why, who is he?'

'That's Lord Lonsdale, lad, one of the richest men in the north of England and the man who pays for all these type of events putting on around 'ere.'

Meanwhile, Lord Lonsdale approached the trainers who were packing up their equipment and asked to be personally kept informed on the progress of young Duggy, who managed to get home even more quickly than he had got to the event, running high on adrenaline and excitement, to show his mam the trophy.

Lord Lonsdale – real name Hugh Cecil Lowther, the fifth Earl of Lonsdale – was an English peer and an avid sports competitor, supporter and philanthropist. He would pour his huge wealth not only into the local wrestling tournaments, but into boxing, rugby, football and all manner of equine sports. He even had his own horseracing stable. To this day, the British boxing champions across all of the weight divisions are awarded the famous and historic 'Lonsdale Belt' – first donated by the Earl in 1909.

The copper candlestick would go on to be one of Douglas Clark's most prized possessions.

As much as Duggy adored his wrestling, it was second in his affections to his beloved rugby. He had attended Ellenborough National School and starred for its team. Upon leaving, he had signed for Brookland Rovers. At just 15, he was a regular for their under-18 team.

After beginning as a folk game played with a mass (any number) of men, the first set of formal rules was published in 1845, stating the teams should be of 20 men each. By the latter part of the century, it had grown in popularity and competitiveness. The Rugby Football Union (RFU) was formed in 1871 and teams were reduced to 15 men for the 1875/76 season. The sports foundations were heavily built around the representative teams of the colleges and universities of the south. It was strictly amateur and rules were in place and enforced around the non-payment of players.

The popularity of Association Football was growing quickly. It had turned professional in 1885 and subsequently invested in training and advertisement to create a true entertainment spectacle and a national league structure of rival clubs. Professional players made for a product of such quality that supporters were happy to part with their hard-earned wages to watch their local team.

With scarcely any students in the north of the country, amateur northern rugby-football teams consisted of men who worked down the coal mines, on the farms and in the cotton mills by day. Naturally fit, strong and rugged, these young men began to excel at the sport and soon, against the expectation of the RFU, Yorkshire, Lancashire and Cumberland were dominating the county championships, the stellar and most lucrative competitions of the time. When those championships reached the latter, knockout stages – which invariably took place in the south – many of the young men competing for the northern counties were forced to take unpaid time off from their laborious day jobs to participate. The one-way travel alone could take a whole day. This was something they simply could not afford to do, such were the levels of poverty in many of those regions at the time. The governing bodies of the teams concerned would invariably find a way to reimburse those star players they had asked to make the sacrifice. This went on for a few years and slowly the method of paying players for the 'broken time' of their employment filtered into the club sides as well as the counties.

When the RFU officials found out about this practice, they came down on the teams concerned with heavy sanctions, including fines and suspension from competitions. With many northern teams now heading into the big national matches weakened as some of their most important players could not afford the time off from work, the southern club sides and counties began to regain their stranglehold on the major competitions.

Members of the boards and committees of the northern teams appealed for a 'broken time' law to be introduced where, if a player of full-time employment could prove he would be losing a day's or two days' wages, he could be recompensed by the club or county that he was playing for. The RFU would not budge. Instead, as the 19th century entered the middle of its final decade, it increased the punishments for breaking the 'non-professionalism' rules, despite the protestations that this was simply not a level playing field.

Secret meetings began to be organised by the chairman of the 21 northern clubs that competed at the top level. The clubs were Brighouse Rangers, Batley, Dewsbury, Huddersfield (or 'Fartown' as they were more commonly known – the district of the town in which they played and trained), Wigan, Tyldesley, Broughton Rangers, Leeds, Oldham, Warrington, Swinton, Liversedge, Salford, Hull, Wakefield, Manningham, Rochdale, Halifax, Bradford, Hunslet and St Helens. They discussed various options as their relationship with the RFU officials became untenable. The most extreme of those options, and initially the least favourable, was a complete breakaway from the RFU and to start their own sporting union.

As one favourable option after another was proposed and subsequently quashed by the governing body, the radical option of a split began to carry more and more favour at the discreet meetings held in various hotels, mainly in West Yorkshire due to its central position.

Vice-president of Huddersfield Rugby Football Club, John Clifford, was passionate about defending the rights of the northern clubs and their players, and securing fairness and equality for them. John, alongside his brother Joe, had grown up in Huddersfield as a rugby fanatic and had played for the club – even captaining them in the mid-1880s. Afterwards both he and Joe became involved with the club on an administrative level, eventually becoming vice-president and chairman respectively. They were almost identical in appearance, always immaculately turned out in smart suits and trilby hats, and both wore thick, greying handlebar moustaches.

On 29 August 1895, at The George Hotel in Huddersfield, John hosted the latest meeting between representatives of the northern clubs and decided that enough was enough. On that day, the option of splitting from the RFU was put to the vote. Twenty out of the 21 clubs opted to create the Northern Rugby Football Union. Only Dewsbury were against it. The result was implemented with immediate effect and the RFU was informed. That is widely regarded as the day rugby in Britain split into two codes and the modern-day rugby league was born.

The Northern Union was made up of three rugby-playing counties: Yorkshire, Lancashire and Cumberland. Every season, each county would hold its own league championship and knockout cup competition. Meanwhile, all teams would compete for the two flagship trophies: the Northern Union League Championship and the Challenge Cup. The end of the season would also see representative teams from each of the counties play off in a round-robin to crown the champion region.

The Northern Union began to create its own rules regarding 'broken time' payments and professionalism – and it wasn't just administrative laws that the Northern Union was changing from those inherited by the RFU. It wanted to create an entertainment spectacle to rival not just the rugby-football being played in the south, but one to challenge the Association Football clubs in the north for the hearts, minds and entrance fees of the enthusiastic sporting men in its communities. As the years went by, RFU also got creative with the rules of the game themselves, as it sought to establish itself as the premier and more entertaining code.

The George Hotel, Huddersfield, in 1895, and the plaque that is still mounted there to this day Huddersfield Rugby League: A Lasting Legacy

By 1906, it had evolved the game. Teams would play with 13 men rather than 15. Once tackled, the offensive player would be allowed to 'play-the-ball', instead of pile-ups of players – a scenario in which spectators cannot see the ball or what is happening to it – resulting in a 'ruck' to determine which side would next hold possession. The 'line-out' was abolished. Even the scoring system was tweaked, with the Northern Union determining three points for a try and just one for a goal kick would deter tactical and possession-based kicking and encourage running and dribbling with the ball and flowing passing moves to open up defences.

As attendances rose to see the top teams play in this new, invigorated sport, the clubs were permitted to pay players professional salaries.

Representative teams from England and Wales would compete against one another, and there were rumours of a Great Britain side one day competing against touring squads from Australia and New Zealand.

Huddersfield was still regarded as the home of the new code of the sport. The Clifford brothers wanted to build a team to reflect that heritage. They had finished bottom of the Yorkshire League in the opening Northern Union season and things had not improved dramatically in the decade since. They had the infrastructure: the Fartown Ground was named after the small district of the town in which it had been built, the stadium could hold 30,000 standing supporters and was regarded as one of the premier rugby auditoriums in the north, and thus hosted many cup finals and county matches.

With the game becoming more global, Australia and New Zealand embarked on tours of the Northern Union. Closely observing, the Cliffords – alongside head trainer Arthur Bennett – were inspired. They had now seen these Southern Hemisphere teams first hand and, in the case of New Zealand in particular, were awestruck by how they played the game: less kicking; faster running; swift passing moves. It was dynamic, entertaining and, when done well, impossible to stop. They set about building a Fartown team of young, strong and technically gifted youngsters they could mould into playing this expansive style. The first man – or boy, as the case may be – they targeted was a mercurial 15-year-old (actually just 17 days younger than Duggy) from nearby Holmfirth. He played for his local amateur side, Underbank Rangers, and his name was Harold Wagstaff.

Joe Clifford, who always wore a long camelhair coat over a dark suit, approached the father of Wagstaff regarding making the youngster a professional rugby player at just 15. A humble labourer to a local painter and decorator, Mr Wagstaff was sceptical, worried it may all be a little early for his son, who was still growing into his adult form and nowhere near his full potential. He told his son to stay with the juniors at Underbank. But Clifford was persistent; he visited Mr Wagstaff at his home, at his work and also at the Druids Hotel, where he drank of an evening – his brother being the landlord.

'Get yourself brightened up, lad,' Mr Wagstaff said to Harold as he walked in from work in his paint-soaked overalls one Friday evening. 'We're going down to your uncle's to see that chap from Huddersfield. Might as well hear what he's got to say.'

Clifford bought the drinks and his charm began to pay dividends as Wagstaff senior realised just how much faith they had in his son at Huddersfield and how much they wanted to nurture his talent. Sensing he was about to clinch the deal, Clifford reached into his pocket and pulled out five shillings. Harold's eyes lit up and his father offered out his hand to Mr Clifford.

That was 2 November 1906. Just eight days later, at the age of 15 years and six months, Harold Wagstaff pulled on the woollen claret and gold hooped jersey for the first time as he made his Fartown debut. A natural centre, creating and exploiting space came naturally to him. As he further improved his positioning, handling, dribbling and pass timing, he became a devastating and revolutionary playmaker.

Meanwhile, 170 miles north-west of Huddersfield, the new rules were turning the already talented youngster Douglas Clark into a renowned star. With his size, strength and speed, the extra space and freedom for him to run forward with the ball was making him simply unstoppable in his own age groups. In the 1907/08 season, at 17 years old, Duggy was a regular starter for Brookland Rovers in each of the under-18, under-21 and senior/'A' teams. He won medals with all three in that season alone. A dedicated student of the game, he practised passing daily until he could perform it with such hand speed that no defender could react quickly enough. His strong, muscular frame, rapid speed and a perfectly honed tackling technique meant no opponent could get past him.

In the summer of 1908, Duggy achieved peak physical condition as he trained hard for the upcoming season; he had been named captain of the under-21 team and would continue to appear regularly in the senior squad. He used wrestling practice predominantly as part of his rugby training. He was, however, disappointed to find out that the rugby campaign would begin slightly later than usual. His father had seen first hand during the coal rounds just how astonishingly strong and fit his son had become. The later start to the season gave John an idea.

One light summer morning, whilst Duggy sat next to him on the horse-drawn cart, John asked him how would he feel about joining his parents on their annual trip to the Grasmere

17-year-old Douglas Clark (rear, third from right), with the triumphant senior team of Brookland Rovers Elizabeth James & Imperial War Museum

Festival as he now wouldn't be playing rugby on the Bank Holiday.

'Delighted!' Duggy responded, instantly buoyed at the prospect.

'Good. It's a pity, though, we didn't send in your name before the entries closed. Would you have wrestled if we had done so?'

'Yeah!'

'Well that's alright then. 'Cos I've already entered you on the off-chance you were home for the holiday.' John looked at his son with pride. Duggy's face filled with excitement, the delayed rugby season now a distant memory. He would instead be competing in the 'All-Weights' competition of the Grasmere Games – the most prestigious and legendary tournament in the world of Cumberland & Westmorland wrestling.

2

CATCH-AS-CATCH-CAN

August, 1908
The Grasmere Festival
Lake District National Park

AS THE early-morning sun burnt through the low mist that sits atop Grasmere Lake, the adjacent fields were already beginning to fill with food stalls, funfair activities and sporting demarcations. Eager supporters began to filter into the field for the most exciting day of sport in their diary.

Duggy and his family arrived early, along with a rugby team-mate of his, Tom Fenwick, who was also entered in the tournament. They were just two of over 90 entrants in the open-to-all competition.

Not wanting to throw his son in over his head after such a long period out of the competitive ring, John had arranged some pre-tournament coaching for Duggy, which of course he insisted his friend Tom make use of too. William Studholme, an acquaintance of John's and a celebrated veteran and five-time heavyweight champion, was only too glad to give the lads some tips and get them prepared for battle.

He showed them various holds and chips and the countermoves for each. During the try-outs, Fenwick jested with his rugby captain that if they were to meet in the tournament, he would triumph with ease. But on the evidence of the sparring Studholme was seeing between them, the actual result would be very different.

So impressed was Studholme that, despite Clark's young age, he sent a message back through his peers and all the way up to the observing Lord Lonsdale that he believed only two men in the entire field were likely to come out victorious should they meet Duggy. Going by their surnames alone, the two clear favourites for the competition were Little and Pickering, of Kingswater and Carlisle respectively. Studholme was duly harsh on Duggy during the training period, though, concentrating on correcting his flaws rather than allowing him to celebrate his skills and great strength.

As the carnival atmosphere and eager anticipation built, Duggy remained calm. He joked with his parents and played with his younger siblings. A series of preliminary matches reduced the field to 64 and so the main knockout tournament could get under way. Due to the number of contestants and matches required to complete, the Grasmere Games were sudden-death, one-fall-to-a-finish match-ups, which only served to add to the tension and excitement as the grapplers locked up.

Both of the rugby youngsters won their opening-round falls with relative ease against some of the lesser skilled hopefuls that made up the numbers. But in a seemingly cruel twist, each were drawn against the two feared competition favourites: Fenwick would face Pickering and Duggy would battle Little.

Tom lost to the 6ft, 15 stone Pickering and remarked afterwards that he believed he was the strongest man he had ever met.

Duggy consoled Tom, more concerned with his friend than with his upcoming battle against Little.

When the eagerly awaited contest got under way, Little was the initial aggressor – desperate to prove that the young rugby stallion the whole area was talking about was not yet in his league when it came to the wrestling ring. Duggy held his ground and could feel his foe beginning to wane. When he sensed the moment was right, he stepped forward with his right foot, forcing his kneecap into the side of Little's left one. Simultaneously, he lifted his heavyweight opponent clean off the ground and with all the leverage from his planted right foot, he swung his helpless rival back around his body and slammed him to the ground. The crowd, which contained John and Elizabeth Clark and the younger children, erupted for their youthful new hero. Lord Lonsdale, dressed in his familiar full suit, long dark overcoat and top hat despite the hot summer's day, nodded with an all-knowing approval.

A successful 'fall' is achieved amidst the pageantry and beauty of the Grasmere Games

Duggy won again in his last-16 tie to advance to the quarter-finals, where he would meet the overwhelming favourite and Tom's conqueror, Pickering.

Sensing the possibility of an upset, all the so-called experts suddenly gathered around Duggy, giving him their opinions on how he might be able to overcome this next mammoth task. But he remained calm and remembered the advice of William Studholme, who had told him prior to the tournament that, should he meet Pickering, his only chance was to stay firm and allow the Carlisle man to get frustrated when his predictable but terribly effective routine (hank, cross-buttock, inside-click) had failed. Not many could survive all three but if Duggy could do so, Pickering would begin to wonder how he could win and become desperate.

Almost everyone at the festival clambered to find a viewing spot. The knowledgeable supporters knew that it was likely this fall would decide their champion. Silent tension built as the umpire shouted '*En Guard*' to the locked-up grapplers, followed by '*Wrestle!*'

During the first tie-up, Pickering predictably attempted a cross-buttock, which Duggy strongly countered and the grapple was broken. The umpire restarted the men. Duggy allowed Pickering to complete the scheduled repertoire Studholme had informed him he would. Like clockwork, the predictable Pickering attempted another cross-buttock but this one was erratic and desperate. With this, Duggy caught his man off balance and raised all 15 stone of him up on to his chest before releasing him with downward pressure, as if scoring a try on the rugby field. The joyous cheers echoed around the hills of the Lake District and could be heard for miles. Pickering got to his feet and immediately offered a warm handshake to the victor. Douglas Clark would later say of the match:

> [*It was*] *one of the hardest bouts I ever had. At the end Pickering remarked, 'Well wrestled, young fellow,' and gave me a hearty handshake.*

The teenager advanced to the semi-finals to the thrill of the many spectators. There, completely in control of his grapple with Norman, Duggy looked for the finish that would put him into the final. With his opponent hoisted and swung around at leisure, he prepared to slam his latest victim down to the ground. The attempted counter by Norman worked temporarily and forced Duggy into a rethink of his finish. Rather than exercising patience and regaining full control, he showed his inexperience by attempting a reverse swing whilst slightly off balance. In doing so, he dropped to one knee and was so declared felled.

Douglas Clark's first shot at the Grasmere heavyweight championship (more commonly known as the 'All-Weights Championship' as smaller wrestlers could enter for extra prestige) ended in semi-final heartbreak, not just for him and his family but for his new and adoring fanbase. To add to the frustration, his conqueror won the final and the coveted prize with relative ease.

> *I felt well satisfied but not so William Studholme, who called me every name under the sun,' Duggy said. 'In fact, he never stopped until we arrived at Brigham, where he left us.'*

When the 1908/09 rugby season finally did get under way, Duggy went from strength to strength. As well as becoming the perfect physical specimen for the sport, he studied it like a science and his technique and reading of the game was more like that of a veteran. He was a forward but could – and regularly would – play in any position his team required of him. Invariably, he would excel.

The position of forward was, and still is, amongst the more industrious roles in a rugby league team. Whilst centres get to handle the ball and create plays and attacking moves with finesse and the wingers have the blistering pace to get away from defenders and finish off the moves with a try, the others in the team have less prestigious jobs. The generally stronger forwards have the tougher tasks of driving the ball into the opposition and pushing them back, gaining all-important yards. When out of possession, they provide the majority of the tackles and the protection of their own precious yards.

Continuing their Huddersfield project of recruiting the finest youngsters to play the fast, unstoppable style of rugby they dreamed of, chairman Joe Clifford and trainer Arthur Bennett arranged a couple of 'friendly' matches at Fartown, in which a selection of their Huddersfield squad would take on guest teams. First, in February 1909, they welcomed the first-ever touring Australian team. Following a hard-fought 5-3 victory, Clifford signed up the two most impressive Kangaroos: starring young winger Albert Rosenfeld and the versatile Paddy Walsh. That tour, in which the British Northern Union side beat the Australians by two Test matches to nil, was the first-ever 'Ashes' series (adopting the same name of the cricket equivalent contest between England and Australia). The New Zealand All-Golds had toured 12 months earlier, resulting in the signing of brilliant centre Edgar Wrigley. He and Wagstaff were becoming an incomparable pairing.

In April 1909, the Cumberland Colts – a team made up of the best young players from the northernmost county – were invited to West Yorkshire. The match took place just a few weeks before Duggy turned 18. It would be the first meeting of Douglas Clark and Harold Wagstaff. It would be the first time Duggy would set foot on Fartown Ground. It would be the first time he would lay eyes on the claret and gold hoops of Huddersfield. Little did he realise just what relationships he would come to form with each of them.

Duggy knew this was his opportunity. The match had been funded by the Huddersfield money men in their search for talent and he had just been pronounced 'the most promising forward ever to play with Cumberland'. Unfortunately, he had sustained a nasty heel injury that might have kept him out of the match. But he would not miss this chance, so to make his ailment more comfortable, he cut the heel out of his right football boot and played through the match like that.

Joe Clifford was on the look-out for his next recruit with eagle eyes. He feared, with Wagstaff on the field, no Cumberland prodigy would shine through. But he needn't have worried. Douglas Clark shone through like Maryport Lighthouse – despite the injury. He and Harold warmly congratulated each other on their outstanding performances at the final whistle.

The proud people of Huddersfield were desperate for a successful sporting club (Huddersfield Town Association Football Club was still in its first year of existence and was yet to find its place in the Football League). Clifford immediately set about acquiring the scintillating Clark to add to the talent of Wagstaff, who had been playing for the first team for two years and had already played for the Yorkshire senior team.

Duggy and his father were involved in the negotiations. Joe Clifford turned on the charm, just as he had with young Harold and his humble father. He invited the pair, as his guests, to the Challenge Cup Final at Headingley Stadium between Wakefield and Hull.

'How would you like to play in a match like this, at a stadium like this, one day, young man?' Joe mischievously asked Duggy, one month shy of his 18th birthday, who stared silently awestruck around the 24,000 capacity crowd. 'You sign for Huddersfield and the very next final on this ground, you will play in it.'

With his father's blessing, Brookland Rovers were offered the mouthwatering fee of £30 for their prodigy (the equivalent of over £3,000 today, 110 years later) and the sale of Douglas Clark made his semi-professional team financially stable for the foreseeable future.

By May 1909, Duggy was excitedly preparing for life as a professional rugby player, even though the small salary would not be enough to keep him and he would need to find another source of income to supplement it. John would also need to find new help for his coal rounds. John did have his reservations about the move; first-class rugby was a far cry from what Duggy had being excelling at and, similarly to Mr Wagstaff a couple of years earlier, he feared his son might be making too big a jump even for a player of his prodigious talent. John had asked Arthur Bennett to ease his son into first-team action slowly by starting him in the junior and reserve teams when the 1909/10 season got under way.

Duggy found himself a cosy bedroom for rent at the house of a family just one mile away from the Fartown Ground. The family were the Hodgsons: husband and father Alfred was a Tramway electrician. He, his wife Sophia and their six-year-old daughter Kathleen shared the master bedroom. They hired out the three smaller ones in order to make ends meet. Sophia's older sister, Annie, was a permanent resident. She was a tailoress and had a young trainee by the name of Lily, who also had a room. The remaining one had been somewhat of a revolving door, with contract workers and evicted married men the kinds of people looking for a roof over their heads. Polite and respectful, Duggy was a very welcome addition to the family. He offered them continuity as he would, hopefully, be there a long time. It quickly became the perfect home from home.

Duggy got a part-time job in a local cotton mill to keep himself busy and fit during his time away from rugby. Whilst he was delighted to be a professional sportsman and was enjoying the vibrant and growing town of Huddersfield (when compared to Elbra' at least), he did miss his wrestling.

When he arrived for the first day of official pre-season training at Fartown, he was shocked to see 2,000 spectators had gathered to watch – such was the buzz of excitement following another summer of recruitment of some of the game's top talent. Arthur Bennett was strict and professional. Duggy loved it and could feel the improvement in his skills almost immediately.

He did, however, begin to share his father's belief that he may not quite be ready to share the professional field with these great stars just yet. He would stay behind every evening after training to work on his techniques and his sprinting. This hadn't gone unnoticed by the Clifford brothers looking on from their offices, and they informed trainer Bennett. Joe and Arthur approached Duggy as he trained alone in the mud the following night.

'What's this all about, Clark?' asked Bennett.

'Well, Arthur, I am so disappointed with my slowness that I felt I must improve myself.'

'That's right,' Joe jumped in. 'And we are both delighted you are so keen, but don't do a scrap of training more than Arthur tells you in future.'

'Look here Clark,' Arthur said. 'You're doing okay. Your training is bound to feel hard and for a time but until you get stamina, you will never gain pace. Don't forget that rest is as essential as work and without rest you will get nowhere. Now get to bed and see you are there every night when I call at 10pm. I am the trainer and I prescribe the training that every man at Fartown does. Good night.'

Privately, however, the staff were more than a little impressed and, when the campaign got started, they were keen to put Duggy straight into the first team. The youthful group had become close friends off the field as well as a tight-knit outfit on it. Joe Clifford, Arthur Bennett and all connected with Fartown, including the supporters, had high hopes for the year ahead.

Duggy was left at home with the reserves as the senior team got the season under way with a trip to Bramley (there were no substitutes in those days and teams travelled with a bare 13-player outfit).

Even with a comfortable lead and victory secured, talismanic young leader Harold Wagstaff would still not allow an easy score for the opposition. In a desperate attempt at a tackle, he was dragged across a bare patch of the field left over from the cricket wicket that shared the pitch during the summer. Harold sustained a nasty graze, but nothing to worry about nor get properly treated.

It was soon three consecutive opening victories as Fartown defeated Broughton Rangers and then, at Headingley, Leeds via a dramatic last-minute goal kick.

Midweek following that win, one that had begun to make the people of Huddersfield feel they were on the cusp of a special young team that could achieve some glory, Harold 'Waggy' Wagstaff fell faint during training. He soon found himself at Leeds General Infirmary. The gash on his knee had become infected and had subsequently driven down his immune system. He was diagnosed with diptheria and was at risk of severe blood poisoning. He and his family were warned he may not come out of hospital, such was the seriousness of his infections (and the medical limitations of the time).

The mood naturally darkened around the team, and the town. There was no doubt in the mind of Arthur Bennett who should be promoted to first-team action in place of Harold: Douglas Clark.

Duggy was summoned to the chairman's office, where Joe Clifford offered him the opportunity of a first-team place for the upcoming match at Hull Kingston Rovers.

'Well, Joe, I mean Mr Clifford, I'm not good enough, big enough or fast enough. And then there's father,' Duggy nervously replied, lacking self-confidence.

'We think you are all of those things. Come on lad, get on those scales.'

'Thirteen stones and 13 pounds! You are big enough. We'll speak to your dad.'

John was delighted that the staff were so pleased with his son and respected them for asking his opinion. He consented to Duggy being promoted to the first team. (It is worth noting here that the natural evolution of man over the last century or so means we are a naturally bigger species now. And with advancements in training methods and nutrition, you will not find any forwards in the modern-day Super League weighing less than 14 stones – but back then, that was a big athlete.)

Albert Rosenfeld, whose Jewish father had fled from Poland to Australia to escape persecution, was performing superbly and so was moved into Waggy's vital role at centre and the team was shuffled around, enabling Duggy to be deployed as a forward for the away match against Hull KR, where he made his official debut in the claret and gold on 25 September 1909.

Huddersfield sustained injuries during the match and subsequently played most of it with 11 men against 13. Duggy's stellar performance was not enough to lift the spirits of the team to a level to beat their opponents that day, but it was good enough for everyone at the club to know that he was a certain first-team member from that point onwards.

Waggy was on the road to recovery within a couple of weeks and officially out of any mortal danger – to the relief of everyone in the Northern Union. The mood at Fartown lifted and the positive results began flowing in again. Duggy quickly became one of the most important players in the team, his frightening power making headlines and sending shockwaves through the whole of the sport – as was his quiet, gentle manner and great sportsmanship.

Over 28,000 supporters crammed into Fartown as Huddersfield played host to local rivals Halifax in the semi-finals of the Yorkshire Cup. A blistering performance saw them rout the opposition by 20 points to two. The victory meant they would meet Batley in the final – confirming the prediction of Joe Clifford that if Duggy signed for him, he would be playing in the next major final at Headingley Stadium.

Within two months of making his bow in the county, Douglas Clark was a Yorkshire Cup winner as Huddersfield humiliated Batley 21-0 in the final. Huddersfield were a young, swift and scintillating team, and the whole of the Northern Union were on notice.

Harold Wagstaff made a slow return to health, torturing himself by watching his friends and team-mates train and joyously win match after match. His mere presence was enough to lift the atmosphere. Camaraderie between the young group was solidifying, the friendships growing and trust total and complete. Waggy made his return to the first team for the final few matches as the club completed an encouraging season. Such was his positive mentality, he still hoped he would be selected for the 1910 summer tour of Australia for what would be the first-ever away Ashes series for the Great Britain Northern Union team. Duggy played 26 competitive first-team matches in that first campaign, scoring four tries.

With his health put first, Waggy – still only 19 – was not selected for the tour. Great Britain won the Ashes series in Australia 2-0, as they had done the 1908/09 home series. The game Down Under was even more in its infancy than it was in the north of England, but the Australians and the Kiwis had fallen in love with the sport. Their matches were played in front of thousands in packed arenas all over the continent of Australasia, and they were improving quickly.

The end-of-season County Championship was still to be completed. Young Duggy was already the most important player for Cumberland, as was Wagstaff for Yorkshire, who, as a result of their greater geographical area, had the larger catchment region and were subsequently, and by some distance, the strongest of the three. Despite a Duggy try, Waggy and many other of his Fartown team-mates ran out victors at the Dewsbury Football Ground in the 1910 Yorkshire versus Cumberland County Championship match. They gained bragging rights over Duggy, who became emboldened that he would one day break their dominance of the trophy. Dewsbury would be a stadium he would become very familiar with in the coming months.

During the off-season, whilst his team-mates and friends spent much of their summer in the public houses of Huddersfield and Holmfirth, tee-total Duggy got himself a second off-the-field job: he went back to his roots and began to help a local coal merchant with his deliveries. He always maintained this was the best possible physical training for him. He also made the long journey back to Cumberland to see his family and whilst there would engage in a few bouts of wrestling, which he missed dearly.

Joe Clifford and Arthur Bennett continued to add to the progressive roster of players that summer. The most impressive of the signings was Welsh Rugby Union international Ben Gronow, who had already appeared for his country four times but was excited to switch codes and move to Huddersfield.

Soon, the hard pre-season training was back as the team prepared for another long, arduous campaign.

Douglas Clark spoke of his blossoming success at Fartown:

> *Much of the success achieved by our old trainer Arthur Bennett was due to the happy family spirit which he engendered to the men under his care. He was ready and willing to do everything in his power to help his boys at all times.*
>
> *Mrs Bennett rendered great assistance to her husband and the players respected her deeply.*
>
> *Arthur believed in plenty of walking, field practice and track work, followed by the punch ball and skipping, concluding with considerable time spent in massage. He was an advocate of the hot bath after a match and on the day following, the cold water hose pipe on Tuesdays and Thursdays.*

*Another big factor in Bennett's success was undoubtedly
that at this period the players under him were in the best
of their days. Keen for work and enthusiastic and willing
to try any new idea for the discomfort of their opponents.
In those days 'players' meetings' were a strong point, and
many games were practically half won as a result of the
lectures and discussions which took place. It was at a players'
meeting that I first suggested a fixed-pack, and a decided
improvement was noticeable once the new idea became a
set plan. I believe these meetings were (and similar meetings
should be today) just as important as training.*

Huddersfield Rugby League: A Lasting Legacy

As the excitement towards the rugby season ramped up, the
Huddersfield Examiner detailed the wrestling exploits of their
19-year-old forward.

The leading wrestling style at the time, across Yorkshire
and most of the country, was 'catch-as-catch-can'. In this style
– recognised worldwide rather than a bespoke style exclusive
to a particular region or tradition – the grapple continues on
to the mat following the 'chip' and the fall only gained when

the aggressor has successfully pinned both of his opponent's shoulder blades to the ground for sufficient time for the referee to award the fall.

The champion of Yorkshire at the time, Percy Teale, invited Duggy to take part in a friendly exhibition match at Dewsbury Football Ground as part of his pre-season training and to generate some publicity.

About June 1910, I was reading the Health & Strength *magazine when, to my surprise, I noticed a challenge list of Percy Teale of Dewsbury – men he would like to meet, and my name headed the list. I had not wrestled in the catch-as-catch-can style and the only knowledge I had of it was what I had gained from books by George de Relwyskow – the world champion – and the legendary George Hackenschmidt.*

I wrote to Teale and informed him I knew nothing of this style. As he persisted with his challenge, I informed him I would meet him for any amount he wished, best of three falls.

Percy claimed Heavyweight Championship of Yorkshire while Edgar Hayes of Slaithwaite claimed English Championship.

I was fortunate in finding the right instructor in the person of Frank Burns, living in the same street as myself and a really clever catch-as-catch-can wrestler. I was put on to this man by a member of the football team, Arthur Swinden, who had gained a bit of a reputation as a boxer and a wrestler as well as being a very useful front row forward playing for Fartown. I secured a suitable room, bought the mats and my instruction as a catch-as-catch-can wrestler began.

Frank was a good 12-13 stone man, strong, and knew the game from A to Z. I was now around 15 stones, but

Frank could pin me easily in a few minutes. But I soon surprised him. I began to cotton-on to the catch-as-catch-can style. I had some difficulty in convincing him I had never wrestled this style before. As Frank put it – I seemed to know what each throw was before he'd finished explaining it to me. That, of course, was due to the fine instruction received from the aforementioned books.

Frank soon realised that my early training in Cumberland & Westmorland style wrestling made me almost impossible to throw to the mat so he concentrated on the ground or mat work, every known hold for turning and pinning your man.

We had plenty of sparring partners and the time soon came when Frank thought I was now fit to tackle Teale. His challenge for £25-a-side was accepted and the match was to take place at Dewsbury Football Ground – one month to finish training.

For my final try-out I had eight sparring partners. We started at 1pm Saturday afternoon. As fast as one had been disposed of another took the mat. I never rested for a minute until 4pm. I was beginning to feel the strain and I acquainted Frank of the fact. Just at that moment, who should come on the scene but my club mate Swinden, who I had asked to assist me getting fit. I remarked, 'Well, just imagine Arthur, I've been bothering you for weeks to come along and now that you have turned up I cannot take you on as I feel done-up, I've had three hours non-stop!'

'Well,' he replied, 'surely you will give me just one, Clark, now that I've come?'

So we had a go. I realised it had to be a quick one as I was a spent force and Arthur, as fit as myself, was just as strong and far more experienced. So I decided to try a Cumberland Buttock and sure Arthur came down. It shook him so much I pinned him before he could recover. 'Well Doug, that was too quick to be called a wrestle, let's have another go,' he remarked.

However, I had had enough and retired to the bath. My trainer Burns was furious and said I should've wrestled it out. I threw about four buckets of cold water over myself and it acted like magic, I felt so fit and refreshed. I offered to give Arthur another go the moment I got back into the room. He was delighted. We squared up and I secured a headlock from a standing position and lifted Arthur right onto my chest. At that moment his neck gave so loud of a crack that we all thought it was broken. I lowered him to the ground and his first action confirmed our first fears as he started running round and round like a dog chasing its own tail. Although we were greatly alarmed we could not help but laugh but poor Arthur was in pain and I assisted him to the doctor, just as we stood, in our wrestling shorts.

Dr Rogerson lived 300 yards away and you can imagine us two fellows turning up, stripped off, only in shorts.

Dr Rogerson – our Fartown Club doctor – how he laughed when he saw us. It was some time before he convinced Arthur that his neck was not broken, although all of the neck muscles were practically severed. It was some weeks before Arthur was well enough to follow his employment, and I got a terrible fright also.

My trainer Burns had often told me that I was not an ordinary man but a man-and-a-half and I had to be careful and not to use all my strength or I could kill someone.

That week Edgar Hayes published a challenge to the winner of the Clark versus Teale match. As I had no intention of taking the game up seriously it was decided to go and have a chat with Hayes. My coach, Frank Burns, knew that Hayes was a different proposition to Teale. He was confident I could beat Teale but not Hayes, who was considered the best catch-as-catch-can in England.

However, the Sunday afternoon before the Clark versus Teale match we went to call on Hayes, who lived way out in Slaithwaite, Huddersfield, right out on the moors. It was arranged for Edgar to give me a run over on the Tuesday night, but on the distinct understanding that no one was to be present and he was to tell no one, only his pupils, as it would affect Saturday's match gate, especially if I put up a poor showing.

Catch-as-catch-can wrestling was gaining attention and popularity, particularly in the area. George de Relwyskow was a Londoner born of Russian immigrants in 1887. A slight man of around 5ft 7in, he took up wrestling to keep fit whilst studying as an artist. By the age of 20, he had won 35 straight contests and held the English amateur championships at both lightweight and middleweight. He was subsequently selected to represent Great Britain at the 1908 Olympics, being held in his home city, in both weight classes.

George won the gold medal at his preferred lightweight and the silver medal at middleweight, where he wrestled against much bigger men. He was the youngest-ever winner of an Olympic gold medal in wrestling – a record that lived for 70 years.

His fanfare grew and he was soon wrestling his amateur contests in arenas and parks packed with thousands. In 1909, still just 22, he defeated German Peter Gotz to become lightweight champion of the world. The match took place in Pontefract, West Yorkshire.

With his celebrity confirmed, George quickly found himself writing articles and booklets on his training and wrestling methods. Duggy had become a keen follower.

With the ring already set up for the weekend's public attraction of Douglas Clark versus Percy Teale at Dewsbury Football Ground, it was arranged to utilise the facilities for a strictly behind-closed-doors Clark versus Edgar Hayes try-out on the Tuesday beforehand.

3

A NORTHERN UNION

June 1910
Dewsbury Football Ground
West Yorkshire

THE LOW evening sun cast a large shadow on the grass pitch as it set over the wooden east stand. A wrestling ring had been set up in the centre of the pitch. Volunteer staff opened the outer gates wide and set the turnstiles to automatic; the evening was freely open to the public and press to enjoy should they wish, although no one should know it is happening.

When Duggy, dressed simply in a white round-neck T-shirt and black shorts, and Frank Burns got within hearing distance of the ground, they could tell the place was abuzz. They looked at one another with surprise and suspicion.

As they walked through the wide-open iron gates, Frank – dressed smartly with a knitted grey jumper over a white shirt and black tie and wearing a tweed trilby hat – recognised one of the press men from his reporting of the Fartown matches and dashed over to ask him what everyone was doing there so early.

'Hayes has been spreading the word all week,' the journalist responded, removing a cigarette from his lips, 'really been stoking it up, he has, especially in Slaithwaite – he's brought half of the village with him.'

Duggy could hear what Burns was being told as he craned his neck to see through a gap between the stands. He could see Hayes, wearing a luxurious-looking velvet robe, showboating to the crowd of people, who were laughing at his gesticulations as he flexed his muscles and imitated Doug.

The pair had been relaxed and were looking forward to the evening just moments earlier as they joked during the journey, but Frank walked back to Duggy to find a very different expression on the face of his youthful athlete – his eyes staring intently into the distance.

'But, we agreed to a friendly, Frank – I told him we couldn't risk a serious match, and why would I?' a dismayed and disheartened Duggy rhetorically asked Frank in his soft voice.

'I think we've been a bit naive, lad. He has hijacked this as a publicity event for himself. We'll have to say you're not fit, and let him wrestle Teale on Sunday instead of you.'

'Not a chance, Frank. I'll wrestle him, good and proper.'

'No you won't. If you wrestle him in front of all these people, Clark, then I have finished with you,' Burns angrily responded, worried about one of his students embarrassing him with a heavy defeat.

'Okay. You're finished, Frank. Just now.' Duggy stormed towards the ring with authority, his ample neck and shoulders filling out the T-shirt more now as it appeared to be ready to rip open at the seams.

The ever-growing crowd parted at the presence of Duggy, eagerly awaiting his response as Hayes began waving and gesturing towards him. They believed they were watching a spring lamb make his way towards the slaughterhouse. As he passed, he heard a man say to his friend, 'The winner of this challenges Teale on Sunday, apparently.'

Duggy, always calm and collected, felt a rare rush of anger: Hayes had conned these people into believing they were here to witness a title eliminator – and potentially created one for real.

Gentlemanly ahead of his 19 years, Duggy entered the ring and approached Hayes, who immediately stopped his pantomime act as the young behemoth walked towards him.

'What are you playing at bringing these people here all the way from Slaithwaite, Edgar?' Duggy calmly began. 'This was supposed to be a try-out.'

'These are my pupils,' Hayes mischievously responded with his arms spread wide.

Duggy nodded. 'Come on then, Edgar. Strip,' he said as he ripped off his T-shirt.

'Erm, actually, I have decided that one of my students will be tough enough to handle you,' Edgar said in a suddenly less confident tone.

'No Edgar. It's you, or nobody.'

Realising he would lose enormous face should he call it off, Edgar finally removed his robe.

With Frank Burns having stormed off, Duggy was alone against the best wrestler in the country, having never had a competitive match in the sport and with a partisan crowd – now over 2,000 people – against him.

One of Hayes's entourage suddenly emerged as the referee and informed the men they were to battle it out in a first-to-three-falls contest: this was yet another ruling designed to nullify any chance Duggy might have, as he would now need to gain three falls in the alien style to be victorious. The referee then told the two men to head back to their respective corners and prepare for battle.

The two bare-chested men turned to face one another. In this style, the wrestlers began apart and engaged in the grapple themselves, rather than the referee only allowing the contest to start once the two were in a strict and fairly balanced lock-up, as was the case in Cumberland & Westmorland.

When the so-called referee shouted *'Wrestle'*, the two tentatively edged towards the centre of the ring. Hayes went on the offensive as the crowd fell into silent tension. Duggy's raw strength meant he could quite comfortably stay on his feet, despite all the efforts of Hayes to force him to the ground. As the men jostled for leverage, suddenly Duggy found himself in a very familiar grapple position, and his confidence grew. He maintained patience and could tell the perspiring Hayes was growing frustrated. When the time felt right, he hoisted his antagonist high in the air before slamming him to the mat. He kept downward pressure on to the shoulders of his winded and struggling rival, whose self-appointed referee was forced to award the first fall to Duggy. The match was a mere two minutes old.

Duggy sprung back to his feet and the crowd audibly switched their allegiance to the talented young underdog. With adrenaline coursing through his body, the pain sensation he felt in his ribs failed to properly register. More at ease, he strolled back towards his corner in the very same easy manner he had initially approached the venue.

In total, the contest lasted only nine minutes, with Duggy comfortably dismantling Hayes and securing two more pin-falls. The awestruck crowd believed they had seen truly superhuman strength. After the final fall, he helped the shellshocked Edgar back to his feet and warmly shook his hand.

As the adrenaline wore off, Duggy realised that he had injured his ribs. This time, he compromised and sent word to Percy Teale that their upcoming match would need to be postponed. He could not risk further injury so close to the rugby season.

To confirm just how impressive Duggy's performance had been, some time later Hayes and Percy Teale met in a competitive catch-as-catch-can contest and Hayes defeated the champion by two falls to nil.

Whilst Duggy's sore ribs meant he wasn't quite as explosive as he otherwise might have been, his ailment paled in comparison to what Harold Wagstaff had been through. Waggy was still weak and struggled greatly to get back fully fit. With some other minor injuries and illnesses added into the squad too, the exciting season Fartown believed they were in for got off to a bad start – and continued that way for the first half of the campaign. They lost 14 of their opening 21 contests in all competitions, including the final of the Yorkshire Cup they were defending against Wakefield.

As the cold winter made the surfaces hard, sharp and unforgiving, and the freezing evenings made late training sessions unpleasant, it would have been easy for the players' confidence to drop terminally low. With that in mind, the Fartown board called a meeting with all the players and coaches. Joe and John Clifford were harsh in their summary and insisted things would be changing – and told the talented young roster it was up to them to choose how. They were going to actively scout and recruit new players during the festive period, a warning to individual squad members that if their form didn't improve, they would be replaced in the team. The Cliffords were like father figures to many of the young players, and they ended by telling them that they believed in them and their abilities.

The pep talk worked and coincided with the timely recovery from almost all of the injuries, illnesses and ailments the players were carrying. Duggy was back to his best – a thought that sent fear around the Northern Union. A bigger relief was the recovery of the scintillating Waggy, who was now an even more impressive specimen than before the sickness that had plagued him for over 12 months. He and Duggy had formed a tight friendship. As well as being possibly the two best players, they were also two of the quietest members of the squad and subsequently gravitated towards one another.

The Huddersfield recruitment drive had been more than just a threat, though. They identified that the weakest point of the underperforming line-up was in the pack, so they sought out the finest young player they could to bolster that position. They identified 20-year-old forward Fred Longstaff of Halifax.

Welshman Ben Gronow, 23, had also just settled into his new surroundings as well as the new version of the sport he had been learning on the job, and was finally showing the brilliant skills that had made him a Wales international.

The inevitable happened, with poor Bramley the victims. Fartown clicked, both individually and collectively. From that point onwards, they were unstoppable. They lost just one more match all season – in the Challenge Cup against Wigan – and soared into the top half of the Northern Union league table. They weren't just winning matches, they were crushing their opponents with pace and power and providing the style of rugby that Joe Clifford and Arthur Bennett had dreamed of since taking over at the club. Despite finishing the campaign without any silverware, they were now the most feared club team in the whole of the sport. They became the first team to score over 800 points in a league season – with almost 600 coming in the second half of the campaign. Duggy, Waggy, Ben Gronow and Albert Rosenfeld were the talk of the Northern Union. Those scoring statistics would be sensational in the modern game, with each successfully converted try earning 50 per cent more points than it did back then.

Duggy found time during the summer off-season to go home to Ellenborough and visit his family. His parents loved it when he returned home with personal tales of sporting heroism. Elizabeth would feed him up with all the home-cooked favourites he was missing, and the portion sizes would be huge – after all, this was the off-season. While back in Huddersfield, Duggy continued to work in the cotton mill and deliver coal.

As the 1911/12 season was about start, the Fartown boys were purring. They had been eagerly awaiting getting back together and catching up. They knew that if they could go into this season fully fit and in form, unlike the last one, they could be an unstoppable force. Arthur Bennett put them through the training drills to hone their skills and techniques and patterns of play as Joe and John Clifford looked on like proud parents.

By November, they had regained the Yorkshire Cup with a 22-10 victory over Hull Kingston Rovers in the final and were sweeping all before them in the league. Week after week, over 10,000 fanatical supporters would watch their heroes play the finest rugby the Northern Union had ever seen. The feeling across the sport was that nothing could stop Huddersfield winning all the competitions they were entered in – the fabled 'All-Four' feat achieved only by the great Hunslet team four years previously.

As the bitter winter came once again, the north of England was a harsh place to live. Money was scarce and to make matters worse there was a coal miners' strike taking place. Travelling a journey of any reasonable length was tough, so when Fartown were drawn against their top-of-the-league rivals Oldham in the third round of the Challenge Cup – with the winners to become overwhelming favourites for the prestigious competition – thousands of obsessed Huddersfield fans trekked the 20 miles over the Pennines through the driving wind and rain on foot to be there. Supporting their new, all-conquering heroes every week had become one of the few times they could escape their woes.

Despite the magnificent upturn in fortunes, the board could not ignore what they had seen in Fred Longstaff. Now 21, he had developed into possibly the strongest forward outside of their own squad in the Northern Union. They brought him on board in December and in the middle of January 1912 he joined the Fartown revolution. Fred was extraordinarily talented, but also enjoyed the 'dark arts' of the game and was never one to retreat from an on-field fracas. Duggy and Waggy, recognising how important Fred could be to the turnaround of their season, took him under their ample-sized wings and made him feel instantly at home at his new club. He duly settled in and quickly appeared as a popular and morale-boosting personality within the changing room. He had been a part-time rugby player with Halifax, supplementing his income as a full-time labourer at a saw mill. Forever wearing a beaming smile, he was an instant hit at Fartown. His perfected Yorkshire accent and no-nonsense traits were matched by a naivety and simplicity that endeared him to all.

Fartown had qualified for the Challenge Cup quarter-finals following a 33-6 away win at Leigh. A match reporter wrote:

> It will be long remembered in Leigh how they were put out of the Cup in 1912. Clark was ubiquitous, and surely four tries for a forward in a cup-tie must be somewhere near a record. What a player he has turned out to be! For some time he looked unhappy when put on roving duty, but since he got the hang of the thing he has been a perfect wonder, and has fully justified the judgement of the committee in selecting him for a position in which he has no rival. I have an idea that it is a much pleasanter job to admire his progress as a spectator than to try to check that progress, and probably Bolewski, who is a fine tackler, will agree with me. It was not Clark's tries alone which made him the hero of the match. He dribbled splendidly more than once, and was always working like a horse.

At Oldham, The Watersheddings was a cauldron of animosity – the highest rugby ground in the country, the wind and hail feeling like it could tear the wooden stands down.

Oldham were a team of big men. It was the slick skill and speed of Fartown against the brawn of Oldham, and the conditions meant no one out there enjoyed the affair. Frustrations and tension set in and skirmishes began to break out regularly. Bob Robinson, the referee, warned all the players that the next one guilty of violent conduct would be dismissed from the game. Fred Longstaff, eager to impress his new team-mates, was pumped up and having an excellent defensive game, breaking up potential Oldham attacks. He was proving a real thorn in the side of the home team and they were determined to put a stop to his influence, taking every opportunity to stamp on his feet and to nip him. Eventually, he lashed out – nothing *too* violent but enough to push the patience of referee Robinson too far – and he was dismissed.

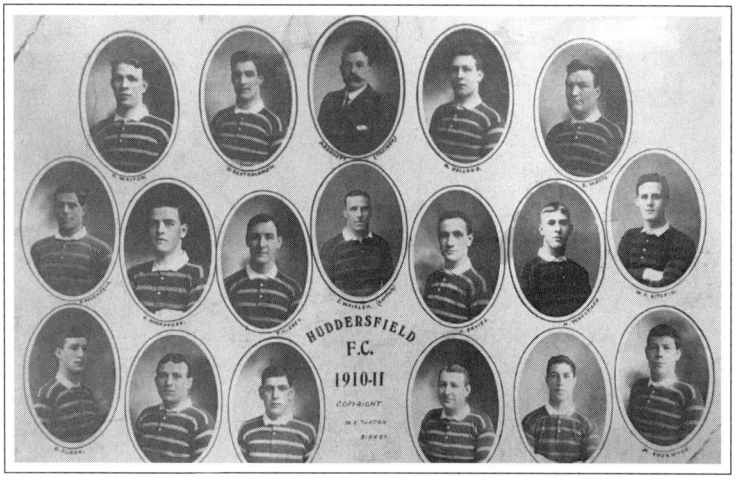

Huddersfield Rugby League: A Lasting Legacy

A long and miserable afternoon for Fartown ended with an astonishingly tight defeat by just two points to nil – one of the lowest-scoring games in rugby league history.

There would be no clean sweep of the four trophies, but the fact they had been dreaming of it meant it had now become the holy grail for the team of seemingly unlimited potential. They soon shook off the disappointment and returned to winning ways, dismantling their opponents with a barrage of attacking and free-flowing rugby. They won both the Yorkshire League and the Northern Union League Championship – which was settled via a play-off of the top four positioned teams – beating Wigan 13-5 in the final to win the coveted title for the first time, and with relative ease.

The young team had come of age and Huddersfield were the pride of the game. Waggy was the talisman and the graceful centre that orchestrated the team. Duggy was the powerhouse that drove them forward, and he returned a reasonable 12 tries that season. But that paled in comparison to the extraordinary tally of Albert Rosenfeld – the Australian winger scoring a sensational 78 and setting a new record. Fartown also set a new point-scoring landmark of 1,196, while conceding just 283.

Duggy's proudest moment, however, came in the County Championships, which had been dominated by Yorkshire for so long. Cumberland beat Lancashire at Warrington and so it came down to the tie with Yorkshire at Millom. Cumberland raced into a 16-0 lead – with star player Duggy on the scoresheet. With just minutes left to go, a Wagstaff-inspired Yorkshire got it back to 16-13 and were eyeing a dramatic victory. But Duggy and the rest of the Cumberland forwards would simply not allow it, defending their line with all their might to win the championship in front of their home crowd.

That 1911/12 campaign had also seen the return of the touring Kangaroos in the latest edition of the Ashes series. Obsession with the sport had driven the talent Down Under up dramatically. The squad selection had been opened out to the whole continent of Australasia, so that they could include four impressive New Zealanders, in an attempt to ensure they could at least win their first-ever Ashes Test match following two consecutive 2-0 series defeats. This series would be a best-of-three, with the tourists spending almost six months playing against all of the Northern Union teams as well as representative teams of each of the three main counties and other random friendlies – a total of 36 matches.

Before the first Test, the Australasia squad played 13 warm-up games, losing just one of them – against Wigan at their Central Park home in front of a huge crowd of 25,000. It was a close, low-scoring match, which Wigan won by seven points to two. But this Kangaroo side was impressing all who saw them.

Surprisingly, Duggy was not selected for the first Great Britain showpiece match of the tour: only Waggy and Ben Gronow from the dominant Fartown were in the team that started at St James' Park, Newcastle. Luckily, as they had zero chance to see him play, superstar Albert Rosenfeld was not selected for Australasia.

Whilst the Great Britain players had been playing competitive Northern Union rugby against one another, Australia were training and playing warm-up matches together. They had developed into a superb outfit, and they secured their first Ashes victory with a 19-10 scoreline.

Another ten tour matches would take place before the second Test at the Tynecastle Stadium, Edinburgh. Duggy would get his first taste of playing against the Kangaroos in November 1911 as he represented Cumberland at his hometown Athletic Ground, Maryport. This gave him a chance to go and see family, and the rare opportunity for them to see him in action. He didn't disappoint, putting in a brave, all-action display as his small county lost to the gigantic continent by just five points to two. He would need to wait less than two weeks for his second chance as the Australasia tour rolled into Fartown.

After each tour match, a formal dinner would be held at a local hotel for all the players, coaches and dignitaries of both the Australasians and their hosts. At each of these events, Mr Charles Ford, the manager of the tourists, would give a speech in thanks of the opposition. In his address at The George Hotel, following the encounter at Fartown, he described Huddersfield as 'the finest club side in the world.' He had seen his team dismantled by 21 points to seven, with 17,000 adoring supporters cheering on their heroes against the stars from the other side of the world. He talked in awe of the second try scored by the men in claret and gold, a flowing 12-pass move that featured nine players, including Duggy, Waggy and their very own Rosenfeld.

It was mid-December when Duggy finally made his Great Britain Test match debut in Edinburgh. Excitement and tension had reached its first unbearable high in what was the birth of one of sport's great rivalries. The Australasia victory in the first match of the series had really put the pressure on the Brits. Subsequently, Duggy and Jim Davies had been added to Waggy and Gronow from Huddersfield following their destruction of the new enemy at Fartown.

Despite the bitter Scottish climate being the very opposite to what the Kangaroos were used to, their team were once again magnificently prepared and stoically held out to confirm that they would certainly not be losing the series, as the two sides shared 22 points for a rare draw. The Ashes would be decided on New Year's Day at Villa Park, Birmingham.

A very similar Great Britain line-up was selected to the one that had battled so hard in Edinburgh, including the same four Fartowners. Determined and motivated not to be the first British team to lose a Test match series, they started aggressively and took the game to Australasia. Duggy was instrumental in setting the pace and his power was now well known to the opponents as he was playing his fourth game against them in less than six weeks. He broke the deadlock as he scored his first try for his country. Alf Wood added a second as well as a conversion to take the hosts into an early eight-point lead. But key prop Dick Ramsdale suffered a bad injury and had to retire from the match, leaving Britain a man light (no substitutes in those days). There was still over an hour to play. This lifted Australasia and worried the home side, who instantly felt the pressure. When the tourists ran in a try soon after having a man advantage, they knew the match was theirs to lose, and so it proved. They swarmed Great Britain with wave after wave of attacking rugby and scored nine tries and 33 points to take the Ashes on the month-long sea journey home. It would be over two years before the Northern Union men would be able to make that journey to try and bring them back.

A conscious effort had been made by the Northern Union officials to take the Test matches outside the northern corridor in which they were already so popular, in an attempt to broaden their fanbase. But from a sporting perspective this had backfired as the smaller, less vocal crowds failed to raise their team as much as the packed grounds at the likes of Wigan and Fartown – with both those teams subsequently managing victories over Australasia.

With so many matches played that winter and so many epic encounters, by the end of the tour the Australia (and New Zealand) players and their British counterparts could not have had any more respect for one another. They became the best of friends off the pitch as well as the bitterest of enemies on it. That deepest of rivalries in which each team feel they simply must beat the other survives to this day, well over a century later.

The Fartown momentum rolled on into the 1912/13 campaign. They had taken a tour of South Wales pre-season and came back with the signing of a third Welsh star to add to Ben Gronow and Jim Davies in the diminutive but speedy half-back Johnny Rogers. Major Holland, a 25-year-old full-back from Halifax, was about to start his fifth season with Huddersfield but seemed to have found another gear – he was now the main goal-kicker and had hit brilliant form.

They once again began to go through their opponents like a juggernaut. So too, however, did Wigan and a duopoly was quickly set to establish who the dominant force of the season would be. When Wigan, featuring 38-year-old New Zealand superstar Lance Todd, were welcomed to Fartown for the first meeting of the two in the campaign, it was an eagerly awaited contest. Wigan raced into a 10-3 half-time lead but surprisingly came out defensively in the second period, hoping simply to hang on to their lead. Forty minutes was a long time to hold the Fartowners at bay and they soon scored and converted to make the score 10-8. The Wigan defence held strong. The second-half tactics of Wigan revolved around their best player, Lance Todd, sacrificing himself to perform the main defensive duty – stopping Waggy from dictating play. Todd never left the side of Wagstaff and wrestled him to the ground every time he got the ball. At every scrum, Duggy would win the ball and offload it to Waggy, who would only gain a couple of yards before Todd launched himself straight into the tackle with everything he had.

With a late scrum on the Wigan 25-yard line, Waggy asked how long was left. Arthur Bennett screamed 'Three minutes!' back at him from the touchline. Harold had an idea. He told Major Holland to push further up the field and create an extra attacking presence – there was nothing left to lose. He told Duggy to ensure he won the ball from the scrummage and to play it to him as usual. Duggy did his job. When Waggy received the ball, he instantly spun and ran diagonally rather than forward, leaving Lance Todd in his wake, and the whole pitch opened up. With Todd finally out of the game, Fartown had a man over. That soon turned into two with the onrushing Major Holland finally receiving the ball as he sprinted down the wing to go over and score the try that broke Wigan hearts. It gave the passionate Fartown crowd yet another wonderful winning moment.

The high of that victory came at a cost the following week as they laboured to rekindle any kind of form in the opening round of the Yorkshire Cup in an away match against Hull KR – a game they were expected to win in a very comfortable manner. But Kingston Rovers rose to the occasion and knocked out the defending champions, once more ending their dream of becoming only the second team to win 'All-Four'.

The great team would once again have to settle for three out of four, which, to the delight of everyone concerned and the supporters, included their first-ever Challenge Cup win as they beat Warrington in the final.

The earlier win over Wigan had deflated the Lancastrians and Fartown swept them aside 29-2 in the play-off final to win the Northern Union Championship once again – with Duggy earning the rare distinction of a league championship play-off final hat-trick as he once again proved an unstoppable force.

With the Challenge Cup victory, Douglas Clark had won every honour available to him for both club and county – most of them multiple times over – at just 22 years old.

Albert 'Rozzy' Rosenfeld unbelievably beat his own 78-try haul from the previous season with a tally of 80 – a record that still stands to this day. But the humble Australian gave all the credit to his team-mates, claiming scoring tries was easy in a team featuring the likes of Wagstaff, Longstaff, Gronow and Clark – who himself amassed 20 tries.

Many of the young team had won almost all the sport had to offer them by their early twenties. But they were creating a legacy; they were changing and evolving the sport. Harold Wagstaff, at 22, was widely regarded as the game's greatest exponent. He epitomised what the Cliffords and Arthur Bennett envisaged and enacted it on the field; now captain, he ensured his team did too. They became known as 'The Team that Never Kicks', and if one of the team did punt the ball upfield without due course to do so, he would surely be reprimanded by Waggy. It was here where the true differences in tactics and the subsequent aesthetics between the two codes of rugby emerged. In union, plays regularly and deliberately end in a kick – be it a drop-goal attempt, a penalty or a simple hoof upfield to gain territory. This is largely frowned upon in rugby league, where bamboozling the opponent with swift passing and blistering pace and power to score a try is seen as the only honourable way to play the game.

It was soon time for yet another pre-season as they prepared for the 1913/14 campaign. Again, the Fartowners swore that this would be the time for 'All-Four'. This was a season that would lead to the next Great Britain Ashes tour of Australasia, so all the squad were keen to be in top form and secure their place on the ship. They again raced into a strong position on all fronts, and soon had both the Yorkshire trophies safely back in their ever-expanding cabinet.

As the campaign accelerated towards its finish, excitement was building towards the squad announcement for the Australasia tour. Every player was desperate for the potential once-in-a-lifetime opportunity and to be a member of the team that could wrestle the Ashes back for Great Britain. The first five names selected and assured of their places on the boat were announced. Three of those five were Douglas Clark, Harold Wagstaff and Freddy Longstaff. In the full squad announced shortly afterwards, the tally of Huddersfield players was increased to six as Johnny Rogers, Jack Chilcott and Stanley Moorhouse were added. There was elation from those included but apprehension over an injury in the meantime costing them their place; there was also deep disappointment for those who had missed out.

Who can say which, if any, of the aforementioned feelings influenced the slight downturn in form that followed. They still lost extremely rarely but did unexpectedly lose two key matches – the semi-final of the Challenge Cup against Hull and the play-off final of the Northern Union League Championship against huge underdogs Salford. Yet again, the 'All-Four' had eluded Fartown. Six of the squad, however, could put the disappointment behind them as they headed Down Under.

Little did they know, the peaceful country they were leaving would not be the same once they returned.

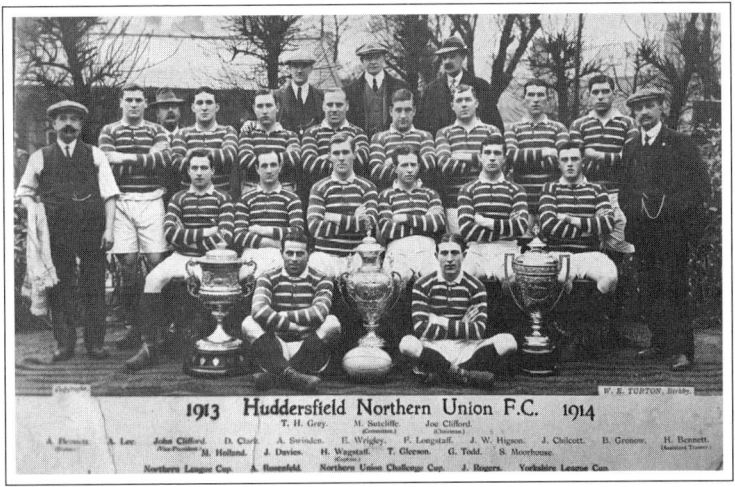

Fartown proudly display their three-trophy haul. Douglas stands alongside his wrestling sparring partner Arthur Swinden

Elizabeth James & Imperial War Museum

4

FREDDY & WAGGY

The 1913 County Championship
deciding match
Cumberland versus Yorkshire
Workington
Cumberland

A game which shall stand at above the rest amongst the
County matches was Yorkshire at Workington 1913.

Longstaff stayed a week with me at home, before the
match, and Wagstaff came through midweek.

Freddy thought he would like a swim in the river Ellen
so into the river Ellen we went.

'Doug, Doug, quick!'

'What's the matter, lad?'

Freddy had grounded upon a hawthorn bush and
it took a few minutes to get him off – that finished his
river swim, so off we went to the sea. Freddy was the first
stripped. He had just got up to his ankles when another
great yell saw Freddy jumping about and racing to his
clothes; a piece of seaweed had got round his feet and
Fred thought it was a crab, remarking: 'I don't want
to swim today.'

Wagstaff and Longstaff stayed with me at Ellenborough
the day before the match. A friend took us to Silloth where
we had dinner. Wagstaff took over the job of cutting the

bread. The knife slipped and caught his finger and gave him a nasty cut to the bone from which he lost a lot of blood – that spoiled the dinner. Coming back at night the motor ran out of petrol and we had to push it up the hills – a really splendid finish.

On Saturday mother wanted to know what we generally played on. I told her, 'Plenty of steak and be sure to get plenty for Waggy and Longstaff, anything from one to one-and-a-half pounds each – they are big fellows you know mother, and they can eat.'

I told Freddy and Waggy that if they didn't want to offend mother they were to let her see that they enjoyed her food and her cooking.

Dinner arrived, mother put them about one-and-a-half steaks each on their plates. Half an hour afterwards I came down and saw old Waggy nearly black in the face.

'Doug, I cannot eat any more – I'm full.'

'For heaven's sake Harold, eat it up or mother will be cross!'

After a struggle Waggy managed it, of course. Freddy soon polished his share off. Then Waggy wanted a shave, but with his injury to his finger he couldn't manage, so I volunteered to do the job for him. I shaved one side when I noticed we only had 15 minutes to catch the train and a mile to go to the railway station, so I left it at that and made a run for the train. Waggy took a tumble, and said, 'I believe you planned on giving me all that steak so that I cannot run!'

We met the Yorkshire party coming through from Carlisle and didn't they laugh when they saw Waggy with half a beard and the dried soap still on his face. The Yorkshire party were very confident of success; anything from 20 to 30 points. We brought Tom Fletcher into the centre position to watch Wagstaff; he was 47 years old and

The 'Prince of Centres' Harold Wagstaff
Elizabeth James & Imperial War Museum

performed his task manfully and scored a splendid try, playing a great game.

What with Fletcher and the steak, poor old Waggy had a hot time. It was very amusing for me to hear the Yorkshire lads discussing before the match what they were going to do with their medals. Carmichael of Kingston Rovers was going to give his to his wife, others to their sisters.

I, to the amusement of all, reminded them that 'there is many a slip 'twixt cup and lip'. They did laugh, they hadn't seen me sitting there. They said, 'Now Duggy, surely you don't think you have a chance today?'

'Wait and see,' I said.

Cumberland had a players' meeting before turning out. I informed them that Yorkshire thought they had a soft job on.

We decided to make it a forward game, keeping the ball in the second row. We absolutely walked through the Yorkshire pack time and time again.

Poor old Freddy, I think, swore as he had never done before and used anything but complimentary language to his colleagues. The crack Yorkshire back never saw the ball, consequently Cumberland gained a great victory that is still talked about until this day.

'A Few Training Hints'
by Douglas Clark

Training for football should be commenced, particularly in the case of a heavyweight, two months before the opening of a season, and for a middleweight, six weeks. In the case of the former, it is a risky business to become too far out of condition at any time, especially if nearing the end of a career.

Up to the age of say 32, the cartilaginous muscles between the ribs are soft and pliable and permit an easy expansion of the chest. Beyond that age, however, these cartilages become hard, and set.

One of the main things to cultivate at all times, therefore, is a regular practice of deep breathing. Form the habit of walking heel to toe with body erect. Swing arms from the shoulders in breathing slowly through the nose. Fill the lungs to their fullest capacity, then release the breath slowly through the mouth, making sure that the lungs are absolutely empty before again in-breathing. Gradually increase the distance walked, keeping up the breathing exercise. This is a fine thing, even for businessmen, who have passed the time of life when active participation in football is possible. Having made sure that the lungs are now in good order, the more serious and exacting side of training may be commenced. First, put on, next to the skin, some heavy woollens. Jog-trot a mile round the track. Then walk quarter-of-a-mile (follow breathing instructions as before), and afterwards trot another quarter-of-a-mile. Perspiration should now be flowing freely, and this should be encouraged by a not too vigorous exercise, and then the use of the hammer.

Obtain a hard log of wood, having its surface say one foot from the ground. The hammer should weigh about two pounds. Swing the hammer full length of your right arm, hitting the log a hard blow, at the same time stepping forward, with right foot. Change hands, stepping back a yard. Swing hammer full extent of left arm, from behind, over stomach. Continue this exercise until tired (not exhausted). Then retire to the dressing room, which should be warm, and remain there resting until perspiration ceases.

The whole length of time taken up by this method of training, from the jog-trot onwards, should be about one-and-a-half hours. Continue these exercises three times per week for three weeks and add physical 'jerks'. A Turkish bath at this period, once a week, until within fourteen days

Douglas Clark proudly represented his beloved Cumberland
Elizabeth James & Imperial War Museum

of the season, is very beneficial. Then become accustomed to running in pumps. Knock off supper. This is the meal that often causes most damage to a man in training. There is often enough a tendency towards fat-producing as a result of supper, the body afterwards, in sleep, being in repose. Drink little or no liquid during a meal.

Continue sprinting in pumps until it is possible to do three sprints, say of 60 yards, all out. From the Thursday (the last day of the week for training) take matters easily.

When fit and playing every week, men following an everyday occupation require very little training. Personally, I prefer to be a little under rather than over-trained. In the former case a player improves as the game proceeds. In the latter case, a man needs rest in plenty. As the season approaches, players should be on the field on Tuesday evenings (light permitting) practising passing and repassing, covering two or three times the length of the field. The forwards should practise dribbling, and the goal-kicker is very often a match winner. Try any new methods suggested at players' meetings.

On the Thursday, three 60-yard sprints, in spikes and a good 220 yards, followed by a few minutes with the punchball, should complete training.

One more point, and a most important one. When away from the ground, see to it that you refrain from doing anything which would be likely to undo any of the benefit you have derived in training. An hour of careless living can upset a week's hard training and make a man a weak link in his team. The meal before a match should be of a light nature and taken, say, about 12.30 to one o'clock. Fresh fish or a small steak or chop with cold toast. If fish is partaken of, then tea to follow, and after a meat diet, then coffee.

Make a practice of retiring to bed in decent time. This is the most important rule to observe.

5

RORKE'S DRIFT

4 July 1914
Australia versus Great Britain
Sydney Cricket Ground
New South Wales
Australia

GREAT BRITAIN captain Harold Wagstaff and Douglas Clark walked side by side down the long, dark tunnel – the light at the end of which was blinding. The sound coming from behind them was of their 11 team-mates; the metallic clapping of their football boot studs against the concrete floor. Ahead of them, the roaring crescendo of 35,000 frantic Australian supporters echoed down the tunnel as they sang along to the live band who were playing out their boys in their (then) traditional claret and blue jerseys to 'See the Conquering Heroes Come'.

Each proudly wearing the British red and white hooped shirts, black shorts and red socks, the 13 men remained in the tunnel, silent in stoic concentration and resolve.

'I've never been so thrilled for a game, Doug,' Harold said, breaking the silence.

'Me either, Waggy. We simply have to win.'

The singing stopped as the song faded out and the cheering turned into chants of 'Blue, Blue, Blue'. The band then struck up the introduction of 'Boys of the Bulldog Breed' – the British lads' cue to enter the fray. The cheers turned to boos. Nervous chills ran down the spines of the players as they finally walked out and the bright sunshine forced their eyes to squint and the cauldron of noise exploded into their ears.

It had all started very differently almost three months earlier, when the team delegation set sail on two separate ships – the Fartown players on a later boat due to their domestic cup final commitments. There was one more warm and familiar face for the six Fartown players – John Clifford, the Huddersfield vice-president, had joined Joe Houghton of St Helens to make up the tour management team. For many, this was the first time they had left the north of England, and it was effectively a world tour.

I know we were like a lot of schoolboys; curious, excited, bubbling over with joy of healthy youth and always in for an innocuous lark whenever the opportunity arose. There is always a leg-puller among a party of tourists and we had many.

Our club team being in the finals, we had to stay behind and take part in the match; the rest of the touring party having sailed some ten days before us in the charge of Mr Houghton.

Our party consisted of Mr John Clifford, team manager, captain Harold Wagstaff, Moorhouse, Rogers, Longstaff, Chilcott and myself.

We had a fairly good crossing, I remember before leaving Dover we were keen to know the nationality of every ship in the harbour. One ship's colours puzzled us. Suddenly poor old Freddy Longstaff called out, 'I know 'em. Amber and Black – it's Bradford Northern!'

The railway journey from Calais to Paris was very enjoyable, also the few hours in Paris, then the ride along the Seine Valley through the beautiful vineyards.

Of course, the main object of the trip is to play football and jolly hard football it is, against opponents as fit as it is possible to get men – hard as nails and keen as mustard. I have often heard our lads remark how sore they felt the day after a game with the Aussies. Oh yes – they like a bit of the rough stuff right enough. When such games are played on the hard Australian grounds, he is a lucky man that leaves the field with a whole skin.

The boat stopped at Naples, where the team visited the ruins of Pompeii. They watched in nervous silence as they passed the violently active volcano Stromboli in the dead of night.

They docked at Port Said, Egypt for a few nights before being awestruck heading down the Suez Canal – one of the great engineering feats of the 19th century – which connects the Mediterranean and Red seas. These were young men who were destined to be coal miners and factory workers were it not for their skill with the oval-shaped ball. Now they were wandering through the desert markets, bartering with the Egyptian stall-holders for lightweight clothes suitable for the warmer climes they had never experienced before.

'What a wonderful education travel is,' Harold Wagstaff would later say when talking of the trip.

The players invited the other ferry passengers to join in the sporting leagues they had organised for the month-long journey to keep themselves active and their competitive instincts lucid. They would play cricket and blindfold boxing on the deck and billiards and card games in the bar. Cabaret acts performed of an evening and the members of the team who fancied themselves as crooners would soon be on stage with the entertainment.

Colombo, Sri Lanka was the last stopover before the ship finally docked in Australia.

The tourists were afforded a couple of weeks' training to work off their sea legs and acclimatise to the heat and humidity.

They were even offered up an amateur South Australia representative side as cannon fodder, and they duly ran in 101 points against them to get their confidence up. But they were still not fit enough and felt sluggish. The first two tour matches were disastrous defeats in front of huge crowds, who jeered and taunted the struggling Brits.

John Clifford, Joe Houghton and Harold Wagstaff held a meeting and decided to double the training sessions to morning and afternoon rather than one or the other, and have lunch brought to them in between. Not only did this serve to lengthen and intensify the training, it kept the team all together and meant the management could choose what the players ate.

Understanding that they could come away with embarrassingly heavy losses in the Test matches if things didn't improve quickly, the players raised their levels accordingly. With the troubled beginning of the tour mostly put down to travel and logistical issues outside the control of the British delegation, they asked the New South Wales Rugby League (NSWRL) – the Australian Rugby League authority in charge of the tour – if they could postpone the first Ashes match by one week to give themselves a chance of being fully fit. The request was granted and it was assumed that the second Test match would subsequently be put back. It wasn't – leaving the two games just two days apart. With such a limited-sized squad up against an association with a whole nation to choose from, this was a major disadvantage to the tourists. The third and final Test was scheduled for mid-August, once Great Britain had returned from the New Zealand leg of their tour.

Performance levels improved and they gained comfortable wins in the next four warm-up matches. But the tour was already taking its injury toll as the opponents in these so-called warm-up matches took their opportunity to help their nation's Test team by depleting the strength of any first-choice Brits they happened to come up against. When the day of the first

Test match arrived, 27 June, both regular full-backs, Alf Wood (broken nose) and Bill Jarman (fractured rib), were unavailable.

Five Fartowners (Duggy, Longstaff and skipper Waggy, as well as Stanley Moorhouse and Jack Chilcott) swapped the claret and gold for the red and white as 40,000 jeering Australians welcomed them out at the Royal Agricultural Showground, Sydney.

After mere minutes, Great Britain were awarded a penalty kick just inside their own half of the field. Fred Longstaff placed the ball in preparation for an audacious attempt at goal. The crowd scoffed at what they deemed arrogance to even consider the shot. But their jeers turned to silence as Freddy sent the ball high into the sky and 40,000 faces looked upwards as they watched the ball zero in on the sticks before sailing through the centre of them.

With the spectators disarmed and the British team in full flow, there was only going to be one outcome: a relatively untroubled victory. The Huddersfield contingent scored 15 of the points in the 23-5 triumph, with Duggy scoring one of the tries. But the 1-0 series scoreline was going to be tough to defend as it had come at the cost of further injuries and, with the second Test just two days later, there was no hope of recovery.

The following day, long political tensions in Europe erupted when Austria-Hungary heir Archduke Franz Ferdinand was assassinated whilst on a diplomatic visit to the Bosnian capital, Sarajevo.

Back in Australia, a Great Britain team was scraped together made up of those who still were able to stand. They took to the field at the Sydney Cricket Ground for the second Ashes Test match. A resilient and battling effort saw them lose 12-7. The series was level and would all come down to the deciding Test on 14 August at Melbourne Cricket Ground, once they returned from the New Zealand leg of the tour. It meant a whole six weeks for many of the injuries to heal.

But before setting sail to New Zealand, the relentless schedule continued. On the Saturday following the back-to-back Test matches, 4 July, they were to play a tour match against New South Wales – again at the Sydney Cricket Ground. In between, on the Thursday, they were obliged to take a team on the 260-mile round trip to Bathurst, where they would play against a NSW Western Districts team. It was decided that John Clifford would take the freshest 13 men remaining from the beleaguered squad to honour that commitment, while Joe Houghton would stay in Sydney with the rest of the recuperating first team. Clifford's men would be gone Wednesday to Friday, and some of those travelling would be forced to play again on the Saturday.

Whilst the touring party were comfortably putting Western Districts to the sword, Joe Houghton received a telegram back in Sydney. He simply could not believe what he was reading as the text in front of him, from NSWRL, announced that the Saturday match versus New South Wales had been directly swapped with the final Test match. The Ashes decider would take place in just two days' time. That meant that the entire series – the jewel in the crown of the five-month tour – would have taken place over just one week. In that time, the already injury-ravaged squad would have played four matches. Two of the three Tests would have been played at Sydney Cricket Ground, the favoured 'home' of Australia, where they get the most vociferous support.

The rage of Clifford and Houghton cannot be underestimated. They begged for compromise, offering logistical solutions on both date and venue, but their requests were rebuffed. The Great Britain management duo made their annoyance heard and, subsequently, NSWRL secretary Ted Larkin felt the need to telegram his Northern Union counterpart, Joe Platt, so that their side of the increasingly heated debate was known back in England. He explained that in August there was the Australia versus New Zealand Rugby Union tour and the Australian Rules Football carnival taking place; he didn't want the deciding Test to be overlooked by the supporters and the press.

The management and players knew the truth – the NSWRL had underestimated the wave of public attention on a potential deciding final Test when planning the schedule, and were now worried about the financial revenue of the major event being limited as a result of clashing with the other, traditionally bigger, sports (at the time). But the decision was grossly unfair on a sportsmanship level and hugely different to the way Northern Union felt they had always treated the Australians when they were hosting.

'We confidently anticipate that the best traditions of Northern Union will be upheld by you. We hope that you will expend every atom of energy and skill you possess to secure victory; failing which, we hope you will lose like sportsmen.' John Clifford read out the cabled message from home to his wounded and dejected troops in the hotel lobby. The match would be played.

Barely a word was spoken around the team dinner table that evening. Those injured were inconsolable that they would miss the biggest match of their careers and the chance to bring the Ashes back to Britain. Those who were carrying injuries but playing anyway were worried about letting themselves and the team down while performing at less than fully fit. But everyone around the table was feeling a burning sense of injustice. Duggy was one of the few who had some real fight left in him, and he was concerned about the mental state of his team-mates – they did not seem prepared for the battle that lay ahead of them. This was the biggest and most eagerly awaited match in the young life of rugby league.

When the squad retired from the dinner table to the bar for a nightcap, Duggy sneaked off to the exotic animal shop across the road from the hotel. He had noticed previously that it stayed open late. There, he struck a deal with the eccentric shopkeeper to hire, just until closing time, the huge domesticated snake on display in the window, which measured 6ft 4in in length.

Duggy carried the giant reptile back over the road and through the hotel lobby in a brown sack, which moved sinisterly from the inside. He took his seat at the end of the group, who were mostly quiet and solemnly stirring their after-dinner coffees. With the sack sat on the floor, he guided the snake out and sent it slithering between his comrades. Within seconds, the mighty athletes were screaming and crashing around and climbing on the seats and the tables.

Duggy casually walked into the path of the snake and allowed it to re-enter the sack, which he then threw over his shoulder before turning to his aghast team-mates. 'Those 13 Aussies on a football field don't seem too scary all of a sudden, do they?'

Realising it was a ruse all along, the whole delegation burst into laughter and began to mock one another over their individual terrified reactions. The mood had been lifted.

The following day, the best 13 men available were in the changing room at the Sydney Cricket Ground. There had to be five changes through injury from the team that battled so valiantly in the second Test – Freddy Longstaff crucially amongst those missing.

They proudly pulled on the red and white jerseys. They tightly fastened their dark brown leather boots.

'You are playing a game of football this afternoon,' John Clifford began in a speech aimed at rallying his combatants, 'but more than that you are playing for Great Britain, and even more than that, you are playing for right versus wrong. You will win because you have to win. Don't forget the message from home – England expects every one of you to do his duty.' The men clenched their fists with excitement.

'Yes lads, and she will not be disappointed,' captain Wagstaff followed up, lighting a fire in the bellies of his compatriots. And with that, they made their way to the tunnel.

Australia	Number	Great Britain
Howard Hallett	1	Alf Wood
Bob Tidyman	2	Frank Williams
Wally Messenger	3	Harold Wagstaff (c)
Sid Deane (c)	4	Billy Hall
Dan Frawley	5	William Davies
Charles Fraser	6	Stuart Prosser
Arthur Halloway	7	Fred Smith
Billy Cann	8	Arthur Johnson
Bob Craig	9	Douglas Clark
Con Sullivan	10	Dave Holland
Frank Burge	11	Percy Coldrick
Sandy Pearce	12	Dick Ramsdale
Ed Courtney	13	Jack Chilcott

Of all the footy matches I have taken part in, none stands out as clear as the glorious third and final Test match for the Ashes, played at Sydney Cricket Ground in 1914. Everything depended on this game: the happiness of the tour, all that we had come for was at stake. The position of playing a Test match with many of our best injured had been forced upon us and every man determined that, come what may, England must win – we would play until we dropped.

From the first scrum the Aussies had the ball, found touch in our 25. The second scrum saw Halloway in possession, a side slip and he was through, Coldrick and I tackling him first as he was diving for the line – where the other boys came from is a mystery. Halloway found himself back in his own half. Yes – this was going to be some game.

The evil genius still pursued our team. We had not been playing 20 minutes when we lost Williams with a wrested knee. Poor Frank, he had tears in his eyes as they carried him off. The crowd counted him out boxing fashion: 'ONE, TWO, THREE, FOUR, FIVE, SIX, SEVEN, EIGHT, NINE, OUT! BLUE! BLUE! BLUE!'

The Aussies were having most of the ball.

Williams returned to the fray. We commenced to get the ball and with well-judged kicks to touch Freddie Smith gained us a lot of ground at one period; he was handing the Australians off clean on to their back as fast as they came for him, but the Aussies worked back to our line.

This time lads, we had the ball, all the forwards came away in a body, took the ball and men with them three parts the length of the field, even the shouts of 'Blue, Blue' could not help Australia. We were slowly but surely wearing 'em down. What a game Waggy was playing. He had never played like this, the same could be said of all the boys. Will Hall put a beautiful cross kick over to Davies and Holland, who dribbled straight for the line. It was a race between them, Tidyman, Fraser and Courtney, but Davies dived and scored a grand try, just saving the ball from going dead.

Alf Wood had kicked a good goal from a penalty early on. He repeated it twice, giving us a useful lead of nine points to nil.

Then Australia gave a bit of their best from a short kick; Cann picked up, bowled over one of our forwards, gave the dummy to Waggy, but Waggy made him bite the dust, but not before it went to Halloway, who transferred it to Messenger, who flung himself over at the corner for a great try, but his goal kick failed.

Yes, legendary Aussie centre Wally Messenger scored a priceless try late in the dying embers of the first period to

A young Douglas Clark and Ben Gronow
Elizabeth James & Imperial War Museum

reduce the tourists' surprise half-time lead to nine points to three.

> *Right from the kick-off second half I had the misfortune to break my middle finger while tackling Hallett but managed to keep on.*
>
> *The Australian pack entered the second half as though bent upon winning at all hazards; they looked as though they were going to carry all before them. But our boys stuck to their guns and when they showed signs of tiring we ran to force matters. Tackling – I never saw anything like it – anything above grass had to go down.*
>
> *The sun was terribly hot. When the ambulance men came to attend to injured men, the players squeezed the trainer's sponge to wet their parched lips.*
>
> *Williams had received another nasty knock and had to return off. Waggy asked for a special effort: 'A try will settle them,' he kept saying.*
>
> *The Australian crowd were going mad. Talk about a yell, 'Blue, Blue, Blue.' One could scarcely hear the whistle.*
>
> *We had the ball; Freddie Smith hands Fraser right on to his back and he is through, gives the ball to Hall who, when challenged, gives it to Waggy. The Aussies are all closing in on him. Our captain, with one of his side-slipping wriggles, changed the play right across the field through his forwards – all of them handled. We just failed to score – really the nicest moment of the match, but they can tackle! A case of 'Jack being as good as his master'.*

Early in that second period, following a neat passage of play from the tourists, Duggy appeared to be racing clear towards the try line to extend the British lead. He was unfortunate that the man chasing him was the rapid Australian Arthur Halloway. As Halloway gained ground, Duggy didn't want to perform his usual powerful hand-off, fearing that his broken finger may prevent him from getting enough power behind it to see off his foe. Instead, he decided to put faith in his speed and try to make it to the line before being caught. As he drove for the line, the heroic Halloway made a strong tackle on an off-balance Duggy and the two men crashed to the floor in a heap. As Duggy rose to his feet, it was clear to all that his immense shoulder was not positioned where it should be – it was either broken or dislocated. He was taken to the sidelines but no one could snap the shoulder back into place. Fearing for his team, who were already a man light, Duggy told them to strap it as best they could to keep it stable and he would go back out like that.

Every second felt like an eternity. The Australians were coming forward with wave after wave of attack, but the British defence stood strong and would not allow them over the white line. Every tackle that Duggy made forced the whole stadium to wince at the thought of the agony he was in. Eventually, his captain and close friend Waggy told him that enough was enough. His team-mates carried him away from the action and Duggy sobbed as he had to leave the field of play.

> *I was thrown on to my shoulder and received a badly wrenched shoulder coming into contact with the ground. They counted me out – I tried to play on but I was useless and had to retire.*
>
> *England had only nine points lead and two men down. They were 11 against 13. They were up against it and all that was in them, not merely as players, but as men of mettle, real grit, that quality that won't be conquered and the spirit to face overpowering odds, was to come out.*
>
> *The crowd on the hill had been a bit quiet but suddenly woke up. 'We'll win it yet!' they roared. 'Blue, Blue, Blue. Come on Australia!' What a shout, it shook the stands.*

11 men against 13, they cannot stand up to it, England must be beaten. It was in these moments that the genius of Wagstaff manifested itself – cool and collected as he was in everything. Taking the ball from the feet of the Australians, tackling as though he loved it, giving orders, always doing the right thing at the right time. Waggy had put Johnson on the wing. Our boys had pinned the Aussies on their line. Chilcott grabbed a loose pass sent out by Deane and was almost over when Tidyman relieved him of the ball and kicked for the open.

Within moments, there was more desperate and heroic defending as the British troops crashed in against their enemies, and once again ended as a pile of fallen bodies atop the oval ball. But on this occasion, Billy Hall did not return to his feet – he had taken a blow to the head and was knocked unconscious. Great Britain would have to play the final 30 minutes against the 13 of Australia with just ten men. But one of those men was the imperious Harold Wagstaff. With his team under the most severe pressure and completely enclosed into their own half – and mostly on the very edge of their own try line – Waggy was simply everywhere.

The situation was eerily similar to what they had faced in Birmingham two and a half years earlier, when they capitulated and lost the Ashes for the first time. The same must not happen again.

With 20 minutes remaining, the crowd began to show the first signs of nervous concern that their team may fail to turn the scoreline around. Waggy managed to break with the ball and beat two men before offloading to 'Chick' Johnson, who was still playing out of position on the wing following the early injury to Frank Williams.

Johnson stormed up the wing with the ball. Australia, having sacrificed some defensive positions in piling on the attacking pressure, were caught cold. With defenders finally closing in on him, Johnson dropped the ball to the floor as he entered the Australia 25-yard line and skilfully dribbled it around each and every one and all the way to the try line to score spectacularly. Alf Wood converted to make his fourth kick of the match – all the while sporting a broken nose. The 35,000 crowd were stunned into silence.

Johnson dribbled all the way from the 25, touched down and Wood's kick made England 14-3. Our boys nearly went mad; the reserves and the injured, I mean.

England's period of trial had begun for quarter of an hour. A remnant of a team stood along its line and met charge after charge. Alf Wood was wonderful, the same might be said of all. How they played. At every stop in the game all eyes went to the clock. From a forward rush, Waggy went down with a zig-zag run and took play into their half, and we breathed again.

The Aussies were on our line again, the crowd tried to spur them on with their 'Blue, Blue, Blue.' Australia brought Cann out of the pack, he tried time after time to break through, but Prosser and Freddy Smith brought him down.

The Aussies lost their heads, it was just wildness that spoiled their efforts time and time again. The ten men were doing a wonderful show. Twice Wood had to kick over his own line to save. Fortune was with those grand lads.

England and Waggy – the crowd had come round; they could not but admire our pluck.

The ten-man defensive masterclass continued and the mood completely changed inside the stadium. The astounded Australian supporters began to respectfully cheer every British tackle. A late Sid Deane try only served to make the scoreline even remotely respectable.

When the referee finally blew for full time, Great Britain had secured a 14-6 victory and safe passage for the Ashes back home to the Northern Union.

Fully aware of the spectacular display they had witnessed, the 35,000 gave the shattered team a standing ovation.

JC Davis, editor of the Sydney *Referee*, wrote:

I have never seen the bulldog tenacity, the courage and heroic skill of the Englishmen that afternoon surpassed on the football field. That day Wagstaff, the English captain, played with inspiration that left upon my memory that it was the most wonderful game any man has ever played in the face of colossal odds.

Wagstaff, always a great player, that day became the ubiquitous, and the king of the game.

In 1879, during the war between the British Empire and the Zulu Kingdom, around 150 British troops successfully defended the station of Rorke's Drift against wave after wave of relentless attacks by over 3,000 Zulu warriors in one of the greatest defensive military operations in history. The deciding 1914 Ashes rugby league game is now known as the fabled 'Rorke's Drift Test Match'. It is still talked about over 100 years later and is widely regarded as the sport's greatest-ever match and individual team performance.

Great Britain won every match of their tour of New Zealand, concluding on 1 August with a victory over the Kiwis themselves.

They then returned to Australia to finally play the tour match against New South Wales that had been postponed to make way for the third Test match. A hard-fought triumph rounded off the epic and legendary tour in the middle of August before they set sail for home with the Ashes safely aboard the ship.

Whilst the squad were celebrating their historic achievements, they were blissfully unaware that on the side of the world they would soon return to, something was happening that would change all of their lives forever. Since the assassination of Archduke Franz Ferdinand and following a series of declarations and ultimatums, Austria-Hungary had declared war on Serbia.

In support of Serbia, Russia had declared a mobilisation of forces against Austria-Hungary. German *Kaiser* Wilhelm II responded by issuing an ultimatum to both Russia and France, who he also saw as potential allies to the Serbs, to remain neutral and demobilise. When the desired responses were not received – also on 1 August whilst Duggy and his team-mates were playing against New Zealand – Germany declared war on Russia and implemented their *Schlieffen Plan*, which saw their armed forces split and begin to invade both to the east and to the west. The majority of the German troops would head west to quickly defeat France, then they would join the smaller force that would already have engaged the Russians to the east, defeat them and win the war, expanding their empire in the process. Britain was politically active in the conflict, but far from militarily engaged and yet to formally ally with France and Russia.

On 3 August, the German Empire officially declared war on France as their troops marched towards the country. They had already occupied Luxembourg and demanded an unimpeded path through Belgium – which was refused. The following day, Germany invaded Belgium, whose King Albert ordered his small military to resist their advances and sent out calls for assistance under the 1839 Treaty of London, which forced all of the powerful European countries to respect Belgian neutrality in any future conflicts. Germany was now in direct contravention of this agreement. British Prime Minister Herbert Henry Asquith urged Wilhelm II to reconsider advancement through Belgium. Following what was deemed an 'unsatisfactory response', on the evening of 4 August 1914, the Great War was upon us.

6

THE TEAM OF ALL TALENTS

Late October 1914
39 Clough Road
Birkby
Huddersfield

DOUGLAS CLARK stood and stared at the modest, beige-bricked terraced house that he had not seen since he left it six months earlier full of youthful excitement and vigour. Seeing it once again, he realised how much life had changed since he last stood on that square foot of concrete that formed the entrance to the alleyway that led to the back of the terrace, which the house shared with number 41.

Whilst he didn't feel like one in that particular moment, he had become a national sporting hero. He had seen parts of the world he thought only existed in books and fantasy. He had experienced blistering highs and crushing lows, the kind of which he never thought possible on a rugby field. He believed he had fought and won the most important battle Great Britain would face in that year, and yet he had returned home to a country at war.

He carried a newspaper under his arm as he walked down the dark alley to the back door. He felt a warm, comforting feeling as he heard the usual chatter and homely noise of the Hodgsons from inside the house.

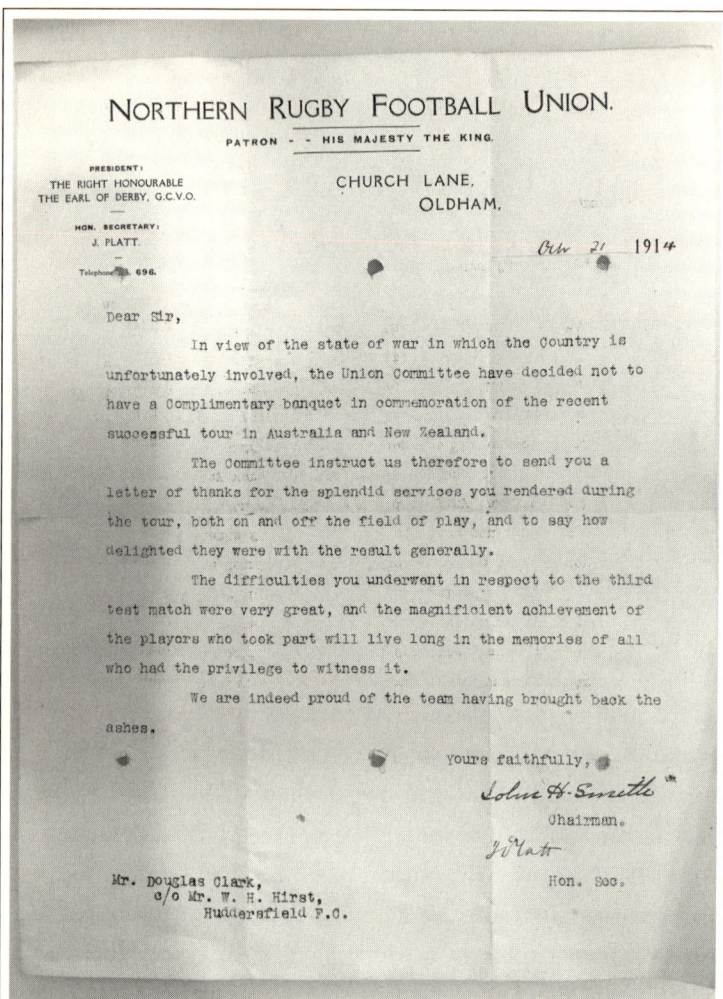

NORTHERN RUGBY FOOTBALL UNION.

PATRON - - HIS MAJESTY THE KING.

PRESIDENT:
THE RIGHT HONOURABLE
THE EARL OF DERBY, G.C.V.O.

CHURCH LANE,
OLDHAM,

HON. SECRETARY:
J. PLATT.

Telephone 696.

Oct 21 1914

Dear Sir,

In view of the state of war in which the Country is unfortunately involved, the Union Committee have decided not to have a Complimentary banquet in commemoration of the recent successful tour in Australia and New Zealand.

The Committee instruct us therefore to send you a letter of thanks for the splendid services you rendered during the tour, both on and off the field of play, and to say how delighted they were with the result generally.

The difficulties you underwent in respect to the third test match were very great, and the magnificient achievement of the players who took part will live long in the memories of all who had the privilege to witness it.

We are indeed proud of the team having brought back the ashes.

Yours faithfully,

John H. Smith
Chairman.

J. Platt
Hon. Sec.

Mr. Douglas Clark,
c/o Mr. W. H. Hirst,
Huddersfield F.C.

Elizabeth James & Imperial War Museum

It had been almost three months since he had broken his finger and dislocated his shoulder, and he had not played rugby at all in that time. He had not wrestled in far longer. His injuries had still not completely healed as he and the rest of the squad had tried – with the limited facilities aboard – to get themselves fit on the ship home, all eagerly awaiting getting straight back into Northern Union action with their club team-mates (the 1914/15 season was already under way). They had all been relieved to hear that, despite the struggles of a collapsing wartime economy closing down many businesses and industries, professional sport had been encouraged to continue as normal – being regarded as one of the few things that may keep up the spirits of the local communities. They were all still professional rugby players – for now at least.

Mrs Hodgson heard him coming down the path and gleefully opened the back door and welcomed him home with a congratulatory hug. Mr Hodgson proudly shook his hand.

The family and current lodgers sat around in the living room with bated breath, eager to be entertained by Duggy's tales of globetrotting, gruesome injury and glory. Mrs Hodgson showed him to the freshly brewed pot of English tea – something he had dearly missed – and the mountain of letters, cards of congratulation and numerous weekly editions of the local newspaper the *Huddersfield Examiner*. As he glanced at them, he couldn't help but notice the headlines paying homage to himself and his friends Harold Wagstaff and Fred Longstaff. They were the pride of the town. He picked up one letter that looked important, the envelope stamped by the Northern Union. It was near the top of the pile, so clearly recent – he desperately hoped they were not cancelling the season because of the war. He was relieved to read that all they were cancelling was the planned banquet for the returning Ashes heroes.

Finally, he was able to read for himself what was going on with his country at war. A cold chill ran down his spine, but he wasn't sure if that was the terribly cold temperature in comparison to what he had experienced the previous few months, or the trepidation of what he was about to read.

He read how the 'Allied Powers' of the British Empire, France and Belgium, had successfully resisted the German invasion into France, but that they were now settling into a violent and bloody battle of trench warfare. He read in horror that almost half a million people had already been killed in the fighting (mostly French soldiers) in less than two months. Germany's 'Western Front' was slowly advancing towards the French border, with the presence of British troops increasing by the day. Relentless shrapnel shell projectiles were the destructive weapon of choice – a missile that could travel over 5,000 metres, with a fuse set to explode the device as it approached its destination in a downward trajectory; upon explosion, around 300 lead balls (effectively bullets) would rain down venomously on the opposing frontline, ripping through the flesh of soldiers and horses and destroying camps and equipment. In addition, there was continuous gunshot fire from rifles and machine guns, and mines were exploding after being strategically placed both above and below ground.

It was harrowing reading for the quiet and gentlemanly Duggy, who strongly believed the only fighting in life should be done in the name of sport – and always end in a friendly handshake.

The following day, Duggy walked the one mile from his Birkby home to the Fartown Ground for training and to be reunited with his old team-mates and the backroom staff. He, Waggy and the other Great Britain tourists shared their anecdotes of worldly travel, sporting heroism and camaraderie – as well as a giant snake – to the delight of their awestruck friends and colleagues, who were grateful for the stars' return, having already lost one of the opening four league games of the season. The training session showed that almost two months without rugby – three in the case of Duggy – had made them a little rusty and lacking fitness and the sharp edge that had set them apart from the rest within the Northern Union. Despite his best efforts, it was clear that Duggy was still injured and was subsequently declared unavailable for the upcoming match. Freddy Longstaff, too, was unable to be selected – he was serving a suspension enforced by the Northern Union following an 'incident' in the final match of the New Zealand tour.

Fartown made the long trip for a tough away match against Barrow that weekend, and slumped to another defeat – with their returning leading men sluggish and unable to reignite themselves to their blistering best. With two defeats already, 'All-Four' was further out of reach than ever.

But once again, the adversity in defeat served as the catalyst the Fartown boys needed. They trained hard, regained their sharpness and went on a magnificent run of form. By the turn of the year into 1915, they had retained the Yorkshire League with ease and the Yorkshire Cup with even greater comfort – thrashing Hull 31-0 in the final.

With the Fartowners in full flow, most Northern Union teams went into their matches with Huddersfield knowing they were already beaten, so would instead attempt to turn the game into a more violent affair. In February 1915, they travelled to Bramley. Frustrated at being embarrassed repeatedly by the skill of Waggy, Bramley's Anderson twice put crunching tackles in on him off the ball, and finally swung a fist at him – all in the first half. Waggy refused to rise to the bait and continued instead to run rings around all-comers. Fred Longstaff, however, looked on angrily and in the second half played closer to Anderson and awaited an opportunity for revenge. The chance arose and Freddy crashed into Anderson to add to his humiliation. Pushed over the edge, Anderson began to rain down blows on Longstaff, who was not so shy about returning fists back at him. Anderson came off worse in that battle too, as well as seeing his team on the end of a 79-0 thrashing.

In the two Northern Union flagship competitions, both of which had eluded Huddersfield the previous campaign, their resurgence had sent them to the top of the league and into the Challenge Cup Final, where they sensationally crushed St Helens 37-3 to regain the trophy – their third of the campaign. 'All-Four' was not just back on, it seemed the only outcome possible as Fartown swept all before them in a blaze of attacking and scintillating rugby. Just as with Great Britain in Australia, Harold Wagstaff was their talismanic captain and genius playmaker, Douglas Clark the powerhouse who drove them forward and Fred Longstaff the hard-tackling defensive rock.

Leeds had found a similar vein of form towards the end of the season, even managing to hold Huddersfield to a draw in their league match and finishing the campaign in third position. Fartown finished atop the league and so played fourth-placed Hull in the play-off semi-final, enjoying another straightforward victory to book a place in the final.

In-form Leeds gave stalwarts Wigan a sound thrashing in the other semi-final to set up a grandstand final at Wakefield's Belle Vue.

Following the draw in the league match and the current confidence of Leeds, there was sudden doubt within the press and the Northern Union fanbase over Huddersfield winning the finale. It was deemed a 50/50 match – with all the pressure on the Fartown boys to complete the clean sweep that had so cruelly eluded them in their recent years of domination.

With less than 20 miles separating them, the grand final between the West Yorkshire rivals became the most eagerly anticipated match in the 20-year history of the Northern Union.

To relax themselves the evening before the final, Waggy and Freddy went for tea together at a restaurant in Huddersfield town centre. Afterwards, whilst slowly walking down the hill of the cobbled high street, many local supporters approached them to wish them luck. Predictably, Harold was getting most of the attention. They were in full-suited attire, as usual. A tailor was busy sweeping the doorway of his exclusive shop when he noticed the smartly dressed athletic pair strolling by. 'Harold, Harold!' The tailor called his hero over and excitedly offered his hand, which was duly shaken by Waggy. Fred offered his hand too, the tailor shaking it but barely diverting his gaze from the eyes of Waggy.

'I tell you what, Harold – if we win tomorrow and you score a try, you can pick any suit from my shop and I will tailor it for you and give it to you for free.'

'That is extremely generous of you, sir. Thank you so very much,' Harold replied whilst going a little red with embarrassment.

'You fellows always think about the backs and never the forwards!' Freddy interjected in jest, throwing his arms out in pretend frustration. 'And what do I get if we win?'

'Okay, okay. Sorry Mr Longstaff,' laughed the tailor. 'Tell you what – the same offer applies to you too. Score a try and win the cup, and any suit is yours!'

The three men jovially shook hands and Fred and Harold went on their way and turned themselves into their beds for a full night's rest ahead of the most important game in their club rugby careers.

In the changing room at Belle Vue, the 13 Fartowners were busy pulling on their beloved claret and gold jerseys and carrying out their own personal final preparations for the match. Arthur Bennett held the team talk in which they discussed the opposition's strengths and how they were expecting them to try and combat their own.

Bennett said he expected Leeds to put multiple men on Waggy and try-scoring machine Albert Rosenfeld, and that those two would be closed down in a flash when receiving the ball from the forwards. Therefore, he told Duggy in particular to hold on to the ball for longer; carry it further forward; take advantage of the extra space created if the Leeds defence were preoccupied elsewhere.

In the opening few minutes of the match, a Huddersfield scrum on the Leeds 25-yard line led to their forwards gaining possession. The ball came to Duggy, who never looked to pass the ball to the backs, as would be the usual play from that position. Instead, he raced forward. The Leeds defenders were in no position to stop a Douglas Clark in full momentum, and he drove over the line to give his side the best possible start.

Ben Gronow converted before scoring a similar try himself and once again successfully kicking between the sticks. After only eight minutes, Huddersfield were leading by ten points.

With their defensive tactics being made a mockery of, the next time Duggy picked up the ball in a similar position, a plethora of Leeds players closed on him. Therefore, this time he knew that his team-mates would have the space. He passed the ball to little Johnny Rogers, who laid it off to Ganley, who then passed it across to Waggy, who raced forward with the ball into the space ahead of him. He had only one player to beat. He toyed with Lewis, the Leeds full-back, feigning to go to his left, then to his right. He knew he had a great chance to score himself when he heard a voice from behind him getting closer and louder with each microsecond that passed. 'Suit. Suit! SUIT!' Fred Longstaff was racing forward to join Harold in attack, and calling for him to pass the ball to allow him to win his bet with the tailor. Waggy popped the ball sideways perfectly into the chest of the flying and hugely popular Freddy, who put the ball down between the sticks to the delight of all of the team and the delirious supporters.

Leeds were already beaten. Huddersfield had their finest hour, enjoying every second as they played rugby to be dreamed of and ran out 35-2 victors. They had finally won 'All-Four' competitions. They became Northern Union legends. They became rugby league immortals. They became the fabled 'Team of All Talents', and are still regarded as the greatest British club side of all time.

Ben Gronow, in his first season on kicking duties after taking over from Major Holland, set a new Northern Union record points haul of 284. Douglas Clark played 31 games and scored six tries that historic season. Albert Rosenfeld continued his blistering record with another 56 tries. Harold Wagstaff cemented his place as the finest player on the planet, and in the history of the game. Fred Longstaff owned the finest suit in West Yorkshire – although Harold scored a final late try to ensure that he too won his bet.

A new song, 'Proud Are We, Proud Are We', was written to be sung on the terraces at Fartown:

In the world of football, rugby football,
There's a team of great renown,
And multitudes all journey to a place they call Fartown,
For it's there behold, the Claret and the Gold,
Keep you spell-bound all the while,
As one and all they juggle with the ball,
In a manner that would make you smile,
And their perfect style of play is on every tongue today.

CHORUS:
Proud are we, proud are we,
Proud of our football team you'll all agree:
We've a real half-back and a splendid pack,
Brilliant three-quarters and a great full-back,
Then shout hurrah, for everyone's a star,
In the Northern Union line,
We're the Champions today and everyone will say
That we shall be for a long long time.

Well you know our Waggy, good old Waggy,
He's our captain, tried and true,
While Douglas Clark is on the mark if there's some work
*   to do,*
Then behind the scrum, our Johnny makes things hum,
In the twinkling of an eye,
He'll dash away and open out the play,
Then Todd is sure to score a try,
And when Gronow plants the ball, ten to one he kicks a
*   goal.*

The euphoria was short lived. The war had escalated and was now officially the Great War as allied forces from across the globe joined together to help Great Britain push the German Empire army back on the Western Front.

The Western Front was a meandering frontline almost 500 miles long, running from the North Sea coastline at the Belgian region of Flanders, all the way down to the Swiss border.

The Germans had concentrated the majority of their forces through Belgium in order to enter France strongly from the north – the direct route to Paris.

Flanders had lain under the sea at some point in the distant past. It is bogland. But the industrious Belgian farmers refused to waste it, and so had constructed a complicated network of drainage ditches in order to utilise the soggy land to cultivate crops. The system requires maintenance and, even in fully working order, a heavy downpour can quickly see the fields become waterlogged. In 1915, it became a hellish, muddy quicksand on which the poor soldiers on both sides were forced into a torturous existence. Soldiers loaded up with equipment and wearing heavy boots simply sank into the quagmire with every step. If and when trench foot set in, a swift bullet from a German soldier – 'Jerry' or 'Fritz' had become their nicknames amongst our 'Tommies' – began to seem like a pleasant ending to the nightmare. Only the thought of one day returning home to their families kept the troops marching and fighting. A generation of young men were being buried in the Flanders mud.

Just when life on the frontline couldn't get any bleaker, 'Jerry' devised a terrifying new weapon: chlorine gas. On 22 April 1915, 150 tonnes of the deadly yellow cloud was sent into the Allied lines with horrifying and devastating effects.

The ancient city of Ypres was one of the few relatively built-up areas of Flanders. It was a quiet home to 20,000 inhabitants – almost all of whom depended on a successful harvest of hops, corn and beet from the fields that surrounded them. Ypres had been built upon due to its high ground protecting it from the regular and certain floods.

Those 20,000 were not in Ypres in 1915; some had been killed during the German invasion and the subsequent cross-fire; the rest had fled and evacuated.

Great Britain and the Allied Powers held the high ground that was Ypres, and it was invaluable land to hold. But the town was situated further east than their frontline, which therefore had to protrude out into the dreaded 'No Man's Land' to encompass Ypres and the precious high land beyond it. In military terms, this is known as a 'salient'. This once picturesque farming town was now a swampy war zone and the most deadly place to be on earth. Depending on your position on the salient, the enemy fire could come from any direction around you. But camp was set up there to maximise the troops and weaponry on location to defend it. Around a quarter of the one million who had already perished in less than 12 months of fighting lay within a few square miles of Ypres. The salient perimeter was formed by the makeshift headstones of those who had been lucky enough to have a burial, and the piles of rotting corpses of those who hadn't.

The daily-updated casualty list making its way back home was unimaginably long. These were not career soldiers and officers who had gone into the Army and trained for years, who had chosen the career knowing it may be the death of them. These were barbers, teachers and bricklayers; they were sons, brothers and fathers. Some were boys under the age of 18, lying about their age in order to qualify to do their bit for their country and because it was their only chance of employment. No matter how blatantly obvious their young years were, they were signed up regardless. These were 'Our Boys', and Our Boys had died, and were dying every day to defend the Ypres salient. Their deaths would not be in vain; for every perished man the salient would be defended even more stoically, even more resolutely. The answer: more troops.

Whilst Huddersfield had been thriving in the sporting arena – as well as the Fartown greatness, the infant Huddersfield Town AFC were climbing their way up the Football League pyramid – there was little else to cheer in the town, or in the whole country. Professional sport was suspended, including the Northern Union. Despite all the glory on both sides of the world over the previous 12 months, the Fartown boys were no longer rugby players. They would need to find other employment where there was none; sooner or later, it was likely they would be going to war.

More and more volunteers signed up. To make the idea more palatable, a whole generation of men from villages, communities or sporting clubs would register together as a group. Their unofficial regiment would be titled with the suffix 'Pals' and their friendship and loyalty to one another would hold no bounds; they were in it together. The tragic side of this romantic policy was that whole communities were being left devastated when a group of Pals were involved in one of the many bloody battles the Allies lost.

Freddy Longstaff signed up to the war effort immediately as part of the 'Bradford Pals'. Many Northern Union players went to war at the end of the 1914/15 season. Others took a little time with their families – with the sickening casualty rate, 'doing your bit' was no longer something one rushed to lightly. There was a very real chance you would not be coming home. But with virtually no alternative employment around, most had no choice. There was, however, the chance that the war could end suddenly, and it may only be a one-season hiatus. Duggy and Waggy were pacifists who objected to what appeared to be a pointless war. With this in mind, they – and many of their team-mates – did not sign up immediately.

Duggy had gone from being a local and national sporting hero – one who had also been carrying out two other part-time jobs in Huddersfield – to being unemployed. He decided to take the opportunity to reacquaint himself with his family, with his hometown, with his wrestling. He returned home to Elbra' to stay in the family home and work with his dad like he had before. He also planned to do a tour of the Cumberland & Westmorland wrestling tournament circuit throughout the northern counties. With a heavy heart, Douglas Clark left Huddersfield.

The Team of All Talents *parade 'All-Four' trophies*

PART 2

'Once more unto the breach,
dear friends, once more:
Or close the wall up with our
English dead.'

— William Shakespeare

7

ROBINSON CRUSADE

June 1915
The Wigton Games
Wigton
Cumberland

CROWDS GATHERED several times larger than usual for one of the regular summer wrestling events. These were weekly occurrences across the northern counties. A series of tents and marquees for food, games, and changing areas for the competitors, were set up in the vast and lusciously green fields. The hills and vast waters of the Lake District made for the most picturesque 360 degree panoramic views.

With the sun rising up towards its apex, the tents serving food and drink could not boil kettles or fry bacon on their fire-driven stoves fast enough to supply the demand. They had so many customers and for one reason: their hero had returned. Following six years of unprecedented sporting glory away from his home county and his favourite pastime, Duggy Clark was back and he was competing.

Lord Lonsdale was among those thoroughly delighted to see the former prodigy return to grappling. Along with everyone else, he thought it would never happen. So crucial was Duggy to the world of rugby that he could never run the risk of injury, but the most awful of circumstance – the war – had brought him back to his beloved Cumberland and to wrestling.

The 'All-Weights' scene, however, was being largely dominated by a relatively small man, in veteran and multi-time champion, John 'Jack' Robinson, who originally hailed from Cockermouth but had since moved and settled in Newcastle.

Quick, strong, with a low centre of gravity and lightning-fast reflexes, Jack was winning most competitions he entered, including the Grasmere in 1913. He used the size of the bigger men he wrestled against them – a true master of the 'hank' countermove Douglas spoke of earlier.

If there were any signs of 'ring rust', the conditioning of Duggy helped him to hide them as he raced through the field and qualified for a place in the final, which would be settled in the best-of-three-falls tradition. He was known to be the strongest man in the Northern Union and was stronger than at any time he had previously competed in wrestling – and his strength had been potent back then.

Douglas himself describes what happened in that tournament final:

> Neither Robinson nor myself will probably ever forget our first meeting. We came together in the final. I was over three stones heavier than he, and I took the first hold. Before I knew what had happened, I felt myself flying through the air. Jack had Hanked me but failed to turn me cleanly. The referee gave a dog-fall, or draw, in spite of Robinson claiming a fair fall. My opponent therefore tried again, applying the hank as quick as lightning. I thought he was falling, and went for him, only to feel once more that awful sensation of falling through space. He again tried to turn me and we both fell to the ground shoulder to shoulder. We were both dazed, and when Jack realised that the referee had given another draw he left the ring in a terrible rage.

I knew myself that I was powerless to counter Jack's terrible hank, and up to now only sheer good luck had saved me from defeat.

Eventually, Robinson returned and the ring was cleared for us. We had scarcely secured our holds when once more I was flying through the air. The next thing I felt was the awful bump, alighting clean on my shoulders. One to Jack.

I confess I would've given a fiver to be out of that ring, knowing full well, as I did, that I was powerless to overcome his chip. 'Come on, Jack, lets have it over,' I cried. A handshake, a hold, and away again right on to my shoulders with such a bang. Robinson was a great wrestler.

Jack was in one of the changing tents shortly after the end of the contest. He was surrounded by his friends, who accompanied him to his wrestling events. 'Why lad, ya fettled that big fella off quickly,' one of his entourage said to him.

'Aye,' replied Jack, 'I'll make him too frightened to come into a ring again.'

Soon after the words had come out of his mouth, the flap that was the tent door began to open. They had been blissfully unaware that Duggy was stood right outside the entrance of the tent, chatting away to some star-struck supporters. He overheard and asked to be excused from the pleasantries. As always, Duggy had changed into smart dress following his wrestle, on this occasion a tweed three-piece suit. The square shoulders of his tailored jacket made his giant frame appear all the more imposing as he ducked under the small entrance to the tent and stood up straight, towering over all the lads from Newcastle, who had gone instantly silent. One of the gang was Robinson's 14-year-old son, Joseph.

'Well wrestled today, Jack,' Duggy began, in his typically calm and gentle manner. 'But look 'ere lad, if you fell me 99 times, I'll still think I can get the hundredth, and I'll follow you wherever you go until I do beat you.' With that, Duggy left the tent the bigger man, in more ways than one.

Duggy was helping his father on the coal round once again and doing all the family chores that required any kind of physical fitness in order to earn his keep – and retain his extraordinary level of conditioning.

In his spare time, he decided to go and train with some of his former coaches and mentors – William Studholme amongst them. He had grown up being the champion wrestler of his age but never reached the open-age elite of the sport to which the likes of Jack Robinson belonged. He needed to get better. He needed to learn how to deal with the Jack's hank.

Duggy spent hour after hour in the old gymnasium and on the fields with the wily old Studholme, who still ran Duggy hard and gave no compliments or pleasantries. They concentrated exclusively on what Duggy couldn't do. Naturally a similar size to Jack and technically just as proficient, William was the perfect man to spar with in preparation for the next meeting with Robinson.

The next event was at Penrith Sports and brought around another tournament. The first person Duggy met on arrival was, sure enough, Jack Robinson.

'Hello there, Jack!' said a cheery Duggy, warmly greeting his rival.

'Hello Doug. Here again, I see,' Jack responded, feigning surprise.

'Yes, old boy. You see you haven't frightened me away, and if you and I meet today, there'll be some fun!' Whilst genuine, Duggy also knew that his cheer and optimism was beginning to irk Jack.

A short while later, Duggy heard a loud cry of 'Duggy!' in a familiar Yorkshire accent from behind him as he was about to enter the changing tent. It was Harold Wagstaff, along with Ben Gronow and Major Holland. The three had come to visit their friend and support him in his latest sporting venture. Duggy couldn't contain his joy at seeing some of his old team-mates, although the absence of Freddy Longstaff was a painful reminder of the horrors that were happening in mainland Europe. Fred had already signed up for the war with the 1/6th Battalion of the West Yorkshire Regiment as part of the 2,000-strong Bradford Pals, who were busy completing their training ahead of deployment to the frontline.

The Fartown boys were not to be disappointed, or surprised, by the wrestling prowess of Duggy, who progressed past each opponent with ease and found himself in yet another final. Between bouts, he was catching up with Waggy, Ben and Major, and informed them of the newly found rivalry between himself and Jack Robinson, who they also watched advance comfortably.

'You've only been back at it a bloody fortnight!' Ben Gronow exclaimed in his strong Welsh accent when Duggy, in his quiet and humble fashion, told them he felt only Robinson could beat him.

The men looked on as Jack locked up with the unfancied Steele, from Brampton, in his semi-final: the winner to meet Duggy for the trophy.

Like Jack, Steele was quite a small contestant of the 'All-Weights' division. Thus, Jack's special manoeuvre was not so effective. Jack became frustrated as the fight wore on. He had overlooked Steele and was already thinking of the final against his new nemesis. In a huge upset, Steele patiently wore down Robinson and slammed him to the ground to advance to the final. Robinson and his friends would return to Newcastle empty-handed this time around.

Duggy was devastated that he would not get the chance to avenge his previous loss and to put into practice all the hours of training he had done specifically for Jack. But he did not let that distract from the job in hand. To the delight of his visiting pals, Duggy beat Steele in the final by two straight falls to win his first wrestling competition for many years.

More intense midweek training followed ahead of the following Saturday's event at Coulthwaite. Duggy and Jack did indeed meet there but in the second round, where only a single fall would decide who progressed.

The grapple went exactly as Duggy expected and the moment he felt Jack go for the hank, he initiated his counter, first by closing his knees together to prevent Robinson's leg being in the required position. From there, he attempted his own lift. But the moment his knees split, Jack thought he was once again in a position to perform his favoured manoeuvre – except Duggy had already begun to lift him off of the ground. Both men were off balance and clumsily fell to the floor. With Jack's shoulders clearly hitting the ground first, Duggy was awarded the victory. Robinson was finally beaten. But, ever the perfectionist, Duggy was far from happy with the manner or style of the win. His disheartenment led to a surprising semi-final loss and once again their fierce rivalry had resulted in neither man coming away with the prize.

More obsessive training and practice followed and Duggy only had to wait one week to try and prove to himself that he could beat Jack almost at will. They met in the final at Carlisle Sports and each of the three falls came down to Jack's hank. He successfully turned Duggy once but the now-perfected counter worked twice to give Clark another triumph.

In terms of his Cumberland & Westmorland career, Duggy's boyhood dreams were to win both the annual 'All-Weights' tournament at the prestigious Grasmere Games and the world heavyweight championship at least once in his lifetime. The world championships changed venue each year and the 1915 edition was held at Kendal. Duggy and Jack met in the semi-final (one-fall-to-a-finish) and Duggy himself describes what transpired between the pair that day, and beyond:

The last three wrestlers left to compete for the prize were myself, Wm. Knowles of Bootle (a splendid type of man: 20 years of age, standing six foot two inches and weighing about 13 stones) and Robinson.

I had wrestled Knowles (who on this day became world champion) six times during that summer and secured five victories over him. I felt very confident of success, but I had first to face Robinson. The latter, early on in the day, had informed me that I had nearly broken his shoulder at Carlisle and begged of me, should we meet, that I would not fall too heavily upon him. My reply was: 'That's all right, Jack, but a fellow who uses the hank must be wrestled to the ground, or the other man is sure to be turned.'

Judge my surprise when Robinson went on to say that he did not intend to use his favourite chip that day, and again requested that I should exercise care should I secure the fall.

Robinson and I faced each other and took hold quickly. We stood well out from one another, and I think we should have been standing on those positions to this day if I had continued to wait for Jack to play. However, I bettered my hold and lifted him for the hipe, and I honestly thought he was falling to the ground, I on top. In order to soften his fall, I was just in the act of loosening my hold when Robbo threw in the dreaded hank and turned me beautifully and I was once more down and out.

Robinson had scored again, and didn't they chaff me when I reached home. Back to the school I must go and master this chip or die in the attempt – I think I succeeded this time!

Duggy had won six of the summer tournaments in the 1915 Cumberland & Westmorland wrestling season, the first in which he had fully competed and following more than five years away from the sport. He did, however, fail to win either of the two major tournaments: the world championship or at Grasmere.

The bitterly cold northern winter began as the wrestling season ended, and subsequently his father John once again required the full-time help of his son to provide coal and heat to the town. Duggy spent the winter keeping fit and doing further training for the 1916 wrestling season to finally overcome Jack Robinson.

> *My next meeting with Jack was in the summer following [1916], at Coulthwaite, and we were drawn together in the third round. On this occasion I waved ceremony to the winds, and when as before I purposely allowed my man to get in his hank, I steadied him and then threw him to the ground with every ounce of strength I had in me. That finished Robbo. He never came down West again. He stated that should we ever be drawn together again he would 'give me the ticket', which meant that I should have a 'walkover'. We have never wrestled together since, but if we do, Robbo will have another pop and before the contest is decided it is quite likely there will be skin and hair flying.*

When that encounter came around, Duggy proved once and for all that Jack was no match for his strength and new offensive tactics and so ended the 12-month long rivalry. It was clear, however, that a very different rivalry had no end in sight: that between the empires of Britain and Germany. The battles were becoming ever more deadly. A thick, vile-smelling smog now hung over much of the Western Front – particularly around the Ypres salient. The smog held the putrid smell of death in the air as the toll of the rotting corpses of both soldiers and horses rose into the millions. More troops were required and subsequently the decision was taken out of many young men's hands. Mandatory conscription was passed into law, meaning that all single men aged between 18 and 40 would be forced to go and fight on the gruesome and deadly battlefields.

The Minister for Sport, as well as the Northern Union itself, confirmed that there would be no 1916/17 campaign and the suspension was now indefinite. With that announcement, Duggy was packing his case once more as he – along with the likes of Harold Wagstaff, Ben Gronow and Albert Rosenfeld – signed up to the Army Reserve and began training in preparation for war despite any moral, political or social objections to the genocidal conflict.

Further south than Ypres, which was still being held valiantly by the Allied forces, the German Western Front had pushed their line forward and were now in French territory. Again, more troops were required to stop them advancing further as they got ever closer to their ultimate targets of Paris and the English Channel.

In December 1915, leaders of the Allies met at French General Joseph Joffre's headquarters to devise their strategy for the year ahead. It was agreed that the key to success against the Central Powers was to stretch their interior lines to the limit – the Germans had impressive transport links between their eastern and western fronts and so could efficiently transport troops and supplies to where they were most needed. So the plan for 1916 would be to coordinate attacks on both sides simultaneously, rendering this advantageous ability of the Germans mute. The dual major offensive strikes would come in the summer, with the British and French launching a significant attack on the Somme region.

New commander-in-chief Sir Douglas Haig was concerned about thrusting his new army – so largely made up of inexperienced volunteers and conscriptions – into such an ambitious and deadly battle. Therefore, he and the British battle chiefs devised a plan: during the spring preparatory months, they would hold the German Western Front at bay whilst

50,000 men secretly dug underground tunnels all the way until they were directly underneath the German trenches to plant explosives. Meanwhile, weeks of heavy and targeted shelling would weaken the enemy line, including 1.7 million shells fired during the week leading up to 1 July alone. Early that morning, the underground mines would be detonated and over the course of that day, commencing at 7.30am, approximately 100,000 Allied (mostly British) men would begin to go 'over the top' and storm the enemy trenches and camps; swarming, capturing and killing the already-weakened Germans and pushing that dangerous part of the Western Front back towards the border. Freddy Longstaff and his 2,000 'Bradford Pals' were amongst that huge number. The objective of the attack on a 14-mile section of the Western Front was to push it back one and a half miles and take the valuable German-held positions such as the town of Bapaume and the Leipzig salient.

Their commanders told them they would be certain to come back heroes, such would be the state of disarray they would find the enemy lines in, with their numbers depleted, their machine guns destroyed or unmanned, their barbed-wire protection broken to pieces, allowing unimpeded and swift access to the German trenches and camps.

So confident were the commanders that they told the soldiers going over to carry with them heavy supplies for setting up their own camp immediately following the invasion, thus confirming the territorial gain.

The first of July at 7.30am would be 'Zero Hour', and so would begin the Battle of the Somme.

8

ZERO HOUR

1 July 1916
The Battle of the Somme
France
Day 1; 7.30am

THE EARTH shook as never before when the explosives – strategically placed following months of painstaking mining – were detonated. One hundred thousand men peered over the parapet of the Allied Forces frontline. They looked beyond the rolls of menacing barbed wire that protected them from enemy invasion; they saw past the low cloud created by weeks of heavy artillery; they tried to ignore the dead bodies scattered in No Man's Land. The regiments were to attack in waves when given their signal, each with a specified target beyond the German line to reach and commandeer, capturing or killing any enemy soldiers that get in their way.

Fred Longstaff peered to his left, and to his right. The endless queue of khaki-clad young men disappeared over the horizon in both directions. He and his 2,000 Pals were among those in the trenches to be going over at the first whistle. At Zero Hour. Their target was the village of Serre.

The summer sun burnt through the smog. Adrenaline coursed through their veins and sweat dripped off their young faces that were ageing decades every day.

Each soldier wore multiple layers of thick uniform, an unforgiving steel helmet and large leather boots. They were carrying rifles with bayonets and bags containing supplies to set up camp once they reached and overthrew the enemy from their target. Also on their backs, they wore a tin triangle as a precaution against friendly fire as they prepared to run ahead of the onslaught of bullets from their own side of No Man's Land.

The whistles blew. Alongside the rest of his regiment, Fred climbed up the sandbag banking that created the trench wall. He manipulated his way through the barbed wire and ran out into the most dangerous territory on earth. A blaze of gunfire sounded from every direction around him. His boots sunk into the thick, heavy mud. His treacherous travel time across No Man's Land would be longer than he had hoped. There was more gunfire coming from the enemy lines than he had anticipated; the area was supposed to have been decimated by the heavy artillery and mine explosions. Friends and colleagues either side of him groaned in agony as they were hit. Fred took cover. The realisation dawned that this was not the scenario his commanders had anticipated.

What the British leaders did not know was that their enemy had protected themselves with 30ft-deep bunkers, and so were relatively unscathed by the relentless shelling. Nor had they taken into account the large number of dud shells that were among the 1.7 million that had been fired – that number having been deemed sufficient to cause the required damage.

When the air artillery had stopped, the Germans had casually come to the surface and launched their own attack – so when the underground mines had exploded, the damage there had been quite limited, too. Hence, the German numbers were not depleted to anywhere near the extent that had been thought, and their plethora of 500-round-per-minute machine guns, which were positioned into overlapping zones so as to cover the whole of this stretch of No Man's Land, still stood and were fit for use in retaliation.

Within the first 60 minutes of that Zero Hour whistle, only 230 of the 2,000 Bradford Pals had not taken fire. Most were dead.

As regiment after regiment were signalled to go over the top of the parapet, the dead and injured bodies of their comrades added to the ever-growing list of obstacles and hardships. It was a disastrous bloodbath and remains the worst day in British military history. Of the approximate 100,000 that attacked on foot that singular day, the British Army suffered 57,420 casualties – 19,240 of whom were brutally killed.

Freddy was one of the lucky few on Day One of the Battle of the Somme. But Day One was the first of many. What remained of the Bradford Pals were forced to retire back into Allied trenches and regroup in Aveluy Wood.

Eight days later, his depleted battalion was asked to relieve the 1/7th West Yorkshire Regiment in holding a recently captured and crucial part of the Leipzig salient. They were told it was 'to be held at all costs'. Knowing that the ridge was now being defended by lesser numbers than the previous battalion, heavy German shelling began almost immediately.

Offence had turned to defence. Day after day brought a new danger. Never had the two sides camped in such close proximity. The limited troops defending their newly occupied and valuable high ground were under constant attack. They looked on in horror as a new weapon was wielded by the Germans: the flamethrower. As instant infernos blazed 100 yards into the air, the faces of the Allied troops shone as they felt the burning heat. The Germans were showing them the terrifying new addition to their arsenal in the hope they would flee in terror. But much like on the rugby field, Freddy and his team would not be deterred; they dutifully held their ground.

By 15 July, they had defended the ground during a whole week of fighting. Led by bombers, the Germans charged, also armed with the devastating flamethrowers.

Fred picked up his rifle and waited in the trench for his opportunity to jump up and strike. For one crucial time in his amazing life, Fred Longstaff mistimed a tackle. As he stood up on to his fire-step and above the parapet, a searing hot flame shot over the ground in front of him. Athletic as ever, he managed to duck back down into the trench as the inferno raged above his helmet. He could feel the blistering heat. Sweat dripped off his reddening face as he heard other members of his regiment squeal in agonising pain – they hadn't been so lucky.

With the battalion on the brink of defeat, they were forced to defend deeper – retreating to the relative safety of the headquarters as the daily shelling pounded relentlessly. Their camp and trenches were turned into a smouldering wreckage.

On 21 July, the Fritz hit their bullseye: the basecamp headquarters. A shell exploded right inside of it and sent hundreds of shards of poker-hot shrapnel jettisoning around what remained of the battalion. One of the jagged darts embedded itself into the skull of poor Fred Longstaff, killing him instantly.

The news was broken to Arthur Bennett via a letter, sent to him at his office at the Fartown training ground. He was heartbroken, and had the sickening job of cascading the news around the Huddersfield rugby family. As the *Halifax Courier* and *Huddersfield Examiner* broke the news to their sombre townsfolk, it became common knowledge that their local lovable young hero had perished like so many others on the frontline.

Second Lieutenant A.L. Vaughan of the 6th West Yorkshire Regiment wrote on 11 August 1916:

> *It was during 'stand to' in the early morning that an odd shell landed on 'B' Co's headquarters – Longstaff*

with others inside. He and another man were killed instantaneously, and five others were wounded. A piece of shrapnel caught his head, and he had absolutely no pain. I cannot say that I knew him very well, but from the very first, I, like everybody else, took a great liking to him. I am assured by his two closest friends – Sgt Turner and Cpl Duff – that the big, good-hearted fellow was the pet of his company, and I know for a fact that his death has been a great blow to the battalion. He was buried in a little cemetery just behind the firing line by our chaplain. Only yesterday a cross was placed over his grave, which stands about four feet high, and is painted white with black lettering, giving his name and regiment.

Fred had played 135 games in the claret and gold of Huddersfield, and had represented Great Britain on the 1914 tour of Australia. He was just 25 years old when he answered the call of king and country, but had won every honour the sport could offer and was one of the most popular and respected men in the game.

His grave lies at the Blighty Valley Cemetery on the banks of the River Somme alongside 1,026 others who died in the battle, which eventually ended after four and a half months and in excess of one million casualties. The Allies gained six miles over a 20-mile stretch of their frontline.

The heartbreaking news soon filtered around and reached Fred's grief-stricken team-mates, many of whom were just beginning their military service.

Douglas Clark and Harold Wagstaff had enlisted just in time to be available for selection for a representative North of England Military XV rugby union team to take on an Australia and New Zealand equivalent in a high-profile charity match at Headingley in April 1916.

Duggy had very little experience in the 15-man code; Harold Wagstaff had never competed in it at all, claiming that he had only ever seen one game and wasn't even sure of the rules. Fartown's Australian Tommy Gleeson – Waggy's best man at his wedding just over one year earlier – lined up for the opposition.

Waggy held on to the ball after being tackled in the first half, which disgruntled some of the Australasians but amused some of his team-mates, and proved that he was being truthful when he admitted he wasn't sure of the rules. He was subjected to much of the infamous Aussie 'sledging' as the two teams trudged off at half-time. With his team a couple of points behind and time running out in the second half, Harold received the ball and sensationally ran half the length of the field, skipping past all defenders who came in with an attempted tackle. Each was destined to fail as Waggy scored a brilliant try to win the match.

After such an impressive introduction, seven serving Northern Union players were selected for the team again one month later for another charity match, this time against the Welsh at Goodison Park – home of Association Football giants Everton FC. Fifteen thousand fans saw an outstanding battle as the North England outfit narrowly won 5-3.

Inevitable pressure was subsequently put on the RFU to allow Northern Union players serving during the war to be considered for selection for all the armed forces rugby union matches and in their competitive league structure, in which teams from every naval and military base across the country competed. On 4 October, they announced:

> *Northern Union players can only play with rugby union players in bona-fide naval and military teams. Rugby union teams can play against naval and military teams in which there are Northern Union players. These rulings only obtain during the war.*

Major Stanley, a respected and senior officer within the Army, was also a member of the RFU committee. He was the commanding officer of the Army Service Corps (motor transport) unit at Grove Park. He immediately headhunted the best of the Northern Union players now available to his military unit – that was anyone who was currently signed up and held a driving licence. Douglas Clark, Harold Wagstaff, Albert Rosenfeld and Ben Gronow were all swiftly recruited by Major Stanley and would not only begin training to serve in the motor transport unit, they would also represent Grove Park in the competitive military rugby union leagues. Major Stanley had done the same headhunting with the most outstanding of the serving rugby union players he knew so well to create the first combination-code all-star dream team.

Grove Park also held a catch-as-catch-can wrestling tournament between the resident troops. This would become Duggy's second peek into that style following his singular match and destruction of Edgar Hayes over six years earlier. He won the tournament and was awarded a golden trophy by Major Stanley.

They practised their rugby skills daily and, alongside their military fitness training, honed their abilities and physical attributes to the best of their careers. Ever the natural leaders, Waggy and Duggy often took charge. Wagstaff ignored the fact that he was new to the sport, and insisted the experienced rugby union players come around to the Fartown way. He would later say:

> *The rugby union men in the side learned that it paid to cut out kicking and to rely on passing and the result was that all sorts of movements were developed.*

In his memoirs, Harold Wagstaff would state of his good friend, Douglas Clark:

His weight was true, his strength prodigious, and, with it all, he was fast. Clark's strength was so great that there were times when, I believe, he was afraid to use it on the field. Indeed, I know it is correct to say that only very occasionally did he go all out.

I used to hope that something would happen early in a match to get him going, there were times when I would kid him [on] to make him go a little more. He was, I firmly believe, afraid of his great strength.

A perfect example of this came whilst playing for Grove Park ASC, as told by Waggy:

We were playing Oxford University Cadets at Grove Park and in their pack they had a bustling sort of a forward who weighed no more than 11 and a half stones, but who really was a nuisance.

One of those fellows who always had his hands swinging about; in the 'lines' he was an aggravating sort of fellow and he was just as troublesome in the loose. He caught me with a blow in the face and though I knew he did not intend it, I was a bit worried as to what should be done about him.

Eventually I said to Douglas, 'I am surprised at you letting that little lad have things all his own way – look at the way he is throwing his hands about. Isn't it about time you reminded him that he is playing with men?'

Now, this player had a set of biggish pearl buttons at the neck of his jersey and when Douglas took hold of the jersey collar, and with a Cumberland cross-buttock threw the lad seven or eight yards, the pearl buttons flew all over the place. The collar of the jersey stayed in Douglas' hand. Straightaway the referee ordered Douglas off the field. We were amazed, for there was nothing wrong in what Douglas had done.

At half time, Douglas was still on the touchline with Major Stanley – he was ever so upset at being sent off – and we got the Major to ask the referee the reason for the drastic action taken. The referee's reply was that Clark had struck the Oxford man and knocked out a number of teeth.

The Oxford man turned up smiling to say that he was all right and that he still had all his teeth. Then came the explanation. The referee had seen the Oxford man flying through the air and he had seen the pearl buttons flying through the air as well, and he had jumped to the conclusion that Clark struck and knocked his teeth out. A comic business altogether, but poor consolation for poor Douglas, who had been sent off so unjustly.

The Grove Park ASC rugby union team were a sensation. The Fartown boys involved were no longer just part of the greatest rugby league team in the country, they were now part of the best rugby union team too. They won 25 out of 26 matches in that 1916/17 season, scoring 1,110 points and conceding just 41.

During that rugby season, Duggy had also completed his training and become a corporal in charge of a squad stationed at Grove Park, and began his motor transport unit service – driving all manner of vehicles to deliver ammunition, supplies and food to various ports on the southern and eastern coasts. The end of the rugby campaign coincided with a major troop deployment and the boys would finally be going to the frontlines. Albert Rosenfeld went to Iraq to join the Australian Army; Henry Wagstaff was posted in Egypt; Ben Gronow and Douglas Clark would go and join the Western Front, with Duggy to be based in the most dangerous place of them all – the Ypres salient.

Meanwhile, following the Battle of the Somme that had claimed so many lives, including that of dear Freddy, both the Allied Forces and the Germans licked their wounds and counted

A. S. C. TEAM, GROVE PARK.
TOP ROW—Mellor   Jones   Holbrook   L. Corsi   Clark
J. Corsi   Gabrielle   Alexandra   Gronow   Pavine   Brown
Ware   Cockell   Neal   General Burn   Major Stanley   Wagstaff   Nixon

Huddersfield Rugby League: A Lasting Legacy

the cost of the battle, whilst commanders and politicians back home planned the next offensive.

A number of troops were allowed home for Christmas and found that northern towns like Huddersfield were being terribly affected by the war, with food shortages and depression making it the bleakest of winters. The scenes damaged the morale of many troops, who bravely and stoically fought in the hellish conditions in the belief they were the ones suffering and that life for their loved ones and their communities back home was relatively unaffected, but now they could clearly see that was not the case. After three years of war, the Allied countries had an estimated three million casualties – dead, wounded or captured. Any flag-waving patriotic excitement that may have existed had gone. Seemingly, every family had lost a loved one.

Both sides had come to realise that the attacking army lost more troops in almost every battle. With this in mind, German field marshal Paul von Hindenburg decided to concede ground and build a new defensive frontline, designed to be completely impregnable, with three rows of barbed wire, strategically positioned post-mounted machine guns, fortified craters and deeper, wider trenches. They would call this the Siegfried Line, but the Allies would refer to it simply as the Hindenburg. Defence was the new form of attack for the Germans, who formally began the retreat on 22 February 1917.

The Allies had to advance quickly to take advantage and attack the Hindenburg whilst it was still in its infancy – allowing the Germans time to set up there unimpeded would only strengthen their new position. With each advance forward, the infrastructure and supply lines of roads, rails and bridges had to be built. The manpower required, particularly of the Royal Engineers, was huge – as was the delivery of supplies and materials.

In conjunction with all of this, field marshal Douglas Haig also planned a series of offensive manoeuvres on some of the valuable high ground being held by the enemy, hoping to seize upon them as the majority of the German frontline troops were busy forming and retreating to the Hindenburg. The 'Arras Offensive' to attack and take control of Vimy Ridge and Bullecourt began on 9 April. The battles were casualty-expensive but ultimately successful, as the final German troops were driven out of Bullecourt on 17 May. With the Allied frontline edging forward towards these German strongholds, some of which were becoming attackable salients as they retreated to the Hindenburg, the various bases of the two sides had never been closer. This led to ambushes and many thousands of soldiers being captured and taken prisoner.

The next ambitious offensive plan of Haig was to take Messines – a village heavily occupied by the Germans since 1914 and being used as a vital base and the strongest position on their frontline. A vantage point above the valley of the River Lys, it was previously seen as unobtainable, but the retreat to the Hindenburg had left Messines a little more exposed. The first target was the nine-mile long ridge running north from the village, towards Ypres – taking that would smooth off the Allied line and take the vulnerability away from the Ypres salient.

Foreseeing the value of Messines well in advance, the British had spent 18 months digging tunnels that led to chambers packed with explosives under the German base positions along the ridge that protected it. In a similar tactic to the initiation of the Battle of the Somme, heavy and constant shelling would begin on 21 May and last for 17 days. In the early hours of 7 June, the bombardment would stop. The weakened Germans would expect a charge; instead, the explosives they had no idea were below their feet would be detonated.

Duggy arrived at munitions depot 7th Siege Park on the Ypres salient in the middle of May. Following a stellar training period, he was made a non-commissioned officer (sergeant) with the 352 Siege Battery Ammunition Column of the Army Service Corps motor transport unit, delivering supplies – mostly ammunition crates – to the 352 battery base, amongst others when necessary, on the frontline. Fully dressed in his khaki uniform, he was shown by the commanding officer of his unit, a welcoming and friendly-faced 'Mr Preedy', the fleet of motorcycles and trucks he was now in charge of, and the supply stores he would load up from. The trucks were open bedded, many with no doors on the driver and passenger sides for quick and easy access. He quietly assessed and understood his role.

Mr Preedy was a slight-statured man. He wore a moustache and a perfectly arranged officer's uniform, which included a beige-coloured shirt buttoned up to the top and a dark brown tie that disappeared into his khaki blazer. Duggy's large frame, now over 14 stone, dwarfed Mr Preedy and also had him sinking into the soft Flanders bog.

He kept a diary of his time on the Western Front. His first entry simply reads:

*I shall never forget Messines as long as I live, the bombard-
ment simply awful.*

*I got knocked off motorcycle, graze my arm and get
it dressed at Bailleul Clearing Station. Shell destroys
over eight men.*

At 02.50 hours on the morning of 7 June, the bombardment
stopped; at 03.10 the British detonated 19 mines containing
450 tons of explosives – killing 10,000 Germans. As the British
troops advanced, they could see nothing ahead of them but the
smoke and flames they had created. Many of the Fritz that had
survived began to stumble out of the mayhem towards them,
disorientated and wounded.

Duggy recorded:

*At 3am British blow up Messines and open bombardment
for successful advance four miles behind Messines. I watch
bombardment from roof of shed. Have my arm dressed.
Hospital full of English and Fritz wounded.*

German wounded say no troops living could stand it.

On Friday, 8 June, *The Times* ran with the headlines:

'MESSINES RIDGE CAPTURED. ATTACK ON
NINE-MILE FRONT BRILLIANT BRITISH
SUCCESS. OVER 5,000 PRISONERS.'

The following day, field marshal Sir Douglas Haig received the
following congratulatory telegram from King George V:

*I rejoice that, thanks to thorough preparation and splendid
cooperation of all arms, the important Messines Ridge,
which has been the scene of so many memorable struggles,
is again in our hands. Tell General Plumer and the Second*

*Army how proud we are of this achievement, by which in a
few hours the enemy was driven out of strongly entrenched
positions held by him for two and a half years.*

Holding the ridge was yet another challenge as every attack
was returned with counter-attack over the days and weeks
that followed. Land possession changed hands and was won
back again. Dead bodies and detached limbs piled up and
smouldered in the hot summer sun.

Despite the blistering heat and heavy uniform, the work
ethic and supreme physical conditioning of Duggy meant that
he made for an impressive motor transport soldier, with other
troops amazed by how quickly he could load, unload and
deliver supplies down to the frontline. The supply roads were a
dangerous place to be as the Germans had increased their use
of spotter planes and observation balloons in order to target
vehicles with long-range artillery – stopping them reloading
and strengthening the British Batteries on the frontline.

Whilst loading up one particularly searing afternoon, Duggy
heard a familiar song that brought back memories, as a regiment
from Huddersfield arrived back at the base from the Battle of
Messines. Despite many being badly wounded, their spirits
lifted when they saw their old hero lifting ammunition crates
into the back of his truck. They sang 'Play up Huddersfield'
and when he turned around and recognised many of them from
his local communities and from in the stands down at Fartown,
they all shared a cheer and a wave.

On 12 June, Duggy was the driver in charge of a convoy of
five lorries delivering ammunition to 156 battery at Ploegsteert
Wood – an eight-mile journey from the Ypres base. They had to
go off road and through muddy terrain when they encountered
one of the roadside fields ahead dangerously ablaze, having just
come under shell fire. They had to wait for the flames to die
down before they could go on. It was so muddy that by the

time it was safe to proceed, Duggy's wagon had sunk down to its axle and had to be abandoned.

When they finally arrived at their destination, the tall sergeant in charge of the battery dashed to greet Duggy. He walked swiftly with a rigidly straight back, his uniform immaculate and boots shining; even his handlebar moustache was freshly groomed. To Duggy's surprise, the sergeant welcomed them furiously. German observation balloons were clearly visible above their heads and ammunition lorries were prestigious targets for enemy fire. The closer to the battery base and ammunition dump they were, the better. A perfect shot at a fully loaded lorry would see all the ammo aboard explode, one crate at a time like a devastating and destructive Catherine wheel, eventually taking out the whole of the battery. Despite his anger at the transport unit making the delivery in the sight of the balloons in broad daylight, the sergeant allowed them to unload their cargo on to the ammunitions dump.

They unloaded each lorry in turn and were just about to start the final one when a shell landed on the dump. The Germans were desperately trying to stop the final wagon from adding to the ammunition at the battery, and now they had their target set they would fire at will until the lorry was destroyed, taking as many casualties with it as possible. Duggy described what happened next in his war diary:

> A German shell landed right on dump, wounding Sgt of battery in back. I would be 100 yards away on open road. Fritz shrapnel bursting all around.
>
> Find myself on ground knocked off footboards by drivers of lorry running to cover.
>
> Fritz is trying to get it. We lay flat in a ditch, shrapnel bursting all over our heads past lorries. Battery want us to remove vehicle, but my drivers refuse. A bit of shrapnel hits door covering my legs. I run to lorry and try to take it to

*cover past our battery, only to receive a curse from officer
for drawing fire on them. I reverse it back to Tree Avenue
and battery men give me a good cheer. Then officer thanks
me. As soon as I get lorry under cover they stop shelling.*

Over the next few weeks, Duggy would spend every day on
these treacherous roads. On 16 June alone, he spent 21 hours
driving to various pick-up and drop-off points. His convoy was
shelled that day too and a car accompanying him was blown
up clean into the air, landing in the roadside ditch. Duggy had
to rescue the driver before towing the car back on to the road
and back to the Siege Park base.

But in and amongst the daily horrors that are his war diaries,
Duggy can occasionally sign off on more light-hearted notes:

June 13: *Cricket ball arrives.*

June 14: *Play cricket. Have a bath.*

June 15: *Received four wickets.*

June 17: *We play 129 Siege Battery at cricket. We were all
out for 16 runs. They got 100.*

June 18: *Huddersfield lads come down to see me, go to
Mesen with them. Frank Hodges is great comic
wrestling. I visit British soldiers' graves fallen 13
Oct 1914. Retire 10:50.*

June 24: *Let all men off for afternoon. I turn in and think
of the good old times past. Our battery go to play
91 at cricket. My knee won't let me, so I write.*

The solidarity and camaraderie between the troops held firmer
than ever. During rest and recuperation, a lot of organised sport
was played, with Duggy representing his regiment, his county
or his country in football, cricket and even chess tournaments
– excelling in all of them. When Germany had occupied the
Ypres salient in 1914, one of their ammunition dumps had

exploded, causing a huge crater. Since taking control of the area, the Allied troops had built rows of wooden benches up and around the edges and a flat central floor at its base. It had become known as the 'Coliseum' and played host to the various sporting and parlour games that took place to keep morale and fitness high. To the entertainment and delight of their peers, there was even the opportunity to use it as an auditorium for some catch-as-catch-can wrestling against the proficient veteran and fellow soldier Frank Hodges.

July 3: *Frank Hodges and Sgt Clark best out of three rounds, Catch-Can. Clark two falls, Hodges one. Finish match under hose pipe.*

July 7: *352 Siege Battery Ammunition Column were moved to a new base, on the southern outskirts of Ypres.*

July 10: *Up at 6am, finish field work. Nasty rumours concerning our new position… we receive our new map position, south a little of Ypres, outskirts of town. I play Cpl Shutt at chess and beat him. 10pm Mr Preedy and I leave park with four guns and four-wheel-drive for new position. Wait in Poperinghe Square til 12:30 to pick up Royal Garrison Artillery men. We arrive at Ypres Asylum. Mr Preedy and I take two guns to their position already prepared over Ypres Bridge on left side of canal. Bridge all damaged, not safe to take lorries over. Fritz give crossroad hell. I go back for the other guns. We get them in position alright. Return to park.*

They soon learnt the rumours were true as the narrow roads leading out of the base were busy and heavily congested, leaving the stationary fleets ominously vulnerable – especially now the Germans had taken to sending gas bombs over these access tracks so that the dreaded chlorine mist hung nightmarishly over the vehicles. Many near-misses forced the initiation of daily gas drills and the issue of new helmets that had integrated gas masks. These new masks were so uncomfortable that even when surrounded by the gas, soldiers would take a deep breath and remove them for a few seconds' respite, or merely to adjust and refocus their vision.

July 16: *I bring out two officers gassed. Feel very bad myself. First signs of gas. Sneezing badly. All curse Fritz for his beastly cayenne pepper.*

July 18: *Battery loss to date: 5 killed, 25 wounded. Cpl Shutt beats me at chess, and I beat Mr Preedy.*

The 352 Siege Battery Ammunition Column of the British Expeditionary Force – 1917 Huddersfield Rugby League: A Lasting Legacy

9

MENIN ROAD

24 July 1917
Messines Ridge
West Flanders
Belgium

DUGGY ARRIVED at yet another battery ammunition dump, leading a convoy of four lorries. He told young Private Williams to pull his vehicle into position for unloading. As the midday sun baked down upon them, the four drivers worked together to quickly pile the ammunition crates on to the dump. Once his trailer was empty, the youthful Williams climbed back aboard his lorry and pulled it out of the way, allowing the next in the convoy to be driven into position and his own to be left facing the correct way for the return trip to base – the dreaded journey along Menin Road.

It was a strongly manned battery on the frontline, with troops milling around preparing for another long afternoon exchanging shell fire across No Man's Land.

The four motor transport soldiers, Duggy included, were unloading the second vehicle when they heard the frightful hissing of an approaching shell. They peered nervously at one another from underneath their newly issued gas mask helmets.

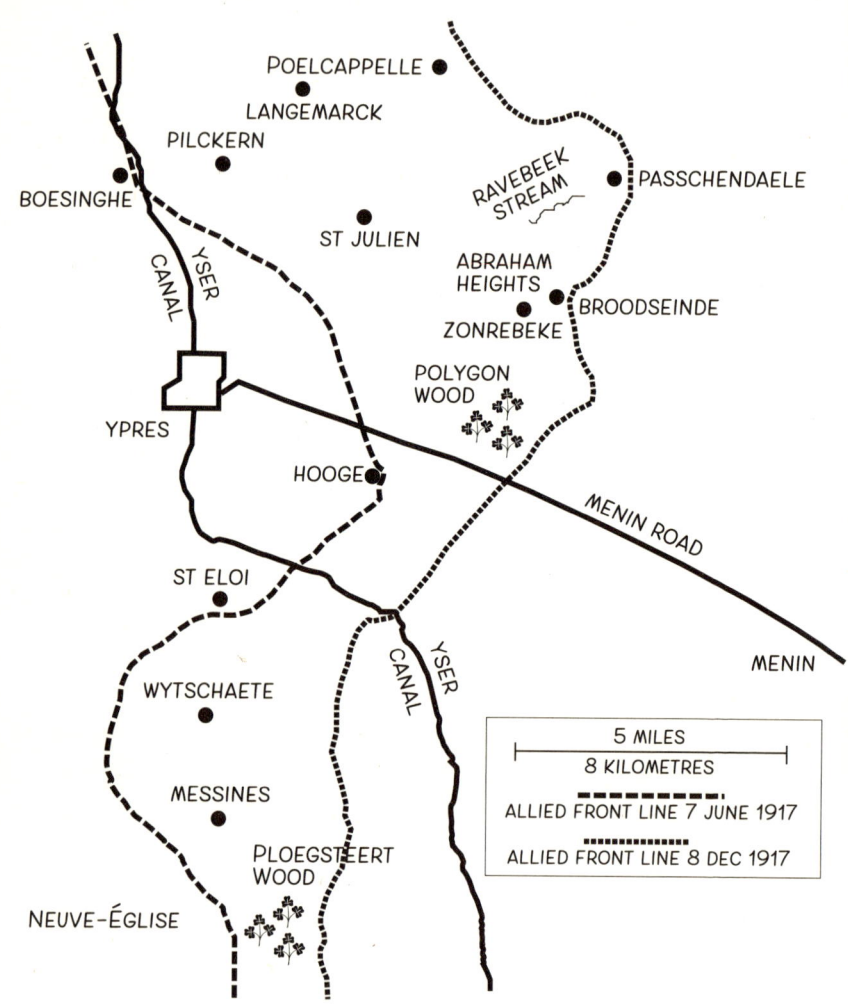

KEY BATTLES OF 1917
MESSINES AND PASSCHENDAELE

The face of Williams filled with terror. The men were flying through the air before they even heard the bang of the exploding shell above their heads.

Disorientated and covered in dust and debris, Duggy stumbled to his feet. It was pandemonium. With his vision blurred and a whistling noise in his burst eardrums, he tried to locate the troops under his charge through the mayhem. Bodies of not only his motor transport colleagues but also of the frontline soldiers who were unfortunate enough to be in the vicinity at that terrible moment were strewn all over the muddy floor.

Undoubtedly aided by the team ethic instilled in him from his sporting life so far, Duggy instinctively acted to save his comrades, regardless of the peril he may put himself in. He followed the muffled, agonised screams that he could only just make out. When he found a fallen comrade, he instinctively wrestled up the body on to his shoulders and ran towards the unloaded lorry – which was facing the right direction for a quick getaway. When he laid the first man down in the back of the open lorry, he was horrified to realise the poor soldier's arms had been blown off, his screaming had stopped as he struggled to retain consciousness. Another frontline soldier rushed to assist and they quickly bandaged up the stricken trooper to stop him bleeding to death.

Duggy ran back and forth through the smoke and horror, sometimes managing one fallen soldier over each shoulder like they were the sacks of coal he used to deliver. Unsure if they were dead or alive, he loaded up man after man into the wagon as shells continued to explode in the sky above him.

Poor young Williams stood frozen: uninjured, but terrified and in shock.

Satisfied he had all the casualties aboard, Duggy jumped into the passenger seat. He had to remove his gas helmet to call out to the fledgling driver, who had the keys for the vehicle.

Huddersfield Rugby League: A Lasting Legacy

'Driver! Driver!' he screamed until Williams finally unfroze and trudged towards the lorry. Duggy hurriedly put his gas mask back as he heard the distinctive and horrifying sound of a gas bomb landing on the dump. The yellow mist engulfed the wagon as the driver finally set the engine running and began to drive away from the ghastly scene. But there was no way he could see through his steamed-up mask and the fog that surrounded them. Duggy noticed they were heading straight towards a roadside ditch so yelled at Williams to stop the lorry – becoming stranded in a ditch at this point would spell certain death for all aboard the wagon.

The two men swapped seats and Duggy once again removed his helmet, risking himself to ensure the swiftest getaway possible for his injured Tommies aboard. With the lorry back on the road, it finally emerged out of the mist and carnage.

Duggy drove directly to the Ypres hospital base and pulled up outside the entrance. Again, he ran back and forth with the fallen soldiers, his breathing becoming heavier and shallower with each trip. He was pale and dripping with sweat. This time he could make out the extent of the awful dismemberment of the casualties – and he knew at least one was dead.

As he placed the final soldier down in the entrance to the hospital, with doctors and nurses now on the scene to assist, he collapsed on to the floor from his own gas inhalation.

July 24: *We are about to unload. Fritz sends over shrapnel. Gets in dump which spreads all over lorries and, of course, we get it. He kills one man and two lose their arms. I am very weepy. We help bandage poor fellow up. He sends over his beastly chlorine gas. We put them into lorry. Driver missing. I take helmet off to call for driver, but have to put it on again. Driver turns up and takes wheel, nearly ditches us. I take off my helmet to drive, manage to get to hospital. Find two of wounded dead. I collapse and taken to gas hospital. Eyes, chest, throat very bad. Sick, sick.*

Duggy required treatment at the hospital at Poperinge for the next ten days.

July 25: *Undergo treatment, feel much better, eyes about alright, chest same. Expect going back to unit tomorrow. Write William and Herbert. Watch first 50 prisoners go back to Poperinghe. Boys to go over tonight. Third battle of Ypres.*

July 26: *Discharged from hospital. Arrive at new park. 1pm receive letter from Wallie. Heavy bombardment opens in front of us on German line. Very intense for one hour.*

July 27: *Take things quiet, afternoon go to hospital, have eyes washed and chest treatment. 11pm hostile aircraft drop gas bombs near park. Wear helmet for one hour. Bombardment sounds like some monster giant wheel crushing everything in its wake. Everybody confident of coming battle, all sorts of rumours regarding retreat of Fritz.*

Whilst at the hospital, he witnessed preparations at the base for the biggest battle yet: what would become the Third Battle of Ypres, but later its infamy would see it take on its own dedicated name of the Battle of Passchendaele. This ambitious and dangerous attack was to capture as much of the German-held high ground beyond the Ypres salient as possible. It would mean a long and costly offence against the Hindenburg. Soldiers poured into the salient in huge numbers, higher than ever before.

The manoeuvre was the brainchild of field marshal Sir Douglas Haig but he had struggled to get it approved by the British Parliament, such was their nervousness at the prospect of another lengthy battle into the winter, like the Battle of the Somme 12 months previously, and inevitably having to declare yet more millions of casualties. With permission finally granted, 'Zero Hour' was set for 03.50 hours on the morning of 31 July 1917.

Duggy recuperated in the tiny war hospital bed, his body almost wider than the mattress, and scribbled in his diary what he witnessed:

July 30: *Eyes not quite as well today. Guns quiet. Royal Army Medical Corps men prepare for 50,000 wounded, marquees all along road. We receive our instruction regarding moving of guns after advance.*

Bombardment to commence after midnight. After dusk, roads full of limbless and Red Cross. 12pm Mr Preedy and myself take up our position to watch bombardment from top of lorries.

July 31: *At 3.50am witness the sight of our lives. 3 mines go off and guns open in full. Such a bombardment the like of which this war has never seen. Then the line just looks white hot and Fritz is soon in trouble sending SOS Green and Red star shells up along the front.*

I have never seen fireworks half so beautiful. We all feel for poor old Fritz. He replies with shrapnel, but soon stops. The bombardment has not ceased for one moment, it is now 11am. We all wonder if it's possible for a human being to live in it.

The left flank of enemy holds fast. We bombard this flank all day. Our men advance. But owing to such bad state of no man's land, we cannot take guns up to support, and our men have to retire and start digging in two miles down. We bombard all night, but rain sets in. Conditions awful, out of question going over.

The Battle of Passchendaele was officially under way; the shelling continued relentlessly in both directions.

Duggy was cleared to return to his duties on 3 August. Immediately, he was back in the perilous line of danger as he had to drive through the once-beautiful and picturesque centre of Ypres. He stared at the once awe-inspiring architecture of Cloth Hall. He wrote:

Mr Preedy and I collect off 7th Group, 200 rounds of pipe. We take pipe to our 352 battery. Return through town of Ypres. It is enough to turn anyone grey, the destruction of this town after Third Battle. All is quiet. Ham shank. Retire 11pm.

August 6: *Horse ditched, we get him out. I receive a letter from home and answered same just to celebrate the good old days. I wrestle Frank. Today was our first rum issue,*

Sergeant Heath takes mine. What a different day this to some of the grand old days. Dear old Cumberland, well you are worth going through fire for.

August 8: *I have a bath. Much to enjoy. A new way to sweeten your coffee, put a sweet in mouth and drink. I write Archibald and Mary. Pours with rain, bombardment commences again at 3am.*

August 10: *I receive dreadful telegram from father – 'Mother dangerously ill, come at once'. I go to signals to send a wire, and to police to get wire verified. Hostile aircraft over our camp. Aircraft guns chase him off, he returns three times, plenty of searchlights and firing.*

August 11: *The most terrible night of my life.*

August 13: *I receive wire from home. Mother fresher. I write back.*

The shelling, or 'rain', wouldn't stop for the next four months. All anyone on the Western Front could see, from the ground to the sky, was grey. The dust from all the devastation hung over the dull, dry mud; it was difficult to distinguish the dust from the smoke of the thousands of shells that exploded every day; the smoke merged into the clouds above, creating a blanket of smog. Grey.

It was impossible to know exactly how much artillery was required to weaken the monstrous Hindenburg line. Duggy would have to drive along the deadly Menin Road, which connected Ypres to the frontline, dozens of times every day.

The Germans attacked heavily on 22 August, Duggy reporting:

Early morning. Great bombardment raging, which shakes our hut just like the end boards on a box cart.

On his very next mission, he was unloading back at 352 Battery base when:

A shrapnel shell burst over my head. I gave myself up as a goner, about 15 pieces hit my steel helmet and my back. I thought of home, but luck was with me and my helmet.

Shrapnel fairly splintered off it and nearly choked me with smoke. Cox was 10 yards from me and gave me up as lost. Pleased to report only damage, a cut on little finger, so I carry on.

Both sides knew this battle could well determine the result of the whole war, such was the importance of the 13-mile front being fought over. There was never a moment of quiet, the bombardment both ways was relentless. An intercepted Zurich telegram said, 'The fate of Germany is now being decided in Flanders.'

September 3: *I go to Poperinghe. I meet Farrigar Stamper. Buy a present for Ma. Meet Cunningham, Dunn, Kirkbride and Ferguson, Nicol and Dick Brown, in fact all Maryport coming. We have a real Cumberland evening, speeches, songs, toasts. I beat Nicol and Dick and Jack Cunnin4gham at Cumberland & Westmorland. People think we have gone mad. Fritz raids all night. No sleep.*

September 30: *Fritz gives us very anxious time, bombs near. I turn in, but Mr Preedy gets me out to find 11 lorries loaded, we are detailed to take 800 rounds to 352. We arrive at Ypres, and fog so thick we cannot see two yards, all traffic stopped. Fritz is counter-attacking. I have to walk in front of lorries on account of fog. We get into Menin Road where Fritz is knocking hell out of. Four motors destroyed, and man's greatest friend the horse, poor beasts, are lying dead or dying on this road this morning. Would turn anyone. We arrive at battery just as bombardment of ours starts. It's hellish awful. I watch the effects of barrage. We hold two ridges. Fritz balloons up, look as near as ours, a beautiful sight indeed. Every make of gun in play, from 15 inch to rifle. Guns everywhere you look blending fire. This is real war, a wonderful, splendid, inspiring, awful sight I shall not forget.*

On 16 October, Duggy delivered a rousing speech to the whole base as he entertained and inspired them with stories of the 1914 Great Britain tour of Australia and the infamous 'Rorke's Drift' Test match. The troops were galvanised, lifted and ready for that equivalent final push to secure victory in the Great War.

October 22: *Air raid, we sing while Fritz bombs. I play Mr Preedy at chess, win two out of two. Selection of group play Australians at soccer, I play left back, we win six goals to nil.*

The final push for Passchendaele, and for the major advantage of overall victory in the bloody war, was under way. The powerful Canadian regiments progressed to within 500 yards of Passchendaele. Many motor transport divisions were sent to reinforce them and keep up their momentum. Duggy was about to get closer than ever to the Hindenburg wall of death and horror:

Death on every side. 12 tanks destroyed. Count 20 horses and 8 dead men. Wounded coming in. Splinters from Fritz shell hit my legs. Flying everywhere.

The Town Hall and Cloth Hall, Ypres, just before the Great War

And the ruins of Cloth Hall after the battles in and around the Ypres Salient

4.30, we see our lot going up, then all guns open up on poor Bosch guns, wheel to wheel. Pours with rain and up to knees in slush, no words could explain condition, still we all see what salient looks like. We return to park.

Have supper and turn in wet through.

That same evening, Duggy had an emotional reunion with his good friend Ben Gronow, who was acting sergeant with the 275 Section Heavy Artillery motor transport. Later, the pair embraced as they went their separate ways – fully aware there was a chance they may not see each other alive again.

I take German bayonet to Ben so it will be forwarded home.

For all of these men, life in the trenches was all they could remember; all they could foresee. They even had their own newspaper named *The Salient*. The following poem, named 'Ilium', had appeared in the Christmas edition of 1915:

Fair was your city, old and fair,
And fair the Hall where the Kings abode.
And you speak to us in your despair,
To us who see but ruins here,
A crumbled wall, a shattered stair,
And graves on the Menin Road.

It was sweet you say, from the City Wall
To watch the fields where the horsemen rode;
It was sweet to hear at even fall
Across the moat the voices call;
It was good to see the stately Hall
From the paths by the Menin Road.

MENIN ROAD

Yea, Citizens of the City Dead,
Whose souls are torn by memory's goad;
But now there are stones in the Cloth's Hall's stead,
And the moat that you loved is sometimes red,
And the voices are still and laughter sped,
And torn is the Menin Road.

And by the farms and the House of White,
And the shrine where the little candle glowed,
There is silence now by day and night,
Or the sudden crash and the blinding light,
For the guns smite over as thunders smite,
And there's death on the Menin Road.

10

HORS DE COMBAT

29 October 1917
The frontline
Passchendaele
Belgium

SERGEANT DOUGLAS Clark was unloading amongst the frontline carnage once more when a major bombardment began from the Germans. The troops of the battery took cover, leaving Duggy even more exposed. The commanding officers were so desperate to get the open-topped truck full of ammunition unloaded that they sent the Grenadier Guards down to assist. But even they soon disappeared from the hellish, deadly fire. Duggy and his companion continued to unload. Every shell seemed closer; every crate heavier; every step more treacherous; every second extra perilous.

> *Fritz starts shelling, simply hellish. We have to unload*
> *ourselves as men have taken cover, horses and men flying for*
> *their lives. Grenadier Guards are detailed to unload us. After*
> *one lorry they scoot and we never see them again. I have never*
> *seen anything as awful as this before, death at every side.*

Each explosion was followed by harrowing screams, some more distant than others as different batteries took fire. As the midday sun burnt through the smog, a shell hit the far side of the ammunition dump Duggy was piling his load on to – the glowing hot shrapnel raining down on the captain of the covering Grenadier Guards and some of his men. As the metal burnt through their uniforms and then through their skin, they wailed in agony – and yet remained confined to the cover they had found.

Duggy attempted to rouse the battery soldiers out from their refuge to assist him with a rescue of the stricken guards. Instead they fled in the opposite direction at the first slight gap in the bombing.

> *Three officers and lots of men refuse to help me, they run like March hares.*

Once again, Duggy set about scooping up fallen comrades – even ones who had abandoned him in danger just moments earlier. Their injuries did not appear life-threatening, but they would surely take fatal fire if left there. Duggy loaded them on to his lorry and, with adrenaline coursing through his veins, threw off the final few crates, on to the ammunition dump, that were required at this drop-off. He then climbed into his cabin and rejoined his convoy on to their next destination: Prazinburk Ridge.

> *I breathe a silent prayer for four hours and think every minute my last. Words fail to express this scene, blood everywhere you look, dead men and wounded. Those fine stretcher bearers.*

The approach road to the Prazinburk frontline was being bombarded to such an extent that it had been deemed too unsafe for horses to take troops and supplies along it; yet Duggy's convoy was required to proceed – their cargo was simply too important to the battle. The frontline soldiers at the battery once again refused to assist with the unloading, as they knew the trucks would be targeted.

There's not a soul in sight excepting men trying to find a better hole.
   You can see shell explode long before you hear the noise of shell travelling through air and explosion.

As he unloaded yet more crates from his lorry full of gunpowder and metal, Duggy reassured his injured but rescued troops in his naturally quiet, calming voice. A shell exploded in close proximity and smouldering fragments landed upon some exposed ammo inside the wagon, perilously close to the stricken soldiers. The crates began to blaze – it was only a matter of time before the vehicle exploded. Duggy ran for cover and desperately screamed at the soldiers aboard to evacuate. Some crawled to the open rear of the truck, but some were motionless. Alone, there was no way he could get all of them out and to a safe distance away before the ammunition exploded. Duggy sprinted around the dump and successfully found a fire extinguisher, climbed aboard the truck – knowing that each second could be his last – and managed to put out the flames before catastrophe struck.

With his load burnt and ruined, he could finally return back to Siege Park and get treatment for the wounded troops.

The awfullest day of my life so far. My lucky star.

Sir Douglas Haig would show his awareness and appreciation of such bravery in his telegram back to England on the progress at Passchendaele, '*Particularly good work … by the Motor Transport drivers who have shown the greatest gallantry and devotion to duty … under heavy shell fire and during long hours of exposure.*'

Each morning, Duggy would wake knowing that this could be the final time he did so, as he spent every day driving on those treacherous roads and unloading on the frontline whilst being specifically targeted by the Germans. For how long could his 'lucky star' continue to shine?

It was a chilly evening just two days later, 31 October, when the whole of 352 Siege Battery Ammunition Column was sent with a major convoy of six lorries that returned to the exposed ridge at Prazinburk. Even commanding officer Mr Preedy joined the fleet. They travelled in maximum numbers to unload quickly, such was the danger.

Duggy rode as a passenger in the lorry at the head of the fleet alongside the driver. Early on that dreaded approach road, they were stopped by the Military Police and warned that the bombardment was at its peak – possibly at its worst intensity in the whole of the war to date.

Duggy got the team huddled behind the cover of his wagon and he and Mr Preedy hatched the safest plan to proceed that they could from the hazardous scenario: they should leave a distance of at least 200 yards between the vehicles; four of them jump aboard the wagon to be unloaded so they were in and out as swiftly as possible; the team behind should wait until the lorry ahead had not just unloaded but had safely returned back past them before they were to proceed to the dump – limiting their time at maximum exposure.

The breeze made it feel cooler than it actually was as darkness set in; the direction of the breeze was altogether more concerning, though, as it came straight over their heads from the German side: perfect for them to send over their horrendous gas.

It is now quite dark and wind favourable for Fritz gas. All guns his side of Bavaria House in action.

With helmets and gas masks fitted, Duggy, Mr Preedy and two other comrades began the slow manoeuvre forward into position.

They soon realised that they were engulfed by gas, which was blowing in the direction of the waiting team. Mr Preedy got out of the cabin and jogged back to warn them, so to ensure there was no complacency with their masks. The vehicle drove into position at the dump. Bare, dead shrubbery lined either side of the road, the far sides of which was bogland in which large stagnant puddles sat on the clay, the water nowhere to escape.

> *Mr Preedy and I rode on first vehicle. We had not gone very far until we found the gas very bad. We pulled up to warn drivers, Mr Preedy going back to following lorries. I took ours forward to unload.*

Duggy and the other two men began to unload. With the masks digging into their perspiring faces and the steamed-up goggles completely blurring their vision, valuable time was being added to the tense, life-threatening moment. Duggy took a deep breath and lifted his mask, taking a valuable few seconds of extra-productive manhandling as he threw crate after crate atop his broad shoulders before hurriedly refitting the mask. Over the next few minutes, he repeated that brave act twice more – knowing all the while that, even with his breath held, particles of the insidious vapour were seeping into his pores. His eyes stretched wide as he struggled to retain consciousness the final time.

> *The place was deserted, so first and second driver and myself started unloading. I pulled off my helmet 3 times, and then the place was turned into hell.*

The thick, heavy sky was now the darkest of greys as night had set in above the smog. Different parts of the frontline sky lit up like a firework-laden nightmare as shells exploded, machine guns fired and crimson blood stretched upwards. The once-bloodcurdling screams were now simply the white noise that made up the backdrop of these brave soldiers' existence.

The luck of 352 Battery ran out: it was the turn of their airspace to light up orange and green as a shell crashed open above them. And then another. Followed by another. They had been targeted from close range. Searing hot shrapnel rained down upon them like a fierce hailstorm from hell. One piece embedded itself into Duggy's left arm.

I doubt if ever Fritz has sent over so many shells on such a small stretch as he did around us, even putting the shelling of the previous days in the shade. I received a nasty wound in the left arm and I thought it certain all would be killed.

'Back to the convoy! Run for cover!' Duggy shouted to his men, as clear as he could through his restricting mask.

The three men made the 200-yard dash up the dusty road and slid behind the trucks, where they found their comrades. Duggy happened to take cover next to Mr Preedy.

'I feared you were toast as I observed that onslaught, sergeant,' Preedy candidly told Duggy.

'Escaped with just a minor wound, sir.' Duggy nodded toward his left bicep. Preedy looked at the severe gash opened up beneath the ripped, smouldering khaki.

'We need to get you back to the hospital, sergeant.'

'We can't leave that wagon in there, sir,' Duggy began, peering around the chassis of the lorry for a gap in the bombardment, 'they'll blow it up and it'll take the whole battery with it.'

I ordered boys to go back and take cover near the other lorries. Here I found Mr Preedy and reported that I was wounded.

He wanted to take me to hospital, but I refused to leave lorries. Shells were falling front, behind and on all sides.

Sensing a crucial opportunity was upon them, as the Germans appeared to be reloading, Duggy pulled down his gas mask and sprinted the 200 yards forward once again. His colleagues watched with awe and anxiety as the giant athlete ran away from them. The blasts in the sky gave their faces a warm glow, their eyes squinted in an effort to see further. Duggy's silhouette disappeared into the wreckage.

Duggy jumped into the cabin of the lorry quickly – grateful for it not having a door on this occasion. He restarted the engine, simultaneously heaving the huge, heavy steering wheel clockwise. Forwards a few yards and backwards a few yards, his wounded arm still powerfully swinging the wheel around one way and then the other. He exited the dump and was back on the road, just beginning to believe he had made it, when the shelling started once again. One exploded low, right beside the passenger-side doorway of the lorry. The force of the blast blew Duggy clean out of the lorry, over the roadside hedges and into a huge puddle of mud and stagnant water, his uniform – including gas mask – ripped from his body as the hot shards of shrapnel pierced into him.

A shell burst, hitting me in the abdomen and chest and throwing me some distance.

He lay there semi-conscious, bleeding heavily from his chest and stomach, smoke emanating from his body, dirty water slopping into his mouth, defenceless against the deadly gas rolling over him.

I was bleeding very heavy from stomach and having lost my gas helmet, thought the end must be near. It's then a

man starts to think of the dear ones at home and I prayed
I might just be able to see them to say 'goodbye'.

On this occasion, it was Duggy's turn to be rescued from certain death. Such was the respect he had within his regiment, the men all ran into the gas – risking their own lives – to drag him from the mud and hurriedly dashed to the hospital, where he underwent emergency surgery to remove 18 pieces of shrapnel from his left arm, abdomen and chest.

The journey left me very weak from the loss of blood, it
was simply murder.

Duggy had succeeded in getting the lorry far enough away from the battery, who went on to have success in counter-bombing the Hindenberg. He woke from his operation at 4am on 1 November. He required round-the-clock intensive care for the next 48 hours. The operation had gone well. The surgeon told Duggy that had it not been for his strong, muscular build and cardiovascular fitness, he would undoubtedly have been killed.

November 2: *A very bad 24 hours. Mr Preedy and Sergeant*
Heath come to see me and bring the mail and promise to see
me tomorrow, but I am sent to the base before they arrive.

On 9 November, Duggy was strong enough to be transferred to the large hospital base at Boulogne.

The following day, the Battle of Passchendaele was over. The Allied Forces took possession of the final ridge and of the town. The Hindenburg collapsed and the Allies were in command of the Western Front.

Almost 600,000 troops died in the battle. More than half of them were Allied and, of those, 275,000 were British.

An assessment of Duggy deemed him unfit to return to duties, and he was 'marked for Blighty'.

By the end of the month, he was at Royds Hall War Hospital in Huddersfield, where he had an emotional reunion with his proud and relieved parents. Whilst recovering there, he also received a telegram from the Army, informing him that his extraordinary heroism was to be rewarded with the Military Medal for bravery.

November 27: *Father and mother visit me. Informed I have been awarded Military Medal.*

He completed his convalescence at Honley District War Hospital. During his discharge assessment, the doctor awarded him a 20 per cent disability certificate and told him that his body was very brittle and fragile and would forever contain many tiny fragments of shrapnel. He was told that it was only his solid, athletic physique and stellar constitution that had kept him alive and that he should not return to his rugby career. He was told never to wrestle again. Wheelchair-bound for the indeterminate duration of his recovery, if Duggy wanted to live a long and comfortable life, he should avoid any form of strenuous physical activity – forever. Douglas Clark had been rendered *hors de combat*.

January 31 (final entry): *Transferred to Honley Con.*

THE BOYS ARE BACK IN FARTOWN

11 November 1918
11am
London

THE MAROON guns that had boomed over London in honour of the war casualties following the particularly deadly battles blasted out once more. The public had heard the rumours and they dared to believe that, this time, the blasts were the positive news that they had desperately hoped to hear for so long.

Swarms of people immediately began to filter out on to the streets from the houses, apartment blocks, offices and museums of the capital city. 'Is it over?' they dared to ask one another, adrenaline completely nullifying the bitterly cold weather.

Confirmation came when the gloriously loud dong of Big Ben echoed around the city – signalling strangers to hug and cry on each other's shoulders with relief and delight; they knew that they had heard the dreadful news of a friend or family member being killed on the frontline for the final time.

Thousands of people worked their way around the cobbled back streets of London that they knew so well until they were part of the huge crowd that had formed within minutes outside the door of number 10 Downing Street, awaiting the formal announcement of Prime Minister David Lloyd George.

The moment the door began to open was greeted with cheer. The Prime Minister emerged confidently, his grey hair swept over and thick moustache neatly combed downward. He stood on his doorstep, with the press fighting with one another for the perfect spot at the front of the crowd. He held his head high and gave a reassuring smile before giving the shortest of statements, 'I am glad to tell you that the war will be over at 11 o'clock today.'

An emotional cheer erupted and the press camera shutters snapped loudly as the Prime Minister gave his delighted people a wave before disappearing back behind the famous blue door.

It was over. Approximately 20 million people had died, with roughly the same number again severely wounded. For what? That was difficult to see, and will always remain so. But it was over.

Duggy – having made a recovery that astonished the Army medical team assessing him – had rejoined his 352 Siege Battery Ammunition Column for a period of time in 1918, albeit on lighter duties and during a period of much lesser bombardment and violence than the horrors of Messines and Passchendaele.

His 20 per cent disability certificate entitled him to a small military pension for the rest of his life for him to live on, should he wish to. But as 1919 arrived, he was already back delivering coal around Huddersfield and once more living under the warm and friendly roof of the Hodgson family.

Professional sport, including the Northern Union, had been suspended for three years but there would be a full calendar scheduled for the 1919/20 season. In the meantime, the officials in Yorkshire were eager to return to normality and so decided to waste no time in getting things back under way, with their supporters and players desperate to return to the battlefield they loved, rather than the deadly one they had hated so much.

And so arrangements were made to squeeze a Yorkshire Cup competition into what little time remained of the 1918/19 campaign.

As they got back to training at the beginning of 1919, Fartown were representative of most of Europe – the Team of All Talents had been decimated by the Great War. Duggy had been told to retire on medical grounds; two members of the legendary team had decided not to return to the game or even to Huddersfield; Herbert Banks had smashed his ankle working down the mines; star players Johnny Rogers, Harold Wagstaff and Albert Rosenfeld were having a reunion all of their own at the Royds Hall War Hospital as each were there convalescing from their injuries of battle; and of course, tragic Freddy Longstaff had been laid to rest at the Blighty Valley Cemetery.

Freddy was one of 69 players to have taken part in that final Northern Union campaign who perished in the Great War. In addition, up to 100 more former players are thought to have died. Leeds alone lost eight of their 1914/15 team and of the legendary 1914 Australasia tourists, as well as Fred, Billy Jarman and Walter Roman failed to make it out of the horrors alive.

In terms of deaths of first-team players, Huddersfield's tally of two was amongst the lowest; the second Fartowner to have perished being young centre Theodore Marshall. With Harold Wagstaff and Albert Rosenfeld occupying the berths in which Marshall longed to play, he was signed as an understudy ahead of the 1914/15 campaign. But with newly crowned Ashes winners and returning heroes missing the opening five matches of the campaign as they sailed the epic sea journey home, there was opportunity. After playing to a high standard in the pre-season games and impressing Arthur Bennett in training, Marshall was the man asked to fill the biggest boots of them all for those five games – those of iconic skipper Harold Wagstaff. The 19-year-old, who hailed from Elland, held the fort dutifully as the weakened squad got off to a respectable start in those five games, with two wins, two draws and just the one defeat. Theodore respectfully and willingly stood aside when the stars returned, but the decent start gave the legendary Team of All Talents something to build on, and they repaid that debt by delivering 'All-Four'. Private Theodore Marshall – just 22 years old – was shot in the head by a sniper on 28 April 1917 during the Battle of Arras. He survived but eventually succumbed to his injuries back in St Luke's Hospital, Bradford on 1 August.

Of the key players from the pre-war team, only Ben Gronow had returned without injury; many others were now the wrong side of 30 and had not played first-class rugby for almost four years.

The tournament draw was made and, ironically, professional rugby would return with a match between the only two teams to win 'All-Four' in the pre-war Northern Union era (now recognised as the 20 years from 1895–1915). Huddersfield would travel to Hunslet in the first round of the Yorkshire Cup. But, based on the training performance at Fartown, an immediate return to the glory days was not looking likely.

A call to arms was made by the old guard; by Jack Clifford and by Arthur Bennett. Rogers, Waggy and Rosenfeld agreed to sneak out of their hospital beds and attend some training sessions and, if possible, the match days. Duggy thought about his future: he had been warned that professional sport could be the death of him, but he had been back to the frontline since his recovery; he had delivered sacks of coal around his community; he felt fully fit; he was a single young man whose passions still lay with his rugby and with his wrestling; the war had robbed him of three years of his life and one of his best friends, but it would not take away his sport. He dramatically returned to training at Fartown to the hero's welcome he deserved.

Little Welsh wizard Johnny Rogers felt fit enough to play; Waggy and Rozzy were less certain. Harold agreed to join Rogers and sneak out of hospital for the Hunslet match; Albert would give himself another week to recuperate from the severe injuries he sustained in the Mesopotamian front of the war.

On 26 April, the band were back together. Major Holland, Harold Wagstaff, Stanley Moorhouse, Johnny Rogers, Ben Gronow and Douglas Clark were among the 13 men who once again pulled on the claret and gold at Hunslet. Rogers and Wagstaff – playing with hospital wristbands on – both scored tries and Ben Gronow converted twice as Fartown won 16-5 to advance to the quarter-finals.

One week later, they travelled to Hull to play against the Kingston Rovers. The same team turned out except this time legendary Aussie try-scorer Albert Rosenfeld made his emotional return, allowing Waggy to stay in his hospital bed. They won 19-4.

In the semi-final on May 10, Hull would come to Huddersfield as Fartown hosted their first professional rugby match since the final weeks of the 'All-Four' season back in 1915, before the horrors of war.

All of their hospital beds would be empty on this occasion as the full team emerged from the tunnel to the sheer delight of the fanatical sell-out crowd: the boys were back in Fartown. 'Proud are we, Proud are we,' and 'Hurrah for the claret and gold' rang around for a joyous and nostalgic 80 minutes. It was a sight none of them thought they would ever see again and the stars of the show didn't disappoint, running out 23-13 winners to secure a place in the final.

The same full-strength team ran out at Headingley Stadium against Dewsbury seven days later in the final. The boys regained the feeling of lifting silverware with a 14-8 win. The victory was immediately dedicated to Fred. Maybe the Team of All Talents, despite the injuries, age difference and aftermath of the war, could still be the team to beat in the Northern Union.

In yet another bid to get back to normality and show further unity with war allies Australia, the Northern Union announced there would be another Ashes tour of Australasia in 1920. All the players once again galvanised themselves for a stellar 1919/20 season to earn the lucrative ticket to board the boat.

Fartown were unstoppable once again. Bolstered by the signings of Gwyn Thomas and Arthur Sherwood and inspired by the dream of sensationally defending all four trophies five years apart, they tore into the new season as if they were all still in their mid-twenties; as if the war had never happened.

The Yorkshire Cup returned to its autumn slot in the calendar. The tournament draw did not do Huddersfield many favours, but wins over Halifax, Hull and Wakefield set up a reunion in a major final as they were pitted against local rivals Leeds. Stanley Moorhouse ran in four tries in a 24-5 rout as Fartown won the cup for the second time in just six months.

With 29 wins from 34 matches, they secured the Yorkshire League trophy and went into the play-offs as clear leaders of the Northern Union. The lucky men who would be travelling to Australia received their invitation letters, and five Fartowners would be aboard the ship: Harold Wagstaff would captain the Great Britain tourists once again, the other four being Welshman Gwyn Thomas, Johnny Rogers, iconic goal kicker Ben Gronow and, of course, reborn star forward Douglas Clark. Should, as expected, Huddersfield overcome fourth-placed Widnes at home in the play-off semi-final, the five star players would set sail before being able to play in the final.

In the meantime, they had also bulldozed their way into the Challenge Cup Final at Headingley— once more against arch-rivals Leeds. Duggy scored one of the five tries as Fartown defended the prized knockout competition and made it three from three in their quest to defend 'All-Four' in Fred's honour.

At the end of January 1920, the home league match against the Rochdale Hornets was selected as Harold

Wagstaff's testimonial match. A crowd of 18,000 crammed into the Fartown stadium to pay their respects to the 'Prince of Centres'. Afterwards, they held a dinner party, with the esteemed dignitaries of Huddersfield present, as well as the whole Fartown brigade. There were also representatives of the Huddersfield Town Association Football team, who looked certain to achieve promotion to the First Division just a decade after being founded and were in the FA Cup Final, where they were to play Aston Villa at Stamford Bridge. It turned into a celebration of the fact that the small cotton mill town of Huddersfield appeared to have become the sporting epicentre of England.

Widnes gave Fartown a tougher test than expected in the semi-final, but Fartown dug deep for a 7-5 win, a place in the final and the chance to create yet more history.

'Town' did secure a place in the top tier of the English Football League pyramid, but lost 1-0 in the first-ever FA Cup Final to require extra time.

With Stanley Moorhouse injured and the other five star players aboard the ship headed Down Under, Fartown struggled to field a team for the final against Hull, who had finished as runners-up in the regular league campaign. With some youngsters who would be playing their first-ever professional game called upon, an unrecognisable Fartown outfit fought and battled hard in the tightest contest imaginable, and owing to a solitary drop-goal were ahead by two points to nil going into the final few minutes, when Billy Batten heartbreakingly scored a try to snatch victory for Hull. The youngsters lost the final by just three points to two and with it the Northern Union crown they had held since before the war. Thirty-one-year-old Batten had an additional reason to celebrate his cup-winning try: as an 18-year-old he had been part of the Hunslet team to win 'All-Four', and the Huddersfield dominance was diminishing their achievement. He had had a career to match anyone of the era – Fartowners included. Having been a Test match regular, he rejected an invitation on the 1914 tour and so was overlooked in 1920. That omission proved very costly for Fartown.

Nevertheless, it had been an outstanding return campaign. Ben Gronow established new Northern Union scoring records with 147 goals and 330 points.

Just two years after being told he would never play rugby again, Douglas Clark had played 36 professional matches for Huddersfield and a further two in the Cumberland colours. He had scored 12 tries, won four major trophies and was aboard the ship for yet another adventure in the baking-hot southern hemisphere.

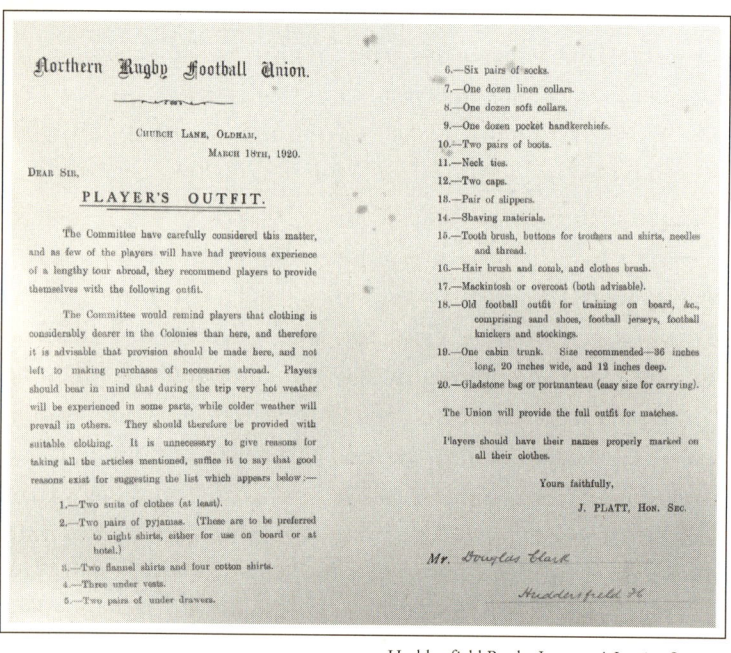

Huddersfield Rugby League: A Lasting Legacy

12

BACK TO ROOTS

14 August 1920
New Zealand versus Great Britain
The Basin Reserve
Wellington
New Zealand

THE 1920 Australasia tour had been a huge disappointment. With the world still recovering from the Great War, the return of major sporting events was truly welcomed but also viewed with perspective and objectivity. This was particularly true in the case of the Great Britain Northern Union team, who were desperately trying to rediscover a squad of genuine international class. So many of the brilliant pre-war squad were now beyond their prime, or even worse in the case of poor Freddy Longstaff. A whole generation of young talent had been missed, with young men sent into battle rather than the sporting arena.

The tour had been scheduled to last less than three months, with the number of warm-up matches greatly reduced. But as well as the Ashes Test series against Australia, 'The Lions' – as they had become known – would also play a best-of-three Test match series in New Zealand.

Six hellish years had passed since the legendary 1914 Rorke's Drift tour, and the Australian supporters were feverish with

Fartown's 1920 'Lions': Ben Gronow; Harold Wagstaff; Johnny Rogers; Gwyn Thomas; Douglas Clark Huddersfield Rugby League: A Lasting Legacy

excitement to see more of the same. Every stadium was packed out – many with more than 60,000 screaming fans.

In just their third tour match, which saw them return to the site of their greatest victory – the Sydney Cricket Ground – Great Britain had been humbled 42-6 by an empowered and confident New South Wales representative side.

The Test matches began a fortnight later, with talismanic veterans Waggy and Duggy leading out the team, supported by Welsh Fartown team-mates Ben Gronow and Johnny Rogers. They had put in a stellar performance to win the final Test, but the Ashes had been handed back to Australia, who had won the series by two victories to one.

They then sailed to New Zealand, where they played one warm-up match against Auckland before challenging the Kiwis in the three-match series over a two-week period.

With confidence low, they lost disastrously and embarrassingly, 24-16, to Auckland. This led to the leaders within the squad angrily challenging their team-mates to pick themselves up and battle for one another, and for their country, once again. They not only had to beat New Zealand but win all three Test matches if they dared to board the ship back to Britain with even an ounce of dignity and pride.

The ultimatum seemed to work as they dramatically improved and defeated the Kiwis with relative ease in the first two Tests.

Clark & Rogers: Johnny Rogers proudly poses with the coal wagon
Elizabeth James & Imperial War Museum

With the series won, the squad were warned not to let their standards drop. They had to prove to each other, and to the nation back home, that they could still beat a team such as New Zealand at will.

This inspirational message was somewhat irrelevant to Duggy – he didn't need it. He proudly pulled on the red and white jersey and then quietly and thoughtfully fastened the laces of his boots in the changing room before the match. He knew he had lost a very slight edge, with all that his body had been through. He had lost a touch of that blistering pace, if not any of his superhuman power. Some soul-searching on the tour had led him to the conclusion that after almost six years away from home – either rugby touring or at war – he wanted to return to some sort of normality as he neared his 30th birthday. He wanted to spend more time with his family; to settle down back in Huddersfield, the town he had grown to love; to achieve his wrestling dreams as he had already achieved all he possibly could in rugby. If he was able-bodied enough to play this sport as his profession, he was able-bodied enough to wrestle for a hobby. And what if it shortened his rugby career?

This was going to be his final Great Britain tour and, in all likelihood, his final Test match. If this was the last time he was going to represent his beloved country at the very highest level, there was no way he was going to walk off that pitch on the losing team.

Unfortunately, New Zealand were in no mood to suffer a home series white washing and also came out with a fighting spirit and determination to win. This was no 'dead-rubber'.

The Lions found themselves 10-6 down with just minutes on the clock remaining. With the seconds ticking by, the adrenaline surged through Duggy as he picked up the ball, put his head down and sprinted towards the line. As he gained momentum, he unleashed all of his extraordinary power. One by one, the Kiwi defenders tried to tackle him or barge him into touch; one by one they were sent crashing to the floor as Duggy handed them off or barged them over like a bowling ball striking through skittles. He knew his try had to be converted to snatch victory from the jaws of defeat, so he risked taking on more defenders to ensure his friend Ben Gronow had the best possible chance of making the goal by getting as close to the sticks as possible before he finally put down the ball to complete an astonishing try. A herculean effort by a true Lion.

The score was 10-9 as Ben teed the ball up. It all came down to this kick.

No amount of pressure or jeering home support could ever make Ben Gronow feel uncomfortable when stood over a goal kick, such was the confidence he had in his own ability. He sent the ball clear between the sticks and the referee blew his whistle to confirm the end of the match and the end of Douglas Clark's Great Britain Test match career, which ended with a dramatic 11-10 triumph.

Duggy played in 11 Test matches (six against Australia; three versus New Zealand; two against the combined Australasia team), scoring three tries and finishing on the losing side just four times.

On returning to Huddersfield, Duggy resumed his Fartown career. He also dedicated himself to more wrestling training as he planned to spend his 1920s summers back with his family in their native Ellenborough, competing in as much of the Cumberland & Westmorland calendar as his diary would allow.

Johnny Rogers had broken his leg in Auckland and the 1920/21 season finally saw the demise of The Team of All Talents as the pinnacle of the Northern Union, as they finished a campaign without a trophy for the first time in a dozen years.

Each year, the Cumberland & Westmorland world championship would take place at a different venue as various events in the calendar were awarded the right to host the prestigious tournament. The later in the summer it was, the less chance there was that Duggy could compete due to his Fartown pre-season training commitments, limiting his chances of ever winning the title. At 30, and with his body having endured everything it had, he knew he had a limited number of years to achieve this particular wrestling dream. This put extra pressure on him at the Grasmere Festival as he desperately tried to win the Canon Rawnsley Cup for the first time.

Hardwicke Drummond Rawnsley had been a priest, a poet, a politician and a conservationist. He co-founded the National Trust and was given the post of canon of Carlisle Cathedral. He was adored in Cumberland and had donated the trophy in the early years of the 20th century, before passing away in 1920. Suddenly, Duggy had another sporting landmark in his crosshairs.

Old friends: Douglas Clark and Lord Lonsdale

In the summer of 1921, his first summer back on the circuit since before he had gone to war and only his second as a full adult, Duggy was angry with himself as he failed to compete in either of the two major tournaments.

He knew he would be missing the world championships and so put extra preparation into what was his favourite event. He left the family home at 6.30am and met with a childhood friend from Elbra' who was accompanying him for the day. They arrived at Grasmere so early that hardly anyone else was there. They decided to take a stroll and find somewhere for a light breakfast. The service was slow and Duggy, believing time was of no issue and meticulous as ever about his preparations, insisted on a slow wander back to the venue to allow his food to properly digest. When they got back, long-serving 'Bellman' Dick Howe was already calling the order for the All-Weights division. Duggy patiently waited until the end and never heard his name. So he approached the locally famous Dick – an elderly and comically belligerent man – and asked him who he was up against and when.

'I've blown you out, young Duggy,' Howe casually told him. 'You know the rules, if you're not present when your name is called, you're out!'

Duggy was respectful and, well, he knew ol' Dick was right. So he didn't argue. He would return to Huddersfield for pre-season training empty-handed – in terms of his wrestling targets, at least. But he did return with a beaming smile upon his face as that summer he had met and fallen in love with the beautiful auburn-haired Jane Gate – known to everyone in the area as Jennie.

The couple had a beautiful winter wedding at St Johns Church, just a few hundred yards from Duggy's Birkby home, on 27 January 1922. Duggy finally moved out of Mr and Mrs Hodgson's house after more than a decade of lodging there between his travels. The married couple bought a slightly bigger house in Birkby. They immediately moved into their new marital home, which Douglas named 'Grasmere'.

The sports fans of Huddersfield had much cause for celebration the following summer of 1922. Fartown were back among the trophies as they regained the Yorkshire Cup, Huddersfield Town won their first FA Cup with a 1-0 victory over Preston North End at Stamford Bridge (the newly built national stadium at Wembley would host from the following year) and their favourite adopted son, Douglas Clark, won the Grasmere All-Weights Championship for the first time at the age of 31. Like the rest of the enormous crowd, Lord Lonsdale was delighted to finally see Duggy with the handsome Canon Rawnsley Cup as he awarded it to him with a warm and friendly handshake.

The Northern Union became the Rugby Football League (RFL) and the official name of the sport, which was duly shortened simply to rugby league.

Lord Lonsdale shows off his champions Elizabeth James

The BBC was formed in October of the same year, as was Clark & Rogers coal merchants as Duggy and close friend and team-mate Johnny Rogers set up a new enterprise in preparation for life beyond the rugby field.

The 1923 calendar meant that Duggy could finally make a second attempt at the world championship, on this occasion held just above the Scottish border on Duggy's beloved north-western coast, meaning a relatively short trip of just 40 miles from his hometown – for the summer at least – of Maryport.

Clark comfortably won his way into the semi-finals, where he would meet Matthews, the home favourite of the Scottish crowd, who stood over 6ft tall and weighed in at 22 stone.

As Duggy made his way to the ring, the supporters mocked him with condescending grins, describing him as a 'poor wee laddie' in premature tones of pity and commiseration. It was rare for Duggy not to be the firm crowd favourite. It was also uncommon for him to be the smaller man in the battle.

The man mountain Matthews bulldozed his way to the ring through the partisan crowd, who cheered in support of him. As the two men shook hands and went face to face, the size difference was even more distinct: Matthews taller and much thicker set. As the umpire manoeuvred them into their opening clinch, it was difficult to see how Duggy could overcome this particular foe.

But he had spent so long studying the hank of Jack Robinson in order to calculate the perfect counter to it, that he too knew how to perform the ideal 'chip' as the smaller combatant himself. With the semi-final still one-fall-to-a-finish, it was over as quickly as it began, Duggy felling Matthews with a textbook hank, shocking and silencing the Scottish audience.

Duggy proceeded to the final, where he would meet the tall and clever Liddell, of Hexham. Liddell went on the offensive first in the best-of-three falls tournament decider. But his attempted swing-and-hipe was countered perfectly by Clark's outside-stroke. One fall to Duggy and surely he was about to complete his dream and become world's champion.

With the pair clinched up for the second fall, Duggy himself attempted the swing-and-hipe but, unbelievably to the aghast crowd, this time Liddell countered with the outside-stroke to fell Duggy in an exact reversal of the opening grapple.

It all came down to the final fall. With both men tiring after a long day of wrestling and a tight, tense and gruelling final so far, it was a much more untidy affair. The scruffy ending saw Duggy heartbreakingly felled and the title once again slipped through his grasp.

But at the end of that same summer, the following article was written by former Grasmere Games chief-umpire Mr Tom Stainton, following the latest edition of the famous event that August:

> *I have seen many Grasmeres and all of the famous wrestlers during the last half-century, including Steadman, Ralph and Tom Pooley, Lowden and Hexham Clarke, but never in the whole issue have I seen a man enter on his task like the renowned international footballer, Douglas Clark. Determination was outlined on every feature, and his disposal of the celebrated Routledge, of Wylam, with a beautiful swing-of-the-breast gave us a taste of what was to follow. The second round brought him up against Davis, of Tarraby, one of the most scientific wrestlers of his period, but the ex-lightweight champion was quickly placed 'hors de combat', and then another doughty exponent of the art was faced in Tom Taylor, of Hawkshead, a very prolific finalist and a master of all the tricks of the sport. After a terrific struggle, contested every inch by the Hawkshead wonder, a 'sliphold' ensued and the bout recommenced again in deadly earnest. Of no avail, were the clever tactics of the tricky Taylor against the muscular Douglas, who brought his man*

to the turf absolutely exhausted to immediately receive the sympathy of the big-hearted Cumbrian.

This brought the natural successor of George Steadman against Steele, of Brampton, the hero of many North Country contests and the winner of scores of heavyweight exhibitions. By this time the semi-final had being attained, and the redoubtable international was wrestling superbly. The brawny Steele was made to look very impotent, for after getting into holds, a terrific wrench by Clark brought him to his knees, and a proud look on Douglas' features proclaimed him one of the finalists.

In the final, one of the youngest and certainly one of the cleverest wrestlers of the current generation (Edgar Hayhurst) had attained his place. Hayhurst was schooled in the Milnthorpe Academy and was a member of that celebrated wrestling family which has produced some of the most brilliant wrestlers of the 20th century. Though in stature he was no match for the Cumbrian, Hayhurst was one of the strongest of wrestlers, scientifically and physically, and we were not disappointed at the remarkable manner in which the Westmorland youth evaded the embrace of his heavier opponent. After several slipholds, however, the crowd's yell heralded 'they're hod', and then ensued a mighty struggle. A terrific Cumbrian cheer heralded the fact that Clark had gained the first fall with his favourite swinging-hipe, after a very tough struggle, in which the two finalists displayed wrestling worthy of all-time Grasmeres.

After their gruelling time, it was wonderful to see how fresh these doughty Dalesmen faced the second venture, but all the play of the clever Hayhurst was of no avail against the muscular Douglas of Elbra' fame, and getting his favourite neck-hold-grip, he felled his man with a mighty wrench, and applying the outside-stroke he once more became the

proud heavyweight champion of the famous Grasmere
Sports, worthy to rank with any champion I have ever seen.
Good luck to a real honest wrestler! May we see him
many times on the famous turf in the wrestling Derby.

Duggy had become a two-time Grasmere heavyweight champion in 1924.

The summer of 1924 saw Huddersfield Town crowned the champions of England for the first time, less than 15 years after being founded. They won the Football League Championship by the narrowest margin possible – the closest finish in the history of the English league. It all came down to the rules at the time, and to rather complicated mathematics. They and Cardiff both finished on 57 points and with a goal difference of +27; but with Cardiff having scored 61 goals to the 60 of Town, any currently used system would have seen Cardiff awarded the title. But it was then settled by goal ratio – the ratio of each goal you have scored calculated against each one you have conceded. The equation for Town was 60 divided by 33 to give a ratio of 1.818. Agonisingly for the Bluebirds – but to the delight of Town – theirs was 61/34, equalling 1.794.

They also won the League Championship in the 1924/25 and 1925/26 seasons to become the first-ever team to win three consecutive titles and the famous and fabled 'Thrice Champions'. The latter two successes did not have the same level of controversy as the first, as they finished clear winners by several points over West Bromwich Albion and Arsenal respectively.

Harold Wagstaff retired in 1925 and Douglas Clark succeeded him as the Huddersfield captain. That same year, Duggy was awarded a testimonial match. An article in the *Lancashire Evening Post* read:

Next Saturday the Cumberland captain, Douglas Clark,
will take a well-earned benefit. The Huddersfield club – of

LORD LONSDALE'S DOUBLE HANDSHAKE

Lord Lonsdale congratulating the finalists of the heavy-weight wrestling at Grasmere sports. (Right) Douglas Clark (Maryport), winner and (left) W. Knowles (Silecroft).   Photo: " The Lancashire Daily Post."

*which Clark is also captain – have granted him the match
v. Batley, and it is hoped there will be a bumping gate.
No player is more respected than Douglas Clark and it is
doubtful if a better forward has ever played.*

*After the match in the evening a grand wrestling
tournament is to be held. Most of the noted wrestlers from
Cumberland and Westmorland have promised to attend
and I expect Cumberland will be well represented amongst
the spectators at Huddersfield next Saturday.*

William Knowles ended Duggy's stranglehold on the Grasmere
crown when he beat him in the final of the 1925 tournament
– continuing a rivalry for the coveted heavyweight crowns that
would last for the remainder of the decade and beyond.

But the disappointment was short-lived. Still just as hungry
for sporting victory as he had ever been, Duggy worked
participation in the world championships – being held at
Bampton – into his pre-season, causing anxiety to the rest of
the field. They were correct to be worried. Revenge was had of
a former conqueror in the relatively diminutive but very skilled
two-time and back-to-back defending champion Gilpin Bland,
who was thrown to his demise by Duggy in the semi-final,
where he met and would dispose of another former champ in
J. Little, of Haydonbridge, to become the heavyweight world
champion of Cumberland & Westmorland wrestling for the
first time.

Approaching middle age, Duggy continued his education
further. His catch-as-catch-can wrestling hero, George de
Relwyskow, had authored two books since the end of the war,
My Simple Way to Health and *The Art of Wrestling.*

George had been on a wrestling tour of South America
when the Great War broke out. He returned home to enlist with
the British Army. He served as an unarmed combat instructor
with such distinction, he was promoted to Sergeant Major and

Elizabeth James

posted to Australia to train their troops. Later, he would be posted in France to tutor their instructors in the art, before finally, in 1918, returning to England, based at Aldershot to teach more recruits his unique but devastating wrestling styles.

He continued to perform wrestling exhibitions in a variety of packed-out theatres throughout the 1920s and was trainer to the 1924 Great Britain Olympic wrestling team.

The first concerning signs since the end of the war that all was not well in Europe had begun to appear. The Treaty of Versailles had imposed economic and military sanctions on Germany, as well as damning blame for the war, and stripped them of land they had previously claimed under the guise of the now-defunct German Empire. It said they were never to hold an army of more than 100,000 soldiers. Many within the historically powerful and proud nation were humiliated and demoralised, and the crippled economy inflicted much poverty.

The far-right nationalist Nazi Party had been founded in 1920 by 31-year-old Adolf Hitler – an Austrian national who had served in the Great War. Having lived in Germany since 1913 and served their empire in the nightmare that was trench warfare, he had become bitterly twisted at the defeat and subsequent sanctions. He installed himself as the *Führer* (leader) of the Nazi Party. His rhetoric was that Germany had been made a scapegoat and was unfairly and overly punished by the bullies that were the Allied Powers, and were now powerless to stop swathes of Jews and Poles taking over their 'Fatherland'. In 1925, he released his autobiographical manifesto 'Mein Kampf' ('My Struggle'), which stated how he saw the idealistic Germany. It was an ingenious piece of evil propaganda that targeted the nationalist underbelly. The hate-filled racist and anti-Semitic aura around post-war Germany was gaining momentum.

Douglas Clark confirmed his global domination of a second sport when he defended his heavyweight world championship crown in 1926.

Diary entry 22 January 1927:

> *Arrive at Cottage Hospital to see poor old Dad, who is very*
> *ill. Jennie and I were very pleased he knew us. He passed*
> *peacefully away at 10pm. He was the best father and dearest*
> *pal a man could have. I loved him when I was a little lad*
> *but it grew so big that now we have lost him, life can never*
> *be quite the same.*

Duggy would remain strong, skilful and committed enough to play for Fartown at the top level of club rugby until he retired at the end of the 1927/28 season at the age of 37. But he returned to help a small but overachieving Fartown team compete strongly in multiple competitions the following season. He played just four matches that campaign, and for the first time since 1920, Huddersfield won the RFL League Championship – a fitting and apt ending to the most wonderful rugby career imaginable.

Whilst out of retirement, the latest Australian tour was taking place in Great Britain, and at the age of 38 Duggy represented Cumberland for a record 31st time against the might of the Kangaroos. He was sensational and inspired his county to a famous 8-5 upset.

He played an astonishing 485 professional matches for Huddersfield – a record that still stands to this day – winning 20 major competitions.

In total, including Test matches and representative games for England and Cumberland, he played 534 top-level games, scoring 110 tries. He inspired Cumberland to County Championship titles and his country to multiple Test series victories.

Whilst his rugby prowess was waning, his wrestling was seemingly going from strength to strength. To the delight of his family and the hordes of followers who watched him there every year, Duggy won back-to-back Grasmere tournaments in

1927 and 1928, taking his tally of Canon Rawnsley Cup wins to four. A fifth would see him awarded the precious trophy as his own to keep.

In 1929, the tournament was won by Joseph Robinson – son of Duggy's legendary nemesis Jack. Joe had turned into quite the wrestler himself. He was a confident young man who carried himself with a swagger. He had won the 1919 Grasmere middleweight tournament as a very young prodigy. A decade later, he was the 'all-weights' champion.

Retirement from rugby meant that Duggy could compete unimpeded in the full 1930 wrestling calendar, including the world championships. It would be his final Cumberland & Westmorland campaign before turning 40.

As well as young Robinson, William Knowles had long emerged as his main competition, and nothing much changed that fine summer. Knowles and Duggy shared the trophies almost equally and came up against each other regularly. Knowles was the younger man, in his prime and without the extraordinary 'miles on the clock' Duggy was carrying after what he had been through during the past two decades. But Clark remained, seemingly, the world's strongest man – a term used to describe him by various sources throughout his life, long before there was an official competition or title to decide whom that may be. His dedication and determination meant that age was no barrier to him.

The 1930 world championships were actually held closer to Huddersfield than they were to Maryport as the event moved further south to Whittingham, Lancashire.

The famous Lancastrian weather meant for a long, tough day of wrestling in the muddy conditions. Duggy's experience and strength would prove vital as he predictably met Knowles in the final and came out the victor. Douglas Clark became a three-time Cumberland & Westmorland world heavyweight champion with yet another tournament win in 1930.

GRASMERE,
45, STORTHS RD.,
BIRKBY,

TEL. 1896

DOUGLAS CLARK,

COAL AGENT,

HILLHOUSE SIDINGS.

HUDDERSFIELD.

He was both a multiple-time winner of the Grasmere and multiple-time winner and current holder of the world championship.

Whilst he was retired from the secure wage that rugby league had paid him all those years, Duggy had already become sole proprietor to the coal merchant business – with Welsh partner Johnny Rogers having left Huddersfield in 1925.

He decided to limit his wrestling to an annual appearance at the Grasmere as he strived for the elusive fifth victory.

When the frosty winter months of 1930 arrived, like his father before him and despite his rugby stardom and being a current heavyweight world champion, Duggy was a full-time coal merchant, and delighted to be one. The neighbourhood loved and thrived on seeing their local hero and deity-like figure each morning. Quiet and humble as ever, he would give them a wave and a smile from the carriage of his horse, and he would rather discuss their heating requirements than his worldly experiences in sport and war. Douglas Clark quickly became the pillar of the community.

Sensing he had accomplished all he could in the late 1920s, Douglas proudly poses with his haul of prizes from his life in sport and war. Little did he know he was about to go 'All-In'. Elizabeth James

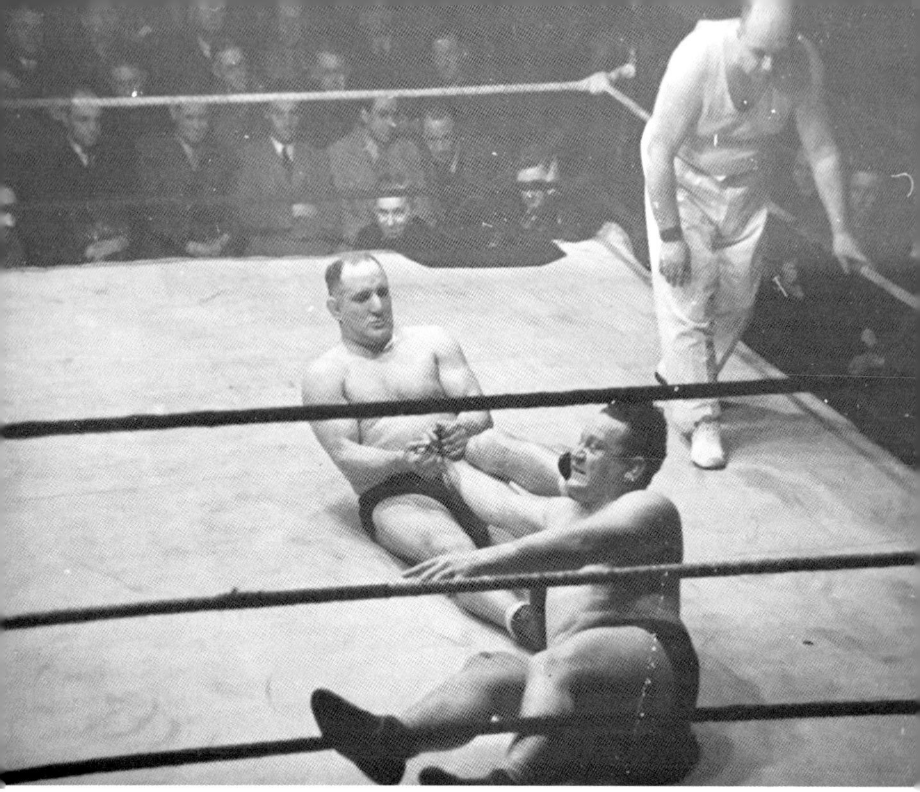

'All-In' action   Elizabeth James

The Clark family. From back left: Archie; William; Mary-Jane; Douglas; Ainsley; Father John; Ruth; Margaret; Aunt Sara-Anne; Mother Elizabeth; Lizzie

Elizabeth James & Imperial War Museum

Loyal friends: Douglas Clark, Jennie Clark and Stanley Pepperell   Elizabeth James

Douglas joins Lord Lonsdale (right) at Grasmere   Elizabeth James

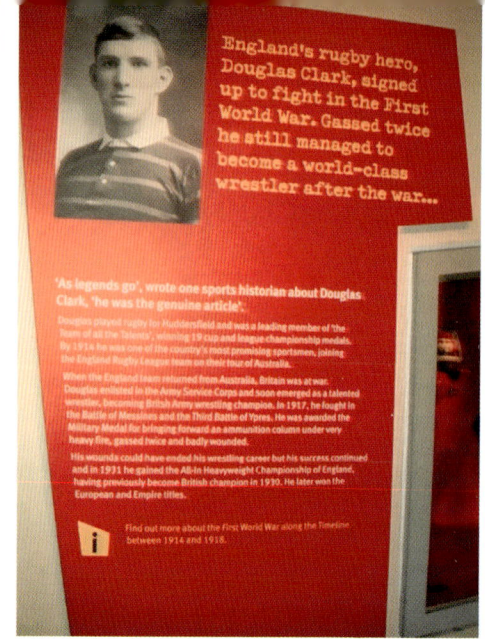

Bust of Douglas Clark commissioned at the John Smith's Stadium in 2010

Huddersfield Rugby League: A Lasting Legacy

The Imperial War Museum North exhibit that inspired this book

Huddersfield Rugby League: A Lasting Legacy & Imperial War Museum

'As legends go, he was the genuine article'

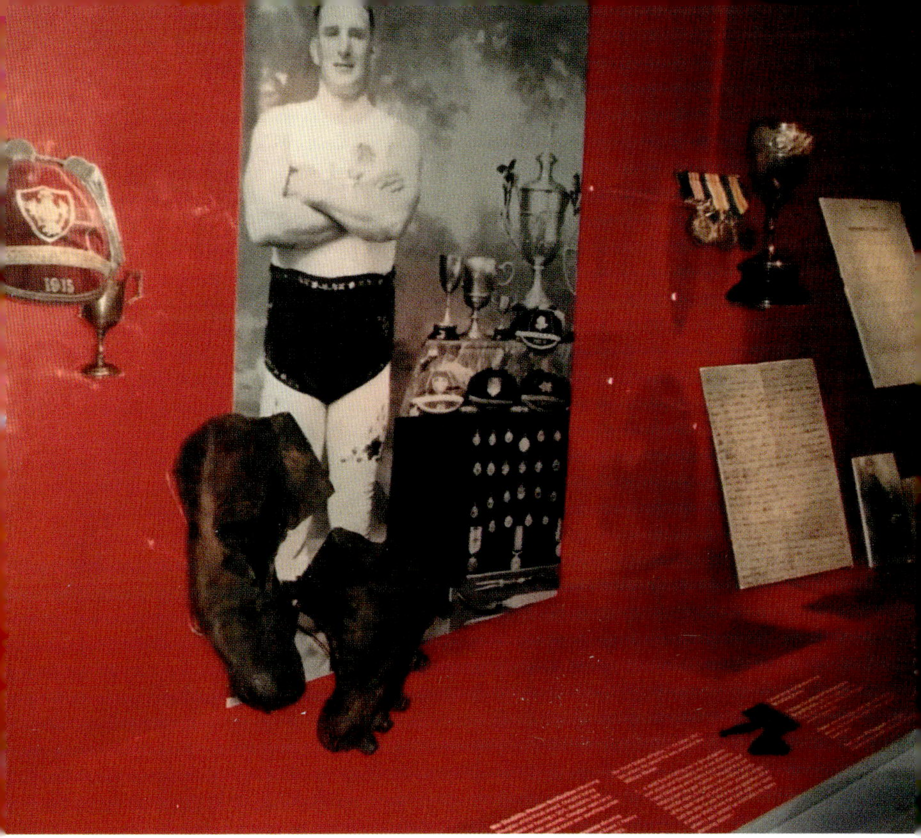
1915

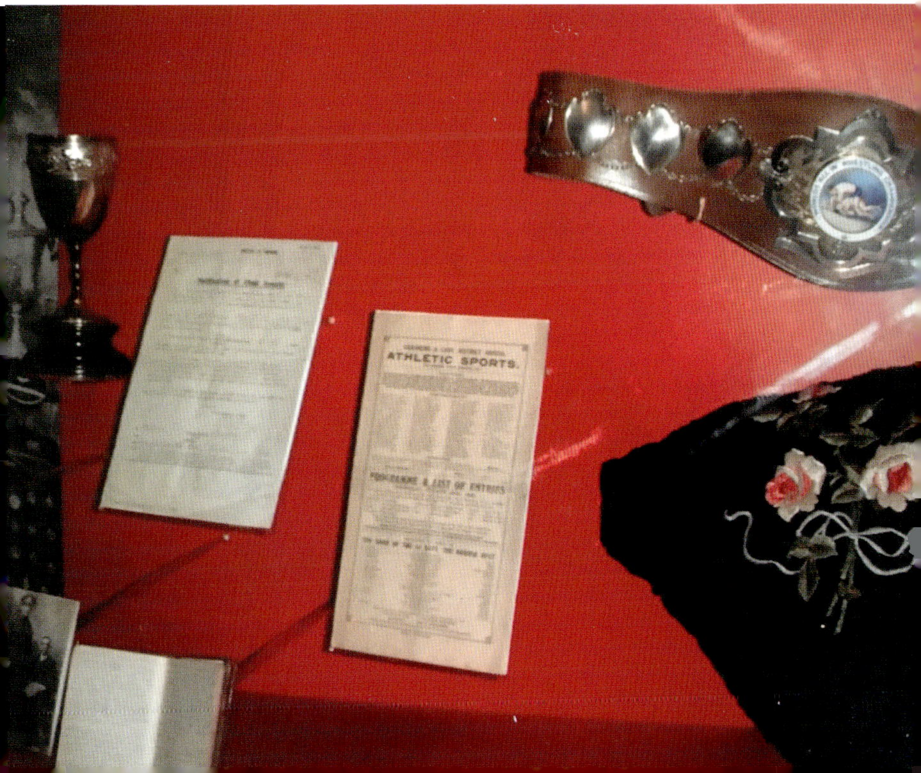
ATHLETIC SPORTS.
PROGRAMME & LIST OF ENTRIES

Rivals? Signed photograph sent to Douglas by Atholl Oakeley in 1931, the year they first faced off in the ring
Elizabeth James & Imperial War Museum

All best wishes to Douglas

Atholl. Oakeley
1931

Rivals? Signed photograph sent to Douglas by Laurent Gerstmans in 1933, the year they twice met for the world heavyweight championship

Elizabeth James & Imperial War Museum

The rebuilt Cloth Hall, Ypres …

… and its 2017 centenary commemorations of the Battle of Passchendaele

PART 3

'If Shakespeare was alive today, he would be writing wrestling shows.'

— Chris Jericho

13

ALL-IN

Six months earlier
June 1930
Islington
London

EDWARD ATHOLL Oakeley poured himself a large glass of milk, one of 11 per day he consumed in a bid to increase his muscle mass. It was working – the 30-year-old walked away from his kitchen standing a little short of 6ft tall, but with a thick chest, broad shoulders and a wide neck. Carrying his glass in one hand and the daily newspaper in the other, he walked out of the patio doors of his well-presented Victorian house and out on to the wooden decking. He was dressed in white, full-length linen pants, pulled up to the height of his naval and secured by braces, the brown straps of which sat over his shoulders alongside his white V-neck vest, where a pair of tortoiseshell sunglasses rested on his chest. He had short, dark hair, heavily greased into a strictly lined side-parting and a strong, square jaw.

Edward was born in Anglesey, Wales, the son of Major Edward Francis Oakeley, a high-ranking Army official. His grandfather, Charles William Oakeley, was the fourth Baronet of Shrewsbury. The family were nobility. Edward junior, who for family simplicity had become known as Atholl, was bullied at school for being 'posh'. He subsequently trained hard to become a fast runner, but also in the art of self-defence, particularly amateur wrestling. He went on to further education at Clifton College before following his family dynasty and joining the military. He graduated with honours from Royal Military Academy Sandhurst and had served as an officer since, albeit in peacetime.

When he moved to London for his Sandhurst placement, he joined the Ashdown Club in order to enhance his fitness to the military standard required and to further develop his wrestling skills.

The Ashdown Club, situated in Islington, played host to boxing and wrestling events and was the training gymnasium to many of both sports' finest proponents. Boxing was professional at the time, with wrestling still strictly amateur. The style was catch-as-catch-can, which he was also getting extra training and practice in with the Army. The contests took place on square, clean, padded mats with ropes around the perimeter to form the ring.

As Atholl placed his milk on the glass, round table on his decking, which overlooked a majestically kept garden, and sat on his wicker chair, he could confidently say he was the best heavyweight wrestler in the country. No one could beat him in the military contests, nor down at the Ashdown, from where he had already returned after a morning of successful grappling. He had showered and was ready to recuperate for the evening.

He opened his broadsheet, snapping it out away from his chest to straighten out the crease as he rested one leg on top of the other and settled into prime comfort. He put the sunglasses on his face as the low spring evening sun cast its rays upon him. Just as he began to read the front-page headline, the heavy front door of his house slammed closed. Atholl rolled his eyes, knowing his leisure time was over before it had even started. It was his young room-mate, Bill Garnon.

Oakeley had met Bill a few years earlier at the Ashdown and seeing him as the wrestling prodigy he was, took him under his wing. He allowed him to live cheaply in his house, which provided easy and constant access to the gym so that he could progress.

At just 22, Bill was already widely regarded as the best middleweight in the country. As he burst on to the decking, dressed in a similar vein to Atholl but with jet-black hair and a thick moustache, his mentor put the newspaper down alongside his glass of milk.

'I've been beaten!' Garnon sighed as he slumped down on the second wicker seat.

'You've been what?' replied Oakeley, lifting the sunglasses from his eyes and on to his crown to reveal a pair of wide, shocked eyes.

'Beaten, this afternoon, at the Ashdown.'

'For heaven's sake! Who beat you?'

'An American that came by, called Sherman. Claims to be the middleweight champion of the world!'

'How long did you go?'

'About 17.'

'He pinned you in just 17 minutes?'

'Well, not exactly. He used a straight-scissors and a neck-bar. I had to quit or get my neck broken.'

'How long has the straight-scissors been allowed when used with a bar?'

'Well, of course, it isn't allowed. But Sherman says that, under the new professional rules, submission holds are now allowed as in Japanese judo. He and his friend, a chap called Irslinger, are here to show us all the new style and introduce the rules they say are taking over. They've arrived here from South Africa on this very business.'

Oakeley sat forward, with his elbows on his knees. 'Who, and what, is Irslinger?'

'Sherman says he is also American and holds the light-heavyweight championship of the world. Anyway, they want to meet you. I've invited them here for lunch, tomorrow.'

Sure enough, the following day – a Sunday afternoon – the two Americans arrived at the house. It was another sunny day and Atholl prepared a light, healthy lunch of cooked meats and salad on the decking. The four men were all dressed smart, in dark suits, perfectly clean-shaven and not a hair out of place. Bill Garnon made the introductions and they exchanged pleasantries. There was wine and water readily available on the table. But Atholl drank milk. The wine went untouched by all.

Henry Irslinger appeared to be the brains behind the duo. Both of them were the brawn. Irslinger chatted openly about how he had been born in Austria of a German father and an English mother. As a 16-year-old he had won an open-age, open-weight wrestling tournament in London way back in 1908 before moving to the USA. Atholl quickly did the maths: this made the man sitting opposite him 40 years old – the age when, invariably, a wrestler's prowess began to wane. The astute Oakeley began to realise what was going on: Irslinger was preparing himself for a career beyond the wrestling mat. He was building his potential empire as a promoter.

Sherman was 28. His boyish good looks told the story of how talented he was – he looked like he had barely broken into a sweat in his entire life. He was from Portland, Oregon.

The finishing up of lunch coincided perfectly with the natural end to the extensive introductions they had all given.

'I hear you're the best prospect over here,' Irslinger said to Oakeley as he wiped the corners of his mouth with his napkin and casually tossed it on to the table.

'Well, that's a matter of opinion. I haven't been beaten since 1928, if that's anything to go by,' Oakeley replied.

'Well, you're going to be beaten now. Sherman wants to try you out. Now. Where can you go?'

'The Ashdown is closed of a Sunday afternoon. The only place is here on the lawn. The grass is soft. Let's go. But, I am assuming you are insisting on these *new* rules applying, under which Sherman beat Bill yesterday?'

'Of course, this is a great opportunity for you, Mr Oakeley. These are not new rules. We are merely sharing "new-catch-as-catch-can" wrestling with the rest of the world. It is more inclusive, as it is a hybrid of several of the forms from around the world. Many of these styles claim to have a "worlds champion", but are only competed in small regions. We will soon have a champion from countries all around the globe. Continental champions. And one, true, Worlds Champion at each weight division. Matches will take place at the biggest venues and pit Europeans against Indians, Americans versus Japanese. And you, Mr Oakeley, can be the first British champion.'

Whilst Atholl listened intently to Irslinger, Sherman was stripped down to his bare feet, trousers – but with the braces now hanging down by his thighs – and his white vest that had previously been an undergarment.

Oakeley stood and calmly got himself into a similar state of dress as his opponent, who was now stretching and limbering up on the lawn.

Henry Irslinger and Bill Garnon pulled their wicker chairs to the perfect viewing position, as they would act as the judges.

'Wrestle,' Henry told them, as he leaned in with a glare. 'But just remember, Mr Oakeley, all holds are legal.'

Sherman ran straight for Atholl, attempting a take-down around his waist. He was smaller than Oakeley's usual opponents and considerably faster, but expecting this, Atholl palmed him away and sent him flipping across the grass. A more cautious approach was then adopted by Sherman, who tried to entice the bigger man into locking up with him, only to evade the grasp of Oakeley and attempt to lock on a submission hold to the loosest limb. But Atholl's strength was proving

Atholl Oakeley Elizabeth James & Imperial War Museum

supreme as he was able to throw Sherman off. Getting used to the style and the speed of his adversary, Atholl began to throw Sherman on to the ground at will, the soil was beginning to cut up and the two men's considerable perspiration quickly turned it to mud.

Sherman landed softly every time and was back to his feet like an Olympic gymnast before Atholl could get close enough to go for a pin-fall.

After around 25 minutes, with both men seemingly tiring, Oakeley attempted to engage Sherman in a standing grapple, but the lightning-quick American ducked beneath his arms and behind him. Before Oakeley knew anything more, Sherman had his legs scissored around his midriff and his right arm wrapped around his face. Atholl was stretched backwards until both men fell in unison. Sherman now had the same hold locked on Oakeley that had forced Garnon into submission just 24 hours earlier. With his body agonisingly contorted, only Oakeley's pride and confidence in his 22-inch neck muscles withstanding the hold prevented him from following suit. But instead, he writhed; he wriggled; he fought. Eventually, he managed to separate Sherman's ankles. He could sense his opponent's grip failing and his body shaking with fatigue. Enough sweat formed in the grip around the face and Sherman broke. Atholl twisted to finally gain the leverage on the ground.

'Time!' called Irslinger. 'I've seen all I need to see,' he said turning to Bill, sat beside him. 'Mr Garnon, how about you make us all a nice pot of your legendary English tea?'

'These new rules are going to bring wrestling back on top all over the world,' Irslinger told Atholl, who was towelling himself off alongside Sherman, whilst pouring black tea from a pot into a china cup, placed perfectly on its matching saucer.

'And what matters at your time of life, Mr Oakeley, is money.' Sherman took his turn on what Oakeley and Garnon began to realise was a rehearsed sales pitch, possibly one that had been used several times already in other countries.

'This is your big chance to make use of what you have learnt. You have the ability, the looks and the physique. If you turn pro now you can train every day, wrestle a few times each week domestically in packed-out venues and as long as you keep winning, you will earn the big bucks and fly all around the world, competing against the biggest and best legends of the sport. And you *will* keep winning. You too Bill – from what I saw yesterday, I'm sure you can be the British middleweight champion. It's up to you guys.' Sherman had really found his voice. Meanwhile, Irslinger quietly sipped his tea and admired the sun-kissed scenery, his sunglasses preventing Atholl from reading his eyes. 'Here's the thing,' Sherman continued, 'if you turn this down now, Henry and I will be on our way. But if you want to give it a shot at being full-time professional wrestlers, Henry will promote an open-to-all tournament for the British heavyweight championship. If you can beat all your opposition, as we *know* that you will, you have nothing to worry about.'

Atholl Oakeley and Bill Garnon shot each other a look and a wry smile, before standing and offering their hands out in agreement.

'Ben,' began Irslinger, turning to look at his companion, 'we had best find ourselves some residence in London – we may be here some time.'

Meetings between the four were held regularly at the Ashdown Club, in and amongst training sessions. The two main protagonists of the scheme really emerged in Henry Irslinger and Atholl Oakeley.

Irslinger organised for two acquaintances of his to be flown into London to assist with the training of British wrestlers to the new style and the new rules. First was George Modrich, a Croatian-born New Zealander with family roots in England. He stood 6ft tall and weighed in at 17 stone, with tanned skin and a clean-shaven scalp. He had many years' experience competing in both boxing and wrestling around the world.

He then flew over George Boganski, whom he had met and trained during his recent time in South Africa. Boganski had short brown hair in a slick side-parting and a lean physique. He had fled Russia during the war, finding himself in Australia and then South Africa. As well as becoming a proficient professional wrestler in these countries, he had adopted their love of rugby.

They were deemed by Irslinger to be the perfect men to come and assist with the project. Sherman was placed in charge of the training regime, with Modrich and Boganski the heavyweight sparring partners who would stretch and punish their disciples.

Following trials, the three chosen for the nightly training were Oakeley, Garnon and a local, fresh-faced 22-year-old named Bert Assirati. Bert was Anglo-Italian in ethnicity and had competed in weight-lifting and gymnastics since the age of 12. He had then become a member of the Ashdown Club as he saw wrestling as the ideal career to complement his extraordinary combination of strength and agility. Standing just 5ft 7in tall but barrel-shaped and muscular, Assirati gave the illusion of being wider than he was high.

Boganski taught them the value of the 'rugger tackle' in this new, faster-paced style. On occasion, they should sprint out of their corner quickly, and with a flying grapple, attempt to take down their rival unawares below the waist. Oakeley recognised this tactic from his garden encounter with Benny Sherman.

Whilst the trio were excelling in their regular training, Irslinger plotted how to get news of the new style and upcoming heavyweight tournament around the country. He approached boxing promoters and offered to provide a wrestling match at their events to attract attention.

Mainly around London but also venturing up to Belle Vue in Manchester, any two of the four experienced professionals on these shores – Irslinger, Sherman, Modrich and Boganski – would put on intense, competitive and sometimes violent contests in front of large audiences of thousands. As Oakeley, Garnon and Assirati mastered the trade, they too began fighting each other, as well as the seasoned professionals, at any events that would allow them to. They stole the shows from the boxers and, as the months went by and the end of 1930 came, the supporters and media were tantalised.

By December, there were enough willing and trained participants, many of whom were experienced and successful fighters in a plethora of styles, for 'new-catch-as-catch-can' to officially launch itself to the country. Irslinger booked London's Olympia and Belle Vue once again in the north to hold events simultaneously on the evening of Monday 15, so that the debut hit headlines far and wide across the country. Irslinger himself topped the bill at The Olympia, defeating Modrich in a magnificent spectacle – described as the roughest professional fight ever seen in the capital. Atholl Oakeley and Bert Assirati were trusted to headline in Manchester, where thousands crammed to capacity and hundreds had to be turned away. Oakeley won the bout after a 23-minute display of speed, strength and agility from both men. On the undercards, dozens of wrestlers performed in a variety of styles and techniques against one another. Any heavyweight contests were billed as preliminary qualifiers for the upcoming British heavyweight championship tournament.

'This is the worldwide combat sport phenomenon that we are bringing to you,' Irslinger told the eager press after the event in London. He explained that the style and the rules were an amalgamation of many of the popular regional styles from around the world as he listed American-catch, catch-as-catch-can, Cumberland & Westmorland and Japanese judo amongst them. He told them how heavyweight competitors from any of those disciplines and more were all welcome to enter the tournament he was organising. He casually described those styles as being 'all-in' this revolutionary new sport. The journalists present, each wearing a tweed or herringbone bucket or pork pie-style hat, scribbled down the quotes on their tiny, flip-over notebooks as ash dropped from the cigarettes that loosely dangled from their lips.

One of those journalists was the eminent *Daily Express* sports writer Trevor Wignall. Wignall's passion was reporting on major combat sports, of which boxing was king, but he recognised something special was maybe about to come to the market.

Meanwhile, with the bitter northern winter fully set in, Douglas Clark was working hard to keep the homes in his Huddersfield community warm. He would start his coal rounds at first light. It would be the early afternoon when he would return home to the modest terrace house he shared with his beloved wife Jennie. He would walk into the kitchen, where he knew she would be busy doing her daily chores. On the worktop there would be a bowl full of steaming hot soapy water waiting for Duggy to plunge his coal dust-covered hands into. Following a rinse that lasted just a few seconds, the water and suds would turn the same black as the coal he had spent the morning handling. He could then embrace and say hello to Jennie, invariably giving her a kiss on the cheek that would leave a charcoal mark on her face from his.

He would then wander into the living room, where a full china teapot sat alongside his favourite cup. Also on the table was a plate full of cheese sandwiches, accompanied by the brand-new favourite condiment of the north of England – Branston Pickle. Folded, with the edges neatly tucked under the side of the plate, was a crisp copy of the *Daily Express*.

This was his daily routine, but on the afternoon of Tuesday, 16 December the wooden table and Duggy's paisley-patterned fabric armchair were more central in the small living room to make way for the plastic Christmas tree which stood, littered with tinsel and baubles, in the corner in which he usually dwelled. As he squeezed his huge frame into the smaller space that he would have to make do with for the festive season, a bauble dropped from the tree. With his giant hands, he gently picked it up and re-hung it. With a huge sigh, he pushed his shoulders into the grooves of the chair his 16 stone frame had indented into it over the years. He felt for his newspaper, feathering it out from under the plate. Like every man of his – or any – era, he naturally and unconsciously turned to the back to read the sports pages. The story still dominating the national sport headlines was that of Huddersfield Town's most recent result: following an alarming run of seven games without a victory in Division One, Clem Stephenson's men had regained their form and taken their frustrations out on a sorry Blackpool with an astonishing 10-1 scoreline at the Leeds Road stadium.

Duggy enjoyed reading about the success of his local Association Football team but, as he turned the pages, a story caught his eye. It was a piece by Trevor Wignall. Duggy sat more upright in his seat and shuffled forward as his curiosity was grabbed by the headline 'ALL-IN'. He went on to read about the action from the previous evening in London and Manchester. He read the quotes of Henry Irslinger regarding the fact that anyone, from any wrestling background, could compete in this mixed format. He read that there would be a tournament to crown a British heavyweight champion. As he read that the tournament was open to all, Duggy looked up from the page with a glint in his eye. He put down the newspaper and walked towards his book cabinet, where he gently feathered out a small, paperback book with his giant index finger. He sat back down and began to study *The Art of Wrestling*, by George de Relwyskow.

It was early January and the Christmas decorations were being taken down at the Ashdown Club as Atholl Oakeley

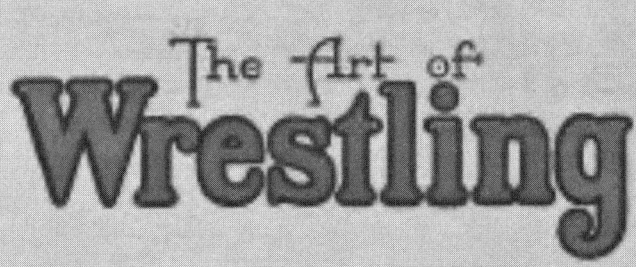

By G. de RELWYSKOW,
LIGHT-WEIGHT CHAMPION OF THE WORLD.
Officially Appointed Trainer to British
Olympic Games Team, Paris, 1924.

GALE & POLDEN LTD
LONDON, ALDERSHOT
AND PORTSMOUTH

PRICE
2/-
NETT.

walked past the open door to the back room Henry Irslinger had taken as his office.

'Captain, get in here,' Irslinger yelled in his mixed European and American accent. Henry had taken to calling Atholl 'captain', and instructed everyone else to do the same. This would be the ring gimmick of Oakeley: the former military officer; the leader; the captain. 'I've made a decision on the eight guys for the tournament, and on who faces who.' He passed a piece of scrap paper to a standing Atholl across his office desk. Scribbled in pencil, it read:

RAHGAT – O'ROURKE
CAPTAIN – L. FRANKLIN
J. ROBINSON – J. HARRISON
G. MODRICH – D. CLARK

'Modrich?! British championship?' queried Oakeley.

'Yeah. He has enough English ethnicity to justify his inclusion. We need some *bad guys* for the audience to jeer. He's perfect – a foreigner gatecrashing the British tournament on a technicality. I've put him against Douglas Clark in the opening round.'

'Clark? He's the Cumberland champ, isn't he?'

'Yeah. But I've read his background on his application. National rugger legend; war hero! The crowd will *love* him, and hate George all the more for it. So when George beats him, and then gets to the final against you, Captain Oakeley will be their hero.'

'Don't you think you're being a little presumptuous there, ol' chap?' Oakeley said, stroking his chin and looking a little concerned.

Irslinger shook his head. 'Clark may be "world" champion in that style only those detached, remote people from the north of this country compete in, but he won't be able to survive one round with George in *our* ring. The same goes for young Joe Robinson. They won't have the techniques to achieve pin-falls and submissions. Plus, Clark's pushing 40.'

The pair had little clue about Duggy's successful couple of forays into catch-as-catch-can before and during the war, nor that he had been a student of the art for a long time, nor the fact that he was *probably* the world's strongest man.

'So, you see myself against Modrich in the final?' asked Oakeley.

Irslinger casually nodded. 'They'll *love* it, Captain. They'll love you.'

'But ...' Oakeley's eyes narrowed as he tried to get Irslinger to realise what he was trying to say without actually having to say the words. He peered around the open doorway to see Modrich in the ring with another young apprentice, who was squealing in pain as George stretched and tortured him to his limits.

'Oh don't worry, Captain, your training has turned you into a formidable foe for anyone. George is well past his best and much slower than you. And besides, he knows what is at stake.' Irslinger stood up from behind his desk and collected his camelhair coat from a hook on the wall in preparation to leave.

'What does that mean?'

'Oh, *smarten up* Atholl. He knows how much we have invested in you becoming British heavyweight champion, and then taking you on the big tour of the US. That's why he's here, after all,' Irslinger said as he tied the belt of his oversized coat. 'He wouldn't ruin that. Oh, and the term *"All-In"* has really caught on. We're going with it.' Irslinger left, leaving Oakeley pondering the situation.

Bert Assirati was furious at his exclusion from the tournament. Henry Irslinger had told him he had been eliminated when he lost to Oakeley in Manchester. But Bert angrily pleaded that he and Atholl had been told to put on a show – an exhibition of sorts – to build the sport, so the result should not count. He had become a feared competitor at the Ashdown. Now, scorned, not even the professionals carrying out the training dared to spar with Bert. His angry demeanour, blistering speed, acrobatic agility and astonishing power in his short, squat frame had made him an adversary to be avoided at all costs. His theory that he had been excluded because he may well have won the tournament and scuppered the long-term plans of Irslinger and Oakeley was difficult to argue with.

By the middle of January, the tournament was set and formally announced. The first round of matches would take place on 18 February 1931 at the London Sports Club. They would be six-round battles, with the rounds lasting ten minutes each. The winner would be the first to obtain two falls by three-second shoulder pin to the mat, submission or the opponent's disqualification or failure to get back into the ring after being ejected from it. If the fall count was tied after the hour-long fight, the decision would go to the judges' scorecards.

The prize would be the handsome sum of £50, a large trophy with the name of the tournament winner engraved upon it, and the new title of British heavyweight champion – his until he was defeated by another British heavyweight.

14

BEST-LAID PLANS

18 February 1931
All-In British Heavyweight Tournament
Quarter-finals
The London Sports Club
London

NORTHERN ACCENTS could be heard amongst the capacity crowd as supporters of their hero, Douglas Clark, had travelled all day by road and rail to see him in action in this new phenomenon.

The northern brigade also joined together to cheer on young Joe Robinson, who managed to overcome Glasgow's Jim Harrison by two clear falls to advance into the semi-finals.

But tension amongst the crowd was palpable. The gentlemanly audience dressed mostly in warm but smart suits and deer-stalker-type hats on the freezing winter evening. They were soon stripped down to their shirts and waistcoats as they puffed on their cigarettes in the smoky, sweltering venue under the low and blindingly bright lights. Their main event was coming soon: Douglas Clark taking on the experienced George Modrich.

Henry Irslinger had promoted the tournament superbly, building the angle of the all-British hero in Clark, a newcomer to the sport at the age of 39, in contrast with the 'foreigner'

THE MAN OF ALL TALENTS

Modrich, a gruff, experienced veteran trying to muscle his way to the British title, despite having only arrived in the country recently. The paying public had lapped it up and were desperate for a Clark upset.

As Joe Robinson walked back into the locker room, Duggy spotted the son of his former rival. 'Congratulations, Joe. Well done.'

'Thanks, Doug. It's tough out there. I've injured my arm, feels really bad.'

Remembering Joe's father wasn't shy about doling out the excuses, and aware that they would meet one another in the semi-final if he did manage to beat Modrich, Duggy didn't indulge Joe too much. He stood to his feet to do the same pre-match routine he followed in rugby. He cut an imposing figure, wearing black wrestling boots – something he was unaccustomed to – and a small pair of black lycra shorts. His metabolism was clearly slowing down in middle age, as a rounding but solid gut protruded above the line of his new wrestling trunks.

Atholl Oakeley was already back dressed in his suit and applying lashings of hair gel to his side-parting in the mirror, having already comfortably won his match to advance in the tournament.

Members of the crowd cut off their friends mid-sentence in order to give full attention to the ring as the announcer stepped through the ropes and on to the mat. Dressed in a full black dinner suit, he began, 'Gentlemen and any ladies who may be present this evening. This is the main event you have all been waiting for. Introducing first. Weighing in at 17 stone. From Croatia. George. *Modrich!*'

In unison, the audience launched into pantomime-style boos as George emerged from behind the curtain and out on to the top of the ramp. Shaven-headed and with his black trunks stretched high above his navel, he dismissively waved the back of his hand towards the crowd, looking mean and angry. He entered the ring and stood in one corner.

'And his opponent ...' the ring announcer restarted, the crowd already beginning to buzz with excitement. 'Weighing 16 stone. From Huddersfield, West Yorkshire. He is a legend of the sport of rugby, a British war veteran and the Cumberland and Westmorland World Heavyweight Champion. Douglas. *Clark!*' The crowd erupted into cheers, whistles and relentless clapping as Duggy emerged from behind the black curtain and through the haze of smoke that was limiting the visibility.

Duggy stepped between the ropes and rubbed the palms of his hands together, sign language if there ever was for 'let's fight'.

The referee waved the two competitors towards each other and battle commenced. They circled each another gingerly, careful not to give the opponent the leverage in the opening tie-up. When the pair did lock up, Duggy used his enormous strength to wrestle the hold into something that resembled the Cumberland & Westmorland style of grapple he was used to. From there, he could toss the bigger man George around at will using his plethora of perfectly executed throws and chips. What he struggled to do was gain a fall; he had no real expertise in ground wrestling or submission holds at this professional level. His only opportunity was to use his strength to pin the shoulders of George to the mat for the referee's three count, but the wily old veteran always managed to wriggle out.

The nervous tension in the arena was causing the crowd to fall silent, until each huge throw from Clark forced them into cheers once more, and they urged him on to gain a fall.

Henry Irslinger, Atholl Oakeley, Ben Sherman and Bill Garnon watched on from ringside – all suited and mafia-like in appearance – amazed by the performance of Duggy and by the vociferous and passionate support of the crowd. Irslinger's masterplan had worked – except for the fact that Modrich was showing no signs of winning. Could they end up with the wildcard that was Douglas Clark in their final four?

Minute piled upon minute as round after round went by. It was a stupendous showing of strength and stamina from the two middle-aged men.

'THREE ... TWO ... ONE' the crowd counted down together before rising to their feet to give the pair a standing ovation. Clark and George shook hands and warmly patted each other on the shoulder in congratulations.

The announcer stepped back into the ring as the arena fell silent with anxiety once again. He got both men to stand either side of him before raising the arm of Douglas Clark in victory, to the delirium of the crowd.

Just two days later, Duggy was back on his coal round. When he returned home there was a telegram waiting for him on the table, too. It was from Henry Irslinger, informing him that his semi-final would take place as top of the bill at an event on the evening of Wednesday, 4 March, once again at the London Sports Club. It said his accommodation had been booked for two nights, as the final, should he make it, was to take place the following night.

Atholl Oakeley's semi-final would take place a couple of nights earlier. Duggy assumed this had been planned in order to give 'The Captain' more time to recover and prepare for the final.

Also, with the final taking place so quickly following the previous round, Irslinger had declared it would be made up of only three ten-minute rounds. Could this be due to the fact that Duggy had proven his conditioning and stamina over the longer format already, whereas Oakeley – against weaker opponents – was only wrestling short matches? Just like so many other times in the life of Douglas Clark, the odds appeared to be stacked against him.

After another long train journey down to London for the

potential double-header, Duggy had naively tried to orient himself around the London Underground – alien to a middle-aged northerner – and arrived at the venue only to be told that Joe Robinson had pulled out with an arm injury. Duggy was awarded a walkover victory and a place in the final against Captain Oakeley – who had, of course, already comfortably secured his semi-final win at an earlier show.

Duggy couldn't help but notice the irony – Robinson Sr having vowed to gift him the win in any bout in which they were pitted against one another after he had mastered how to wrestle him back in 1916 before he headed off to war. With the new contacts he had made, Joe flew out to Cape Town, where he became South Africa's main-event wrestling superstar and made a fantastic new life for himself.

Duggy would have a full night of rest before finding himself in the unlikely position of challenging the aristocratic Atholl Oakeley to be the first-ever 'All-In British Wrestling Champion'.

15

JOHN BULL IN TRUNKS

5 March 1931
All-In British Heavyweight Tournament
Final
Atholl Oakeley versus Douglas Clark
The London Sports Club
London

'NOW. THE moment you have all been waiting for,' the ring announcer began once again as he introduced the main event of the evening. 'The following bout is for the title of British heavyweight champion!' Chills ran down the spines of the tantalised audience.

'Introducing first, from Wales. Atholl. "The Captain." *Oakeley!*'

Oakeley emerged from behind the curtain to a chorus of jeers. His hair was cut short and sharp and, as always, slicked across in a perfect side-parting, Army officer style. He wore white trunks and black wrestling boots, with a rolled-up towel hanging around his huge neck. He swaggered slowly down the ramp as the boos intensified. This wasn't what Irslinger had promoted him as: he was supposed to be much-loved and cheered.

But then, he was supposed to have been up against George Modrich. Instead, he was the man standing in the way of

Douglas Clark, the working-class hero representing the common man, and his destiny.

Henry Irslinger, sat alongside his associate Ben Sherman and Bill Garnon – whose fearsome rise under the 'All-In' rules had seen him gain size and reputation, and adopt the nickname 'Bulldog' – looked on from ringside. Even Irslinger had not expected such animosity towards Oakeley, who stepped into the ring and arrogantly outstretched his arms.

'And his opponent. Weighing 16 stone. From Huddersfield, West Yorkshire. He is a legend of the sport of rugby, a British war veteran and the Cumberland and Westmorland world heavyweight champion. Douglas. *Clark!*' Once again Duggy emerged from the haze created by all the cigarette smoke to a booming reception. He walked with purpose and determination towards the ring.

The referee waved them to wrestle as the two combatants stood apart in opposite corners of the squared circle.

As the tension grew, the buzz around the arena did too. The men tentatively circled each other, slowly coming closer together before finally tying up into a grapple. They wrestled and contorted one another around, each looking for leverage and a preferred position from which to mount an attack. Neither man gave an inch. They wrestled on their feet, down on the mat and from long range – throwing each other against the ropes to try in an attempt to unbalance the other and gain some momentum.

Duggy was coming out on top whenever the two were on their feet, regularly launching Oakeley through the air and to the mat, to the delight of the transfixed crowd. But once he engaged Atholl on the ground, the superior experience and technique of Oakeley came to bare – although the immense strength of Duggy prevented him from being able to gain a pin-fall or a submission. Neither looked like breaking the deadlock as another stalemate emerged. The minutes agonisingly passed by, and soon the third and final round neared its end.

The bell rang to signal the end of the contest and the two men broke the grip they had on one another. It would go to the judges' scorecards. Suspense consumed the arena. Irslinger dashed to the side of the judges, whispering in their ears, peering at their cards as they were collected by the announcer.

The building fell silent as the two men stood either side of the white-shirted referee. The large, square microphone was lowered from the ceiling and taken by the ring announcer. 'After going to the judges' scorecards, we have a draw,' he declared to the aghast audience. 'In accordance with the All-In wrestling rules, we will continue until a pin-fall or submission is gained in order for a winner to be declared.'

A furious Atholl Oakeley stomped back to his corner, whilst Douglas Clark casually strolled back to his. When the referee waved them on to wrestle, the frustrated 'Captain' began to sprint towards his adversary. Duggy saw an opening; a chance. He ran to meet Atholl in the middle of the ring with the biggest rugby tackle of his career, his shoulder crashing into the solar plexus of Oakeley, almost breaking him in half and lifting him clean off the canvas, the two of them landing in a heap. There was no air remaining in Oakeley's body for him to fight with. Duggy leapt on top of him, putting pressure and all of his strength down to pin his opponent's shoulders to the mat as the referee joined them on the canvas to perform the count: *one … two … three!*

The roof came off of the building as the audience cheered and hugged one another in delight. Duggy – seemingly only included in the tournament to make up the numbers and attract some interest – had done it. He was the British heavyweight champion.

Atholl Oakeley angrily stormed around the ring, grabbing the referee and the ring announcer by the scruff of the neck, strongly disputing and denying that he had actually lost, before Henry Irslinger climbed into the ring to guide him away.

Irslinger then begrudgingly congratulated Duggy and awarded him the trophy and the £50 cheque. He took the opportunity to remind the audience that he was not just a promoter but also the light-heavyweight champion of the world, and now that Britain had joined the professional wrestling world they might be seeing much more of him inside the ring.

Douglas Clark climbed back aboard his northbound train with his loot and the invaluable title that went with it, to the excruciating pain of the new London-based wrestling mafia. 45 Storths Road, 'Grasmere' became the first-ever home of the professional wrestling British heavyweight championship.

The British wrestling boom had begun. Promoters who had previously struggled to get events together in small, run-down clubs and dilapidated old gyms now couldn't get big enough venues to fill.

George de Relwyskow, former Olympic and world champion, knew the business better than anyone. He was 44 and recently retired from his own legendary mat career. He analysed the new wrestling landscape and realised that Atholl Oakeley and Henry Irslinger were solely concerned about London and the surrounding areas. But the imagination of the people in the towns and cities in the north of England had been captured.

De Relwyskow turned entrepreneur and quickly started up a rival promotion. His market: the entire country north of Watford. He moved his family away from London and into a mansion in Oakwood, Leeds, which he regarded as a central location for his potential empire.

The first man George de Relwyskow would ask to come aboard was the new British heavyweight champion Douglas Clark. Of course, Duggy was overjoyed to work with his wrestling hero.

Douglas Clark.
The World's Champion Wrestler C & W style and All in Champion, 1930-31

Elizabeth James

As well as his promoter, De Relwyskow acted as Duggy's manager and mentor and the pair became the most powerful team in the industry. De Relwyskow's teachings evolved Duggy into the complete heavyweight wrestling superstar; he already had the strength, stamina and background, but De Relwyskow honed his mat skills to perfection. He became fast and elusive; he knew every hold and the perfect counter to it.

Now retired from the sport, De Relwyskow had begun to fill out a little and he quickly cut a new image as a promoter, appearing by Duggy's side wearing sharp suits and puffing on large cigars. The pair had the respect, the charisma and the British title.

The southern-based promotion spearheaded by Henry Irslinger schemed and plotted for a way to bring the title back to London. Irslinger honoured Captain Oakeley's commitment to the American tour, billing him throughout as the British heavyweight champion, with Atholl still denying to anyone who would listen that he had been beaten by Clark. In his absence, the young Bert Assirati became the south's new top contender and the great hope of Irslinger to bring the title home.

Whilst still working as a coal merchant, Duggy's inadvertent celebrity status was now at its peak as he made multiple appearances at sold-out venues across Yorkshire, while Irslinger and De Relwyskow thrashed out a deal for his first defence against the fearsome Assirati. De Relwyskow held all the cards in the negotiations; he had the champion, after all. Any defence would take place in Yorkshire. The deal was eventually made: Bert Assirati versus Douglas Clark for the British heavyweight title would happen on 13 June 1931.

In the meantime, Duggy decided to capitalise on his wave of popularity and give yet more back to his community and to his loyal rugby club. With the help of De Relwyskow, he promoted a wrestling event at the Fartown Ground, with himself as the main event. After performing in over 200 professional rugby matches at the stadium, Duggy would now attract the same supporters to cheer him on as a professional wrestler. The 8,000 available tickets for the date in May sold instantly.

Chesterfield-based veteran Johanfesson was the number one northern contender. Duggy agreed to put the title on the line as well as a £100 side bet with his latest foe – even though the title being at stake could cost him that next major payday the following month. Negotiations regarding things such as side bets were done via the printed press, to raise awareness of the event and build the tension and excitement around it.

The event was a huge success and the Fartown faithful were delirious as they saw their hero at his destructive best whilst singing his name between renditions of 'Proud are we, Proud are we'.

After dominating his opponents in the earlier tournament but struggling to achieve pin-falls, there was no such trouble for Duggy back on his old stomping ground. Just as he had in the final round against Oakeley, he came out of his corner with momentum and crushed Johanfesson with an almighty rugby-style tackle – to the supreme joy of the fans who had seen him do the same to many an opponent on that very field.

With Johanfesson floored and his ligaments torn clean off of the collarbone, Duggy secured the first fall after just 25 seconds. He helped his opponent to his feet and back to his corner and the referee ordered them to wrestle. They locked up in a grapple but Johanfesson was so badly damaged from the previous takedown that it was a simple job for Duggy – who by now was referred to and widely regarded as the world's strongest man – to force him to the canvas for another count of three. The whole fight lasted little more than one minute.

The media dubbed Douglas Clark the 'John Bull in Trunks'.

Exactly one week later, De Relwyskow and Duggy made the short journey to Wakefield for what promised to be an epic encounter with Bert Assirati, who was just 23 years old but had become the most feared wrestler in the country. With a snarling, angry persona and a squat but immensely muscular physique, he was now known as the 'Islington Hercules'. With many wrestlers ducking Assirati, there were no such antics from Duggy, who gladly put his title on the line.

It was another sold-out partisan crowd supporting Duggy, and they certainly got value for their money. The champion was the aggressor for almost all of the 60-minute bout, but found it simply impossible to pin the strong and barrel-shaped shoulders of Assirati to the mat for a count of three. The fight spilled over into excessive violence as both men and the canvas became a crimson mess. Following the sound of the ring-bell that signalled the end of the match, the referee raised both men's arms and declared the contest a draw. Duggy retained his title but was frustrated that, for the first time in professional 'All-In' wrestling, he would not be leaving as the resounding victor. So, to the delight of the capacity crowd, he challenged Assirati to a rematch – as soon as it could possibly be arranged.

De Relwyskow and Irslinger set about the promotion and immediately announced another contest between the

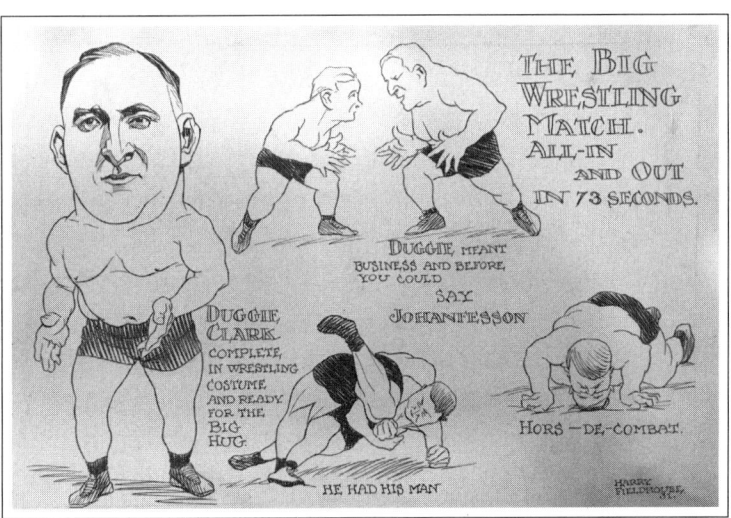

two gladiators the following week, this time at the home of Wakefield Rugby League Football Club: Belle Vue.

At such short notice, the undercard had to be a combination of boxing and wrestling as the promoters scrambled to fill up the event. Still, they managed to sell all 3,000 tickets.

Those lucky 3,000 fans saw a spectacular ending to the Clark-Assirati rivalry, and the result they desperately hoped for. The contest appeared much the same as the previous stalemate: entertaining and enthralling but with no clear winner in sight. After 49 more minutes of blood and sweat from the exhausted but dedicated warriors, Duggy produced a moment that made the crowd gasp in awe and then wince in sympathy. Once more the aggressor and with the leverage in the clinch, Duggy launched the 17 stone Assirati up into the air, over the top rope and down to the concrete floor. A perfectly legal manoeuvre left Bert in a crumpled heap. The referee began the ten-count by which Assirati must be back in the ring, but it was irrelevant. Bert was still struggling to move when the time was up and Duggy was awarded the sensational victory and his title was retained.

Henry Irslinger was incensed. With Atholl Oakeley Stateside, Bert Assirati beaten and George Modrich past his best – and all three now defeated by Douglas Clark – his stable was out of legitimate challengers to take the title back to London. 'Bulldog' Bill Garnon was becoming a beastly figure around the circuit, but was still gaining size and muscle mass on his former middleweight physique and was not yet ready to launch a bid for the heavyweight crown.

With no realistic chance of taking his British championship away from him, all Irslinger could do was attempt to beat Duggy himself in a non-title match. Beating him would at least remove the air of invincibility that revolved around Clark and was being peddled by George de Relwyskow to keep the northern fans flocking into the venues to see their idol. Yorkshire had become the epicentre of the wrestling world, which was not what Irslinger had come to these shores to achieve. He was supposed to be adding London to the professional wrestling global map.

Whilst Duggy continued with his surreal life of coal merchant by day, wrestling superstar by night, De Relwyskow received a telegram from Irslinger asking them to arrange the bout: BRITISH HEAVYWEIGHT CHAMPION VERSUS WORLD LIGHT-HEAVYWEIGHT CHAMPION; NEW ENGLISH PHENOMENON VERSUS AMERICAN LEGEND.

De Relwyskow drooled at the promotional dream. Henry suggested an autumn date to give himself time to get back in peak physical condition for the encounter – he had not competed in the ring for many months now, whilst concentrating on expanding and promoting the sport around the world.

A maximum of 3,000 people could be crammed into the chosen venue of Leeds Greyhound Track, Elland Road. But the most expensive ringside tickets plus the selling of rights for TV cameras (it was one of the first wrestling events to be filmed)

Douglas Clark 'All-In' training Elizabeth James

and media photographers and reporters made this the most lucrative professional wrestling show ever on British shores. It would be a Saturday afternoon open-air extravaganza. The winner would be decided over six ten-minute rounds or the best of three falls. The huge fight was on.

Douglas Clark and Henry Irslinger had three months to increase the excitement for the bout to fever pitch. They both made weekly appearances at wrestling events in their respective northern and southern territories, telling the eager audience how they were going to end the career of their respective ageing opponent. Irslinger vowed to crush the unbeaten record of Clark; Duggy promised to send Henry back to the States with his tail between his legs. It was always done in full view of the public, or even through the press themselves.

Henry Irslinger was training at maximum intensity every day to be in the best condition of his long and celebrated career. He trained in the luxurious gymnasiums and swimming pools of London, and honed his wrestling skills down at the Ashdown Club.

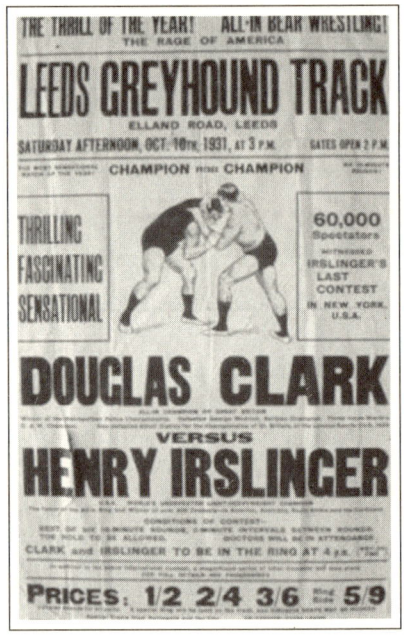

As the cold northern autumnal weather hit, the coal orders began their seasonal boost. With this, Duggy asked one of his employees to take the reins of the horse and cart so that he could roll back the years and do his training by dashing up and down the streets and alleyways of Huddersfield with two-hundredweight sacks of coal upon his back for hours at a time. The ice baths and hot showers were back as Duggy poured all of his life experience into getting himself into premium condition once again. The eyes of the country, and the wrestling world, were on them.

16

GOD'S OWN COUNTRY

10 October 1931
Douglas Clark versus Henry Irslinger
Leeds Greyhound Track
Elland Road
Leeds

THE UNIQUE and unmistakable sound of a full, vibrant and excited sports venue echoed around Duggy's changing room as he sat in quiet contemplation – still dressed in the smart, tweed suit he had arrived at the arena in.

He stared at his wrestling kit, which hung on the opposite side of the dressing area. He considered how it was his latest rival who had given him his opportunity in the sport at the beginning of the year. Granted, he had been expected to lose his first-ever match against Modrich and it could be argued Irslinger had only been using the notoriety created by Duggy's success in his previous careers, but he still could not help but feel much respect, admiration and gratitude for Henry Irslinger.

He stood to his feet, removed his jacket and tie, and changed into his wrestling trunks.

Irslinger pulled up the full-length leggings he had chosen for the evening – the American unaccustomed to the autumn evening open-air temperature of northern England, unlike his opponent. He too stopped to appreciate the noise emanating from the packed audience that awaited them.

His plan of introducing professional wrestling – since termed 'All-In' – to Britain, particularly London, may not have gone completely to the blueprint due to Douglas Clark overcoming the more traditionally seasoned and hand-picked wrestlers. But an evening like this brought to him the realisation that it had gone better than he ever imagined.

The whole country was gripped by the sport and the storyline that was evolving. Rather than resent Douglas and wish for the end of his career, he should be embracing him, and thanking him.

Henry fastened up his wrestling boots and walked towards the door that led out to the ring.

The doors to the two changing rooms – one directly opposite the other on the corridor that led out to the arena where the crescendo of noise was coming from – opened at the same time as the pair inadvertently walked out and almost into one another. As they stood just a tiny distance apart, there was an awkward and silent stand-off before Irslinger held out his hand. Duggy reached out and shook it firmly. 'Good luck out there, Henry,' he said.

Irslinger smiled and nodded as the warm handshake continued. 'Same to you, Doug,' he replied.

As the two parted ways, Irslinger began walking down the corridor towards the ring as the announcer called out his name to a chorus of boos and jeers.

Just minutes later, Duggy followed Henry's footsteps to the bellowing sound of cheers and frantic clapping.

As the two stood in their opposing corners of the ring, the dark cloud and lowering sun was beginning to limit visibility. Suddenly, the floodlights used for evening greyhound race meetings came on with a thud and a glorious light shone upon the ring to the delight of the crowd, who dutifully responded with a crescendo of noise. A unique and groundbreaking sporting atmosphere was created.

The *Yorkshire Post* covered the event and reported:

GREAT BATTLE BETWEEN
CLARK AND IRSLINGER

The first programme of 'All-In' wrestling in Leeds attracted about 3,000 spectators to the Greyhound Racing Track, Elland Road, on Saturday. The principal contest provided many thrills to the crowd, who had taken the exposition of the sport provided by the minor bouts in a rather light-hearted way. But the two 'stars', Douglas Clark, of Huddersfield, the British Heavyweight 'All-In' Champion, many times the All-Weights Cumberland and Westmorland-style champion, and formerly an international rugby league forward, and Henry Irslinger, of America, the Light-Heavyweight 'All-In' Champion of the World, had a gruelling contest over six ten-minute rounds, which ended in a draw of one fall each.

Clark offered at the conclusion of the contest to wrestle for the winning fall, but Irslinger would not agree.

The two men offered an interesting contrast in style. Clark wrestled, as was natural in a Cumbrian, more with his feet and legs, while the American, who has had many more years' experience of 'All-In' wrestling than Clark, was the cleverer with head and arm locks and holds as applied by the arms. While the pair were standing Clark was the more dangerous, but Irslinger was rather the better man on the mat, thanks to his skill.

The following is a description of the principal moves during the rounds:

ROUND 1 – Clark tried a Cumberland hipe and missed. Irslinger attempted a head hold, but Clark countered. Clark rushed his man to the ropes and tried for his favourite Cumberland waist hold, but Irslinger wriggled clear, Clark tried three times to cross-buttock.

ROUND 2 – Clark got a three-quarter Nelson hold, but Irslinger slipped and tried a double wrist lock which Clark did well to evade. Irslinger attacked again with a hammer-lock and then a scissors, taking the upper position, but Clark got out of it well.

ROUND 3 – Irslinger tried two standing headlocks and then falling to bring Clark on his back. With the second he got a magnificent leg-and-arm-lock with bar, which held Clark powerless for minutes until he gave the fall after five minutes 25 seconds.

ROUND 4 – Clark brought Irslinger down with an arm roll and head hold, but Irslinger used his great strength and escaped. The men got to leg locks, and then Clark got a headlock, but Irslinger countered brilliantly.

ROUND 5 – Clark equalised with a sensational fall. He got his favourite Cumberland waist hold, crushed Irslinger to him, and threw him magnificently with the Cumberland inside-hipe in 50 seconds.

ROUND 6 – This was a desperate round, Clark again tried for the waist hold, but Irslinger dropped clear, although he was warned for holding the ropes. Twice Clark got a head hold and brought Irslinger over, but was unable to pin him.

Duggy remained undefeated. Henry Irslinger was satisfied he could leave Britain whenever the time suited him, safe in the knowledge that his objectives had been met and professional wrestling was thriving and in safe hands.

The year 1932 saw Atholl Oakeley return from America and take the reins of the London-based operations. He immediately declared himself British heavyweight champion and, when challenged on this, he justified his claim by saying he had recently won a tournament for it. Atholl had won many tournaments, so that was a difficult thing to disprove. He claimed Duggy was 'catch-as-catch-can' champion and that 'All-In' wasn't an official sport at the time of the tournament 12 months previously. He said he had never been beaten by a fellow British professional, insisting that Duggy had not turned professional at the time of their encounter.

Oakeley was playing semantics. Whilst Duggy continued to take on and beat all challengers, an attempt was being made from London to discredit his championship.

The momentum and popularity of the sport continued to rise, bringing with it a new generation of talent, and businessmen clambered into positions as promoters in charge of regions and territories.

Whilst refusing to accept he was not the champion, and equally refusing to give Duggy the title he had earned, Atholl Oakeley, amongst others, created the International Wrestling Syndicate, based at the London Sports Club.

As for Duggy, the professional wrestling world *did* recognise him as the champion, and as he continued to beat all domestic challengers in packed-out arenas, the mighty powers across Europe wanted a piece of the action that only he and George de Relwyskow could offer.

Oakeley, on the other hand, knew that he had to beat Duggy to legitimise his claim – or at the very least, Duggy had to be beaten.

Duggy discovered a letter alongside his newspaper as he sat down to relax one afternoon. The return address was the London Sports Club. It was an invitation to enter an eight-man tournament – one in which the winner won the right to challenge 'The Captain' for the undisputed British heavyweight crown immediately afterwards. The letter swiftly followed some of Duggy's fine coal into the open fire of the living room. He sent a reply through the newspapers, stating that he would

Douglas Clark and Henry Irslinger battle out an epic
Leeds Mercury & British Newspaper Archive

gladly face Oakeley for the undisputed title, even at the London Sports Club – conceding home advantage – in a straight-up one-on-one contest. He also offered a personal side bet of £100 with Atholl. Neither he nor George de Relwyskow received a response.

And so it continued; every month or so a new invitation would reach either Duggy or George, offering entrance into some form of tournament or other stipulation that dramatically stacked the odds against Duggy. Not once did they acknowledge him as a champion; just another challenger who should be grateful for the opportunity. Eventually incensed, Duggy sent another message through the press, telling them he would never wrestle at the London Sports Club again, so strongly did he feel about their disrespect. His final offer: a one-on-one match against Atholl Oakeley for the undisputed British heavyweight championship at any other venue in the country of their choosing; Duggy would also put a £500 stake down as a personal side bet, but Oakeley only had to put £100 down in return. Again, he never received a response.

Alongside that promotional and political back-and-forth, Duggy spent 1932 defending his title in the north. He defeated respected veterans such as the aforementioned Johanfesson (on a number of occasions) and future legends such as 'The Doncaster Panther' Jack Pye and 'The Black Devil' Jim Wango.

The start of 1933 brought concerning news from Germany as Adolf Hitler and his Nazi Party narrowly won an election and gained power. Hitler became the German Chancellor and no longer just the self-installed *Führer* of his extremist political party, but of the whole country. He soon began to chip away at the military restrictions imposed by the Treaty of Versailles, as he recruited hundreds of thousands more troops and ominously broadcast their marches to an increasingly uneasy Europe.

Duggy's domination of the north but stand-off with the south continued. But there were bigger and more lucrative offers coming his way. He was now also promoting wrestling events himself as well as working alongside George de Relwyskow.

George's son, George Jr, had been taught by his father in the artform since being a child and, at just 18 years of age, he was a prodigy. He appeared regularly in the supporting cast of Duggy's shows.

Duggy took the younger George under him as a mentee in both wrestling and promoting. The evolutionary trio of both George de Relwyskow Sr and Jr and Duggy were now offering the full package of wrestling, promotion and management. They had the recognised championship, and they had the respect.

Professional wrestling was a complete phenomenon up and down the country. There were multiple packed-out arenas, clubs and stadiums every night of the week. The epicentre was the north of England – from Newcastle to Nottingham, almost every major town or city had hugely publicised weekly events. West Yorkshire-based Douglas Clark was the main attraction of the whole industry. He was undefeated in over

100 contests in over two years in 'All-In', he had competed against and beaten the best in the business, and he filled every venue he headlined. He had added the British Empire (now known as the Commonwealth) heavyweight title to his outrageously sized cabinet of sporting awards, trophies, medals, titles and belts.

A newly commissioned 'All-In' world heavyweight championship belt and associated title was vacant and its donor, Mr T. H. Kaye, knew the perfect place to hold the event that would crown his champion. It would come to Yorkshire, and humble coal merchant Douglas Clark would be competing for it. Choosing his opponent was relatively simple – dominant 19-stone Laurent Gerstmans, of Belgium, held the European heavyweight championship and he and his team were interested in a voyage to Yorkshire.

A match between Clark and Gerstmans had been long talked of, but never had the mutual incentive existed for both promotions to finalise a deal. But now, with the world title on the line, the negotiations were easy and completed swiftly: Douglas Clark (British & British Empire heavyweight champion) versus Laurent Gerstmans (European heavyweight champion) would take place on 3 July 1933 at the Headingley Stadium, Leeds. The match would be held under standard championship rules: six ten-minute rounds, two out of three falls, but no points decision, would decide the new world champion. In the event of a tie after the full 60 minutes, a rematch would need to be negotiated.

By now, Duggy had hired a team to take care of the day-to-day running of his coal merchant business, so time-consuming and physically demanding was his career as a professional wrestler. He travelled home to Elbra' for much of his training for the biggest match of his life. He and Jennie relaxed with their families and he trained with his former Cumberland & Westmorland mentors such as William Studholme. He jogged up and down the hills of the Lake District and along Maryport beach. He asked his old coaches to assist him in peaking his already colossal strength so that he could perform his lifts and throws on the monstrous 19-stone Belgian. He was now 42 years old.

Duggy soon found himself pulling weights up and down the muddy hills and throwing heavy rubber tyres further and further as the adrenaline and determination kept him training longer than he should have. Over the family dinner table one evening – following a particularly brutal session – Duggy felt uncomfortable. With his siblings and their own families at the family home for a rare grand get-together, he felt a tightness across his chest. He recognised the feeling from the many times he had suffered the same injury in the past: a broken rib. It was just weeks before the big night.

Ten thousand fans went through the turnstiles at Headingley Stadium on 3 July. To a man, they were there to see Douglas Clark create history. It was another raucous open-air night, on this occasion a mild and light British summer evening.

Laurent Gerstmans was introduced to the astonished audience first. He was a man mountain standing over 6ft tall, with a chest and shoulders even wider than those of Duggy, and a physique that tapered down into an athletic torso. He wore an all-black singlet that had to stretch so far over his colossal shoulders that the straps appeared they may snap like an over-extended elastic band. The respectful Yorkshiremen that made up the crowd had no reason to boo or jeer Gerstmans; instead they just fell silent in awe of the giant before their eyes.

There was no silence from them when their hero was introduced, however. Duggy received his usual vociferous welcome as they desperately hoped they could see him become the first British and world heavyweight champion. He emerged this time as the ultimate John Bull figure, clearly at his thickest set yet following his mammoth training camp in the elusive

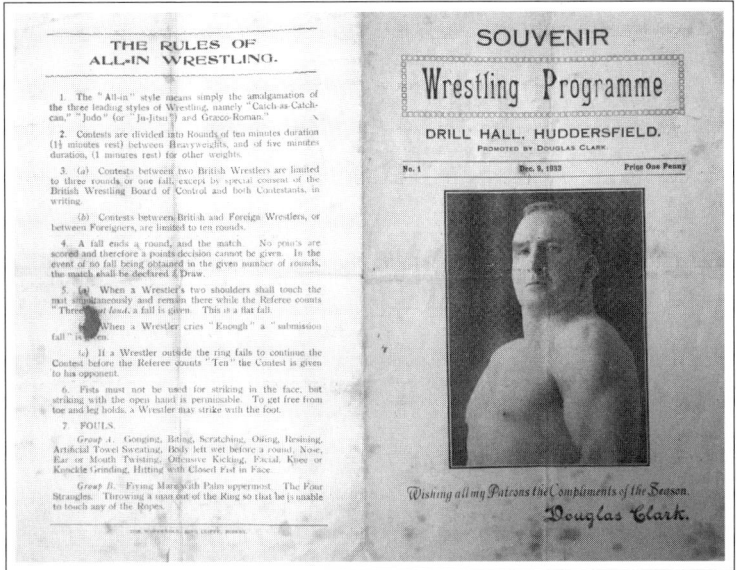

The programme for an event promoted by and headlined by Douglas Clark
Elizabeth James

hills of the Lake District. He wore a bright blue singlet with the Union Jack emblazoned on the front. The crowd went crazy. Unbeknownst to them, the middle-aged man for once in his life actually felt like one; with his broken rib not yet healed, he knew he had no chance of lifting or throwing Gerstmans. With his favoured moves out of the question, it was difficult – even for himself – to see where a possible fall might come from.

Not only a behemoth, but also quick and very nimble, it was easy to see why the Belgian was a formidable European champion. All this led to a rare defensive display from Duggy, who bravely wrestled toe to toe with the rampaging giant and managed to repel all the attempts to pin him to the canvas or to make him submit. The six ten-minute rounds timed out and the epic encounter was declared a draw. They would have to do it all again.

Now that Duggy was also promoting, he could see the dream rematch venue instantly in his mind's eye. He knew

World's Heavy-Weight Championship

ALL-IN WRESTLING

Promoters—BRUNSWICK STADIUM LTD., LEEDS.

MONDAY, JULY 3rd COMMENCING at 7-30 p.m.

— ON THE —

Leeds Rugby League Football Ground

HEADINGLEY

SIX 10-Minute Rounds

LAURENT **GERSTMANS**

(BELGIUM) Heavy-Weight Champion of Europe. VERSUS

DOUGLAS CLARK

(HUDDERSFIELD) Heavy-Weight Champion of the British Empire.

The Best Two out of Three Falls

Elizabeth James & Imperial War Museum

his body and he knew from experience the minimum time required for his rib to heal. But the Belgian delegation wanted the rematch as soon as possible: they knew Duggy was not fully fit and wanted to capitalise.

So Duggy spearheaded the negotiations and insisted on a date and a venue, allowing the representatives of Gerstmans to name all of their terms outside of those two stipulations.

They added that, this time around, the match would continue until a fall was achieved – no time limit; no third fight. Douglas Clark and George de Relwyskow agreed and signed the contract.

On 12 July 1933, the *Yorkshire Evening Post* reported:

CLARK AND GERSTMANS TO MEET AT
FARTOWN ON JULY 24
Arrangements were completed today for the return bout
for the All-In heavyweight wrestling Championship of the

238

world between Douglas Clark, of Huddersfield, the British Empire champion, and Laurent Gerstmans, of Belgium, the European champion, at Fartown, Huddersfield, on Monday, July 24. The pair drew at Headingley last week.

According to a telegram sent from Antwerp [...] the pair will wrestle until a decision is reached.

Since his first bout with the Belgian, Clark has been in training at Solway Firth, Cumberland. Clark has been receiving treatment from Alf Mansfield, the former Bradford boxer, for the injury which he sustained in training for the Headingley match, and he is reported to be quite fit.

17

PROUD ARE WE

24 July 1933
Douglas Clark versus Laurent Gerstmans
World heavyweight championship
Fartown Ground
Fartown
Huddersfield

NO SPORTS fan from Huddersfield was willing to miss it.

The windows and balconies of the surrounding houses and high-rise blocks of flats were bursting with people scrambling to get a view. Ticketless locals had squeezed through the bars or vaulted over the fences. Harold Wagstaff and other former team-mates and sporting friends were in the audience. Both George de Relwyskow Sr and Jr were ringside.

His rib injury fully healed, Duggy stretched and limbered up in the Fartown home changing room just as he had done over 200 times beforehand – the first time almost 24 years earlier. But this time he was wearing his blue leotard emblazoned with the Union Jack rather than the claret and gold of Fartown. The crowd sang his name between emotional renditions of their favourite songs from Fartown's Team of All Talents glory years.

When they knew the final match of the undercard was complete, they all stood to attention. Nerves jangling, they shuffled in anxious anticipation as one last chorus of 'Proud are we, Proud are we' reached its spine-jingling crescendo.

The introduction of the mountainous Belgian lowered the mood's volume and joviality as they all realised just what a mammoth task their coalman had for himself. Gerstmans walked slowly and purposefully down the aisle created by a gap in the temporary seating that sat upon the covered Fartown pitch. The 1932/33 season had recently finished and the supporters were in extra high spirits having seen their team roll back the years to win the Challenge Cup at the magnificent new Wembley Stadium for the first time since 1920 – the season that saw the Team of All Talents return from war, to resume their dominance.

The noise popped to its peak as the familiar local ring announcer began, 'And now, the moment you have all been waiting for! Weighing in at 16 stone. He is a Fartown legend. He is the British heavyweight champion. He is the world's strongest man! Douglas! Clark!'

With the two competitors pacing their respective corners of the ring, the referee held up the prize on offer – a huge dark brown leather belt awash with glistening silver shields and a chain, with an image of two grappling men surrounded by the words 'WORLD'S "ALL-IN" WRESTLING CHAMPIONSHIP'. The belt was passed back to the ring announcer on the outside of the squared circle, leaving just the two behemoths and the man in the middle in the ring. *Wrestle*, they were told.

The pair tied up in a grapple, but the clinch didn't last long as Gerstmans gained some leverage and used it to launch Duggy across the ring and flat on to his back, but he was able to get to his feet before Gerstmans could engage him on the ground. They circled each other for a while before tying up once again, but this time, to the delight of the crowd, it was Duggy who was able to show his extraordinary power and throw the near-20 stone Belgian into the air and to the mat. Gerstmans jumped to his feet and the pair stood firm, respectfully staring one another in the eye as the first round ended with a standing ovation from the transfixed Yorkshire crowd.

Gerstmans was surprisingly quick and as Duggy tried to force the pace by showing some aggression and urgency – something he couldn't do in the first bout due to his rib injury – the European champion showed his great technique by proving very elusive.

It was then Duggy's turn to defend as Gerstmans came forward, and he found himself in a number of worrying and painful-looking holds – but regularly brought the crowd to their feet as he skilfully wriggled out of danger.

A gripping series of holds and counter-holds ensued. It was beginning to appear that an unstoppable force had met an immovable object.

Gerstmans found himself in a headlock but beautifully twisted his way out of it and took Clark's right arm with him as he spun around his back. With a hammer-lock engaged, he showed tremendous strength to almost lift Duggy up off of the floor with his arm seemingly at breaking point behind his shoulder blades. With his free left hand, Duggy tapped on his chest in submission and the referee asked for the bell to be rung signalling the award of the first fall to Gerstmans with just seconds left in the second round.

As the third round began, the sun set over the stadium and the floodlights came on to confirm the epic feel of the event that was unfolding. The dominance of Gerstmans was looking ominous for Duggy, who was carrying his crippled right arm close to his body.

Like a shark smelling blood, Gerstmans launched an offensive blitz, primarily focusing on the injured limb, and was looking to end the bout early. Out of desperation, Duggy performed a move that launched his worried supporters into delirium as he lifted his gigantic foe clean off of the mat and slammed him back to the canvas. The whole arena shook as Gerstmans crashed to the floor.

Sapped of energy, Duggy fell to the floor, which stopped him gaining full advantage of his most effective offensive move so far against the European king. Both men got to their feet, Gerstmans still stumbling. A rush of adrenaline allowed Duggy to run and bounce off of the ropes to gain momentum, and he crashed into the midriff of the champion with an enormous rugby tackle to the delight of the Fartown faithful. He landed on top of his fallen rival and immediately pushed down on his shoulders with all of his might, allowing the referee to begin his count for the pin-fall. The vast crowd counted along with him. ONE. TWO. THREE. The equalising fall was dramatically confirmed two minutes and five seconds into round three. The pair regained their composure in their respective corners and came out ready for the third fall. The crowd chanted their hero's name.

Sudden death brought about a more cagey period following a frantic and gloriously entertaining opening two and a half rounds as both men were wary of the other's strengths and aware that one small mistake could spell the end of their dreams of becoming world champion. There was discernible tension inside the stadium as the third round ended and the fourth began. The two were getting more tired and desperate with each passing minute; with every clinch, move and countermove. At the halfway stage of the fourth round, it looked terminal for Duggy as he found himself face down on the canvas with Gerstmans atop him and a toe-hold locked in. Duggy grimaced in pain and it was surely only a matter of time before he must submit. But out of nowhere, he summoned the energy and supreme power to flip himself around on to his back, leaving Gerstmans off balance and his grip hanging by a thread.

If his earlier diving rugby tackle finish had been the equivalent of a try, Duggy was about to find the conversion his adoring fans were desperate for. With the sole of his right boot, he kicked his target not between the sticks, but through the ropes, sending the giant mass and dead weight of his rival crashing to the floor from the full height of the ring apron. Half of the crowd cheered, half winced at the painful sight and sound of the impact.

The referee began to perform the ten count by which Gerstmans must be back inside the ring or the match would be over. By the count of three, he hadn't moved and the capacity crowd were shouting out every number with the referee. By seven, Gerstmans had shakily gotten to his knees. At eight he was leaning against the ring and up to his feet. The count of nine saw him raise one leg on to the side of the ring, but as he tried to pull himself up the whole of Fartown bellowed 'TEN' and the referee waved his hands to declare the fight over. Huddersfield erupted with cheers. Douglas Clark fell to his knees before being awarded his title belt. He was heavyweight champion of the world.

Offers from around the world began to flood through the door at Duggy and Jennie's address – still the humble terraced house in Storths Road, Birkby. Despite national and even international acclaim, Duggy still returned annually to his wrestling roots: the Grasmere Games. He was the star attraction and his family and friends adored watching him compete there. His loyalty paid off in August 1934, when he finally won his fifth 'All-Weights' tournament and was awarded the cherished Canon Rawnsley Cup to keep as his own.

At 42 years of age he was British, British Empire and world heavyweight champion, devoted husband to his beloved wife, ambassador and mentor at Huddersfield Rugby League Football Club and still oversaw his community coal delivery service. Life was great – although it did still rankle with him that the London wrestling mafia continued to discredit him, with arch-rival Atholl Oakeley still parading and defending *his* version of

World Heavyweight Champion Douglas Clark
Elizabeth James & Imperial War Museum

the British title. This continued into 1934, when Atholl's claim began to weaken as he lost some non-title matches.

Bert Assirati was now managed by a rival promoter of Oakeley in the shape of William Bankier. The pair were screaming out to challenge Oakeley but the match was never made, to the frustrations of the fans and the press. Atholl's position as promoter-come-wrestler-claiming-to-be-champion became untenable after his defeats and the media called for him to retire from the mat. But he would go out on his own terms; Bill Garnon had now gained enough muscle mass to enter the heavyweight division. He was, of course, the decade-long mentee of Atholl Oakeley and had become one of the most technically gifted and well-respected wrestlers in the country.

'The Captain' pitted himself against his good friend 'Bulldog', with his title on the line. He would retire afterwards and concentrate fully on the managerial side of the industry. Knowing the match would garner much attention and directly affect the future of what was going to be *his* business – certainly in London and the majority of the south – Oakeley was determined that the pair would put on a spectacular.

Following a 50-minute contest on 12 September 1934, 'Bulldog' Bill Garnon won their version of the British heavyweight title in what was said to be one of the most violent, bloody and entertaining spectacles in any combat sport ever seen in London. News spread quickly, both of the newly crowned champion and the quality of the live entertainment, and demand for the sport in the capital city reached a new high.

Atholl Oakeley retired from competing and became the overlord of the business in the south. Business was booming, so much so that he promoted one of his assistants, the smart and glamorous Kathleen Look, to the position of a promoter working under him. She was to concentrate on shows outside of Atholl's London bubble.

With a new champion and a new promoter to work with, the De Relwyskow-Clark team were soon in communication and negotiations began for a match to find the undisputed 'All-In' British heavyweight champion and a conclusion to the saga that had rumbled on for over three years.

Duggy stuck to his conditions of a neutral venue and a straight one-on-one contest. He conceded that, as Kathleen Look was the official promoter, he would officially be labelled as the challenger, and Bulldog the defending champion. It was made. The eyes of the whole wrestling world would be on Belle Vue, Manchester on 12 November 1934.

It was yet another packed house, with Duggy's name being sung into the night sky.

Even more so, it was another titanic struggle. The crowd became frustrated as the pair cancelled one another out for the first three rounds. It broke out into a brawl in the fourth as both men crashed to the outside of the ring. Duggy comfortably climbed back in, but a tiring Garnon only just made it back in by the count of nine.

With one minute to go in the fifth, Duggy finally made the breakthrough, ferociously slamming Bulldog and claiming the first fall. A desperate Bill tried to find an equaliser in the final round but left himself open to easy countermoves and Duggy sealed the victory with a second fall.

He was awarded yet another championship belt to signify his dominance of the sport.

It was over. As well as being recognised as a world champion, Douglas Clark was finally the undisputed British heavyweight champion. A near four-year story that started when he gatecrashed the tournament organised by Henry Irslinger and Atholl Oakeley – groundbreakingly told via the press for maximum public exposure – could finally be laid to rest.

THE LION'S DEN

18 July 1936
Tom Lurich versus Douglas Clark
British Empire Championship
Leichhardt Stadium
Sydney, Australia

THE HEAVY boots of four uniformed New South Wales police officers thudded on the floor of the aisle as they dashed down towards the ring amid fears of rioting following a swift escalation of violence in the contest between Douglas Clark and Tom Lurich – violence that was spilling out into the frenzied audience. It was the fourth round. Blood stained the canvas. The referee had lost control of the situation.

It was the seventh time the pair had faced each other in just four months. A bitter and intense rivalry with Australia's number one had evolved during Duggy's latest tour Down Under – 22 years after his first – and it was poised to reach an unedifying crescendo.

The big matches and paydays had continued after he unified the British championship against Bulldog Bill Garnon. Canadian and German champions, Burnett and Froehner respectively, visited the north of England to challenge Douglas for his world championship. They were dutifully beaten, as was Sweden's 'Anaconda'.

Duggy even toured Belgium in 1935 following the successful promotional partnership made with Gerstmans. He continued to face and defeat the premier domestic contenders, too, with the Highland Games champion George Clark, giant Carver Doone, Francis Gregory, Jack Pye and Johanfesson at the fore.

Fartown had signed a fellow Cumberlander in young Stanley Pepperell and Duggy had taken him under his wing, giving him a job on the coal round, assisting him with his training and even putting a roof over his head by allowing him to stay in the spare room of his house. He had become a loyal student and good friend.

Duggy's diary entry 26 October 1935:

Today at 9.45am we lost our dear old mother. God bless her dear soul. She was always the kindest hearted best old mother that a man could have. Truly a terrible day, this awful 26th.

Born 18th of February 1863.

Despite his world title being declared defunct in favour of the American-based one dominated by Ed 'Strangler' Lewis, Duggy was happy with his lot. He was still the undisputed British and the British Empire champion. He was settled in his home life with Jennie, still an ambassador for Fartown and even managed to find time to run his business as a coal merchant. Despite lucrative offers from around the world for wrestling exhibitions and tours, he didn't feel the need to take them up.

That was until the very beginning of 1936 – the year of the next Great Britain rugby league Ashes tour to Australia – when an offer was made that even Duggy could not refuse.

Promoters from Down Under sent Duggy a lucrative contract to reignite his love affair with Australia and New Zealand, as well as his sporting rivalry with them. In a genius cross-promotional extravaganza – a six-month tour – he would be challenged by the finest professional wrestlers on their continent alongside the eagerly awaited latest edition of the intense rugby rivalry he was so synonymous with. Two decades on from his original heroics and at the age of 45, Douglas Clark would be a Great Britain Ashes tourist once more – unofficially, at least. He held legendary status in Australia and the promotional vision to tie the tours together was spectacular. Like Henry Irslinger in 1930, it was Duggy's turn to use his stature to promote the business elsewhere in the world – and, of course, he chose his beloved Australasia.

He accepted the offer, and his ticket for boarding the Orion for another month-long journey arrived. Including the travel time, he would be leaving Jennie – 'Pip', as he affectionately called her – for nine months. Duggy was due to set sail on 19 January 1936. He had still never lost a professional wrestling match in approximately 400 bouts.

A photograph was taken of the couple at the Tilbury docks as they were about to emotionally part. Duggy took the photo with him and, feeling lonely and sorrowful on the ship, wrote on the back of it:

> *One of the saddest days of my life. My poor lil' Pip and I broken-hearted.*
> *'Price of True Love'*
> *Orion 19/1/36*
> *Tilbury*

The epic voyage and heavy heart made Duggy, for once, feel his age. Lethargy and low spirits impacted his preparation, and he was scheduled for a baptism of fire in his first fight of the tour as he was pitted against the Australian number one Tom Lurich.

An Eastern European immigrant, Lurich was known as the 'Russian Bear' and was in his prime. Strong and muscular with

The heartbroken couple say their goodbyes Elizabeth James

a frizzy mop of black hair, he had a reputation for winning with consummate ease in Australia – despite a cluster of talented heavyweights, no one they had to offer could get close to beating him. For once, in Sydney on 15 March, Lurich would be the underdog against a world-renowned veteran in the shape of Douglas Clark, who would then embark on a relentless 30-match tour, wrestling week-in-week-out against the finest competitors from across a whole continent.

The promoters had wanted the British Empire title on the line in each of the superfights between the pair, but there were contradictory reports over Lurich's nationality and therefore his qualification into the Commonwealth. He was billed as Russian, Polish and Australian by different promotions – so the belt was left off of the table. The Ashes tourists were not due to get under way until the end of May, leaving two months for Duggy to build the tension and rivalry to fever pitch.

Several days before it was due to take place, an ominous feel began to surround the upcoming Lurich encounter: an unbeaten star on his home turf and in his physical prime against a homesick 45-year-old. The promoter was worried about his imported superstar. Duggy wasn't himself. A loss in the first match of the six-month tour could scupper the excitement and subsequent ticket sales. He politely queried with Duggy about what was bothering him, and asked him if he could do anything to help.

'Arrange for my wife to be sailed here from merry old England,' Duggy joked.

It was done. So valuable was Duggy's happiness and ability to perform at his brilliant best to the promoter that he sent Jennie a ticket. News that his 'Pip' was on her way lifted Duggy's spirits as he prepared to battle Lurich for the first time.

On 15 March, in Sydney, Duggy entered the ring in a bright blue gown emblazoned with Union Jacks to a chorus of applause from the Aussie crowd that deeply admired him. He and Lurich wrestled an enthralling draw, with the Australian punters satisfied they had seen the greatest wrestling ever produced on their shores, and were left thirsty for more. Lurich left the arena confident he could be the first man to beat Clark in the professional ranks. The match hadn't been without its controversy – Lurich being admonished multiple times by the referee for foul play.

One week later, Duggy defeated George Pencheff before he and Jennie were heartwarmingly reunited. He had a three-week break from the ring to enjoy the country with his wife – but next up was part two of his budding, but potentially epic, feud with the Russian Bear.

On 13 April, following the second meeting between the pair, the *Labor Daily* reported:

Police had to climb into the ring at Leichhardt on Saturday night to quieten Tom Lurich after he had been disqualified for kicking in the fifth round of his bout with British champion Douglas Clark.

The Englishman again provided the Australian champion with a good deal of trouble, and at the time Lurich went berserk, had bright prospects of pinning the Russian.

The intensity of the rivalry continued to rise.

Duggy added Con Grivas to his ever-expanding list of defeated foes, which brought an end to the Sydney leg of the tour. Duggy and Jennie then travelled north to Brisbane, where they would be based for a whole month. He would wrestle six matches in the state of Queensland – three against his new nemesis, Tom Lurich.

At the first of those three meetings, on 29 April, it was more of the same from Lurich, who – frustrated at being unable to fell Clark cleanly – resorted to more of the illegal brawling tactics of kicking and closed-fist punching. The referee was Brisbane's most experienced, known respectfully to all as Mr Rivers.

The crowd turned on their champion and cheered on the popular Englishman, who stood firm and continued to wrestle fairly against the barbaric nature of Lurich's attacks. Following warning after warning, 'Terrible Tom' was disqualified by referee Rivers. Duggy walked away from the ring and up the aisle to a standing ovation.

They repeated the blockbuster main event at the Brisbane Stadium a week later, Mr Rivers again the man in the middle. Worried about a third disqualification, Lurich wrestled smarter and again the bout appeared to be heading towards an epic stalemate as the combatants had secured one fall each going into the final round. Knowing he was probably behind on points, Terrible Tom once again resorted to the dark arts – this time striking Duggy repeatedly in the abdomen with his knee. This was clever and put Rivers in an awkward position: it was all down to his interpretation. Was it a legal strike with the thigh? Or an illegal kick?

Lurich continued to sink the ball of his knee into Duggy's stomach, completely knocking the wind, life and fight out of him. Lurich covered him, assuming he had secured victory – but Rivers never appeared down on the canvas to perform the three count. Whilst he didn't view the knee-strikes worthy of disappointing the crowd with yet another finish via disqualification, he would not allow Lurich to win with such a violent act that was not in keeping with the spirit of the sport; he simply refused to count the pin-fall. Lurich jumped to his feet in a rage and attempted to bully and intimidate him into performing the duty – but the veteran referee bravely refused to obey the brutish behaviour.

After wasting time remonstrating with Mr Rivers, Lurich resumed his aggressive prowl and pondered his next move on his stricken foe. The crowd detested him and let him know it. Before he could dish out any more offence, the bell rang to signal the end of the epic contest. The confused audience fell silent, unaware what that meant for the result. Duggy clambered to his feet and as soon as he was upright, Rivers raised his arm to confirm he was the victor via a marginal points advantage, to the delight of the vociferous crowd. The referee quickly scarpered away from an irate Lurich, who felt he had been robbed of ending his now-desperate obsession with becoming the first professional wrestler to defeat the legendary Douglas Clark.

Four matches into the scheduled seven and Duggy had won three, with one ending in a tie – but all had ended controversially and without the clear and decisive result that Duggy prided himself on achieving.

It was groundhog day two weeks later as the same three men – Mr Rivers included – shared the same ring at the same venue for the third time. Yet again, the tortured fans would have to wait for a conclusive winner; they were left frustrated this time by the final decision of Rivers, who scored the bout

The Russian Bear: 'Terrible' Tom Lurich
Elizabeth James

a draw after the full 60 minutes of action saw one fall awarded to each man. It had appeared that Clark had clearly won the first four rounds, and was a fall to the good going into the final 20 minutes. Lurich finished strongly and scored the equalising fall, leaving the crowd celebrating what was surely another points victory for Duggy – but Rivers raised the arms of both men.

The following day, the *Brisbane Telegraph* couldn't find enough superlatives for the British veteran ringmaster, claiming:

> *Clark undoubtedly did the more impressive work during the first four rounds, his evasion and countering being quite a revelation ... A cross-buttock throw crashed Lurich heavily in the third round and Clark, holding a head-lock, pinned his opponent with a body press for the first fall.*

Just three days later Duggy had to go again, this time against another top contender in Fred Atkins. Another hour-long epic ended in a draw as the relentless schedule began to take its toll on the ageing Duggy; and so concluded the barnstorming Brisbane leg of the tour. The Lurich rivalry had made international news and the gripping action was critically acclaimed. The sixth encounter was ten days later, back in Sydney. The promoters had been wondering how they could keep the bitter rivalry heating up more than it already had, fearing it may have peaked too soon, so they finally had Lurich's Australian citizenship processed and confirmed. The Sydney battle would see the British Empire heavyweight championship on the line. It would also be on the evening of the first tour match of the Great Britain rugby league tour.

On 30 May, just seven days after the Atkins fight, Great Britain beat the Sydney Firsts by 15 points to three at the Sydney Cricket Ground – an arena Duggy knew all too well – before attentions turned once again to the Leichhardt

Stadium. The wrestling was meant to be the support act but now, with the title on the line, it had turned into the headline event.

With a new referee, Lurich needed to find out how far he could push his maniacal tactics. Despite the constant jeering of the supporters and being reprimanded by the referee, Terrible Tom continued to slap, punch and kick. The Sydney crowd were mesmerised as the pair traded holds and countermoves, twisting their ageing but agile bodies around one another, and elusively rolled swiftly and athletically around the mat.

Finally, though, this was one match too far for the incomparable Douglas Clark. The audience were left heartbroken as Lurich had his arm raised and was named the new British Empire heavyweight champion. Duggy, tasting defeat for the first time in over 400 matches, got to his feet and shook the hand of his victor. They would not meet again until the very final match of the Australian part of the tour seven weeks later, when the championship belt would be on the line again.

Duggy travelled to Brisbane with the rugby stars as they defeated Queensland on 13 June, and that evening beat Wong Buck Cheung.

The delegation travelled back to Sydney, where Great Britain were scheduled to play the first and third Test matches at the Sydney Cricket Ground – so notoriously ingrained with the Ashes following the legendary Rorke's Drift affair.

Two days before the first Test they were beaten in a warm-up match against Newcastle, and Duggy battled out another epic 60-minute draw against Haban Singh. The wrestling was proving a revelation.

An out-of-sorts Great Britain team comfortably lost the first Test in front of 70,000 delirious Australia supporters. Despite its relative infancy, rugby league had become their national sport. They had swapped their claret and blue for the now-iconic green and gold, and had an ominously stellar-looking team. It seemed quite certain that the Ashes crown would be staying Down Under.

But there was a shock in store the following week as the Lions rallied to hunt down their Kangaroo prey and brought them crashing down to earth in a tight match, winning by 12 points to seven. Once again, it would go down to a deciding match at the *Sydney Cricket Ground*. The mouthwatering tie would take place on 18 July, and that very same evening at the nearby Leichhardt Stadium – in a once-in-a-lifetime promotional double-header – Douglas Clark would challenge Tom Lurich and attempt to regain his British Empire belt. It would be their final meeting, as Duggy and the Great Britain team would then travel to New Zealand to simultaneously complete their respective tours.

Sensationally, the Lions won at the Sydney Cricket Ground by the exact same score of 12 points to seven that they had in Brisbane, regaining the Ashes once again.

But on Monday, 20 July 1936, the *Sydney Morning Herald* reported:

> Billed as a contest for the heavyweight championship of the British Empire, the contest between Tom Lurich and Douglas Clark at the Leichhardt Stadium on Saturday night was stopped in the fourth round by the police. Neither man had secured a fall and the referee (J. McMaster) gave a points decision to Lurich, a verdict which had a mixed reception.
>
> Clark opened well, and frequently had Lurich in trouble in the first two rounds. Lurich then began to use his fists, but a retaliatory punch from Clark brought the blood from Lurich's mouth. In the third round Lurich threw Clark out of the ring, and it was a double repetition of that infringement in the fourth that led to police intervention.

The most controversial ending of all the seven encounters meant that the British Empire title Douglas Clark had brought around the world would be staying in Australia – despite a winning record over Lurich in their ferocious series (3-2-2).

The Lions and Duggy – with Jennie by his side – followed up with successful and winning tours of New Zealand before boarding the ship for the epic journey home once again.

Duggy may have left behind a championship belt, but he also left behind a legacy. He had elevated Tom Lurich into a global star and put Australasia on the wrestling map. The reputations of those who achieved draws or went the full 60 minutes with Douglas Clark were enhanced beyond recognition. The tour is now regarded as the stuff of mythical legend. So immensely popular Down Under was Duggy that a tour was repeated in 1937 – even without an adjoining Lions squad – but this time, Jennie was on board the outbound Orion. There was no meeting with Terrible Tom this time around – their fabled feud best left in the annals of time. He did wrestle and increase the eminence of more of their top stars – once again leaving a thriving new sport behind when he and Jennie returned to Blighty and Huddersfield for the final time in the autumn of 1937. His support network had come to the fore in his absence: George de Relwyskow Jr had become a world-class wrestler and held the fort as the main-event star in the north of England – even becoming British Empire lightweight champion following tuition in the business from his father and mentor Duggy. Meanwhile, young Stanley Pepperell – leading the way alongside his younger brother Russell, who had also been signed by Huddersfield – looked after his home and his coal business. Stanley became the closest and most loyal friend to Duggy and Jennie in their later life.

The 46-year-old Duggy sustained further losses during the second Australian tour – once more catapulting his victors and the business into superstardom.

But Douglas Clark was *still* the man back in Britain and had once again defended his British title regularly between the tours and on his return. He was finally past his prime. But he knew there was still at least one more major payday available to him back in front of his loyal English supporters.

The intense rivalry goes from competitive to violent
Elizabeth James & Imperial War Museum

19

THE J.S. CONNECTIONS

August 1938
The Grasmere Festival
Lake District National Park

I never meant to wrestle here again. When, four years ago, I won the cup given by the late Canon Rawnsley in the years before the war, I was as proud as I have ever been over winning anything. Altogether, for football and wrestling, I have over 90 medals and 15 cups, and the one I really treasure the most is the Rawnsley Cup. It took me years to win it, because I could not manage to win the requisite three years in succession I had to win five years in all.

I have not been to Grasmere Sports since. Last year and the year before I was in Australia wrestling in the 'All-In' style, and the year before that I was in Belgium.

As I say, I never meant to wrestle here today, but I cannot bear to come and not have a try. It is always helping the sports and keeping up the interest.

Douglas Clark was interviewed as the raucous crowds gathered on the famous turf. His return was the talk of the community. Not even the lashing-down rain and puddles of mud that had besieged this particular edition of the eagerly anticipated event could keep the punters at bay.

Duggy was now 47. It was exactly 30 years since the boy wonder, so full of potential and awe, had made his Grasmere bow and progressed all the way to the semi-finals. He thought he had donned his black velvet over-pants for the last time four years earlier, when he once again defied his age and the odds to win his fifth crown and a place amongst the Grasmere immortals. But he had decided – as he was attending his beloved event anyway – to blow the dust off of the embroidered garment one more time.

There was a nostalgic feel around the village. Not only was Douglas Clark back, but the other veterans of a golden era, such as William Knowles and Gilpin Bland, were also competing – possibly for the final time too.

There was an unfamiliar name amongst the 100-strong entry list for the 'All-Weights' tournament. The name was shown as a J. Spedding, of Newcastle. When the bellman called the name, there was a silence. That was until a man, mingling into the crowd with the hood of his raincoat up, called out, 'Oh, sorry sir. I appear to have listed my middle name instead of my surname. The name is Robinson.' He lowered the hood to reveal his identity: 'J. S. Robinson.'

The wrestlers and supporters alike were silenced as they realised it was Joseph Robinson, who had returned after almost eight years. He had won the event on his last appearance in 1929. Although based in South Africa, Robinson had travelled the world in those eight years and held championship titles in both professional wrestling and in Ju-Jitsu – which he had learnt in Japan itself. He boasted of being friends with legendary American heavyweight boxing champion Jack Dempsey, and flashed a grainy black-and-white photograph of them together as proof. He had spent time in America as he continued his worldly education on all things combat sport-related. He was employed by the South African government to train their police force in self-defence and martial arts, and his 11-year-old son, also named Joseph, was keen to follow in his father's footsteps.

For the first time in his career, Duggy was eliminated from the Grasmere Games 'All-Weights' tournament in the fourth round. He warmly congratulated his conqueror, J. Salisbury, and thanked the emotional crowd as he left their ring for the final time.

Gilpin Bland cheered up the soddened supporters as he rolled back the years to win his sixth middleweight title.

Robinson accounted for William Knowles as he raced to the final without conceding a fall, and duly won the blue-ribbon category in his first time competing in Cumberland & Westmorland in almost nine years.

Joe returned to South Africa to raise his son, who would become third-generation grappler 'Tiger Joe Robinson'. Tiger Joe won the European heavyweight championship in 1952 and later became a successful actor and stuntman, enjoying a 17-year career on the big screen culminating in a role as diamond smuggler Peter Franks in the 1971 James Bond movie *Diamonds Are Forever*.

Ivan Seric had been born in Yugoslavia in 1894. At the start of the Balkans War, he fled to America at the age of 17. An extremely tough young man, he had found professional wrestling as it ascended into its initial boom in the aftermath of World War One. He grew to be 6ft and 18 stone of solid muscle. Skilled and rugged, he had slowly made his way through the ranks under gimmicks such as 'Indian Jack' and 'Alaskan Jack'. The American promoters managing him – Henry Irslinger amongst them – decided to go with the simple name of 'Jack Sherry' and make him their new superstar, claiming him as American born-and-bred. With a curly mop of black hair and a small moustache, he was a serious man of few words, although he had managed to develop a strong New York accent in his time there. He became the man to beat as he felled big-name opponents in quick-fire time, one after the other.

Henry Irslinger contacted old friend Atholl Oakeley and offered to send his new star over to England to help build his growing global fame and to put on some great shows for Oakeley's promotion. Jack Sherry toured Britain in both 1934 and 1935 under much fanfare and obliterated all of the top names, including the great Bulldog Bill Garnon seven times. With his ascendancy and momentum, he was possibly the top heavyweight name in the world, but he was never booked against Duggy on either of those tours. Neither man – or their promoters – could risk ruining their momentum with a much-publicised defeat, so the two had been kept apart. The tantalising but elusive encounter had become the one the world wanted to see.

Sherry finally took the world heavyweight championship from Ed 'Strangler' Lewis following a long and storied rivalry in mid-1930s USA, before taking the title on a three-year tour, starting in South Africa and then to Europe, concluding in England in 1938 (and into 1939).

Duggy was looking forward to retirement, or at least the closest thing to retirement he would allow himself – back to the simple life as a coal merchant he was always meant to have but for the three consecutive, spectacular, pioneering and historic careers in rugby, the army and professional wrestling that had kept him rather busy.

Kathleen Look booked the northern part of Jack's tour and they had him roll over all of the big names, teasing the media and fans with the promise of finally seeing him share a ring with their working-class hero.

'THIS MAY BE JACK SHERRY'S WATERLOO! ENGLAND HAS WAITED FIVE LONG YEARS FOR THIS!', the poster read as the major announcement was made for their long-awaited match at Belle Vue, Manchester on 11 November 1938.

The booking stoked up the supporters to fever pitch once more for the final run of Douglas Clark as a main-event superstar. The world championship match was scheduled for an epic 15 rounds of five minutes each.

After a memorable battle, the referee stopped it in the seventh round in favour of Sherry due to a terrible cut above Duggy's eye – his first 'All-In' loss on British soil.

But this controversial ending meant only one thing: a rematch was required.

Five weeks later, they met again as the Christmas cheer engulfed Manchester along with a frenzied wrestling hullaballoo.

On this occasion, in the same seventh round, Duggy was disqualified for a knee that was deemed an illegal kick. Once again, the conclusion was not conclusive enough: the fanatical supporters demanded there be a trilogy fight.

The promotional team of Atholl Oakeley and Kathleen Look teased them once more, waiting until the very end of the tour in May 1939 to have the final match.

This time, Sherry made short and decisive work of the veteran and legendary figure, who by now had turned 48. Jack subsequently became the undisputed king of the heavyweight wrestling world, and Duggy magnanimously and wilfully retreated from the glare and spotlight that came with being a sporting headliner.

Jack Sherry and Atholl Oakeley had spent most of that three-year period together as Henry Irslinger insisted his star was taken care of on his travels. They became good friends, and *Sir* Atholl (as he would become later in life) tells the following story in *Blue Blood on the Mat*:

> *They were wonderful weeks and we all had a marvellous time in Vienna. One Sunday night Jack was sitting in the Bier Garden. Lovers everywhere were under the trees, and romantic as anyone could have wished for. A violinist came over and played Strauss to him.*

 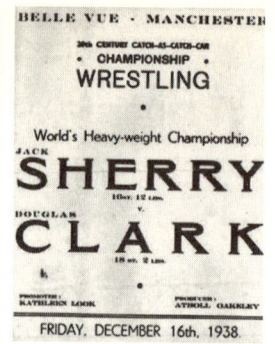 

'Wonderful place Vienna, Jack,' I said.

'Okay if you're in love,' says Jack. 'I gotta wife in New York.'

'I didn't know that.'

'Yeah, I got hooked before I left.'

'Does she write to you?'

'Nope. I forgot to tell her where I was going.'

'Do you mean to say you just left and never told her you were going to South Africa?'

'I just told you. I forgot.'

Jack went back to America three years later. When he later returned to England he told me, 'My wife and I broke up.'

'Why?' I asked.

'I went along to my apartment and let myself in with my key. After a while in comes a young boy. He looks at me and calls out, "Hey, Mom, there's a strange man in the joint."

'My wife says, "Where you been all this time?" I told her, 'England.' She asked me, 'Why didn't you say you was going away?'"

'I forgot.'

'You've been away for three years. Why didn't you write?'

'I sent you regular money. I don't write much.'

'You don't write at all.'

'Who's the boy?'

'That's your son."

I asked Jack why she left him.

'I guess she got bored without me,' says Jack, 'and found herself another guy."

20

THIS WAS A MAN

22 July 1939
Holmfirth Parish Church
Holmfirth
Huddersfield

THE SILENCE of mourning sounds distinctly more silent than any other. The more people are present, the louder that silence is.

Eight large men, mostly balding – in keeping with their late-middle agedness – and each wearing perfectly tailored black suits, walked slowly in unison, carrying the grand coffin of the former team-mate and eternal friend out of the church, following his funeral service. The hundreds of mourners unable to fit inside separated as the former rugby players sombrely took their talisman on his final journey.

A glorious and unique wreath made up of gold tiger lilies and claret carnations – tied together using claret and gold ribbon – sat upon the coffin. It was signed from 'The Boys of the Fartown Football Team'.

The pallbearers laid the casket in the hearse and gently, silently, huddled together. They included Major Holland, Ben Gronow and Douglas Clark.

Three days earlier, the *Huddersfield Daily Examiner* had sadly reported:

Old friends: Ben Gronow and Douglas Clark at the funeral of their Captain, Harold Wagstaff Elizabeth James & Imperial War Museum

> *Sportsmen in all parts of the north of England will learn with great regret of the death of Harold Wagstaff, the 'Prince of Centres' and the former England and Huddersfield rugby league captain, which occurred this morning at a Huddersfield nursing home at the age of 48.*
>
> *Wagstaff had not been in the best of health since the end of last year. More recently he had a bad attack of influenza, and this had left him with heart trouble and in a weakened state. He went into a nursing home on Monday and gradually became worse as complications ensued, passing away this morning.*

The funeral congregation had met at the Royal Swan on Westgate, Huddersfield, where Harold had been the licensee. It is estimated that 2,000 people saw the cortege leave for his final resting place, his home village of Holmfirth.

Police escorted the procession through the town – which stayed still and silent throughout – and all of the six-mile journey. Large crowds of people lined the roads and streets through Berry Brow and Honley to pay their respects. Waggy had been the greatest and most influential rugby league player of all time, and he achieved all that he did despite being so physically brittle. He had spent much of his life battling various long-term and serious bouts of illness; tragically, he had seemed destined to die young.

Harold Wagstaff was laid to rest at Holmfirth Cemetery.

Douglas Clark officially retired from professional wrestling in 1941. But he had picked a good time to bow out of the top level, on his own terms, in that summer of 1939. On 3 September, the country once again declared war on Germany.

Adolf Hitler and his Nazi Party had reneged on all of the sanctions imposed on Germany following the Great War and the signing of the Treaty of Versailles, taking the ultimate step by invading Poland, forcing Great Britain and France to reluctantly go to war with them again. Yet another generation of brave men would have to go and sacrifice themselves, and many, many more heroes like Fred Longstaff would have to pay the ultimate price. Hitler had created a monstrous army, with a determination and drive for world domination.

Professional sport, including wrestling, was eventually postponed in the early 1940s until after World War Two had ended – although small shows were put on by promoters in an attempt to keep some public interest and cash flow.

The British economy suffered worse than in World War One and went into complete depression. It was a time of recession, hardship and food rationing. Families were torn apart as children were evacuated from major towns and cities at risk of air strike from the dreaded German *Luftwaffe*.

George de Relwyskow Jr signed up as a military physical training instructors. With a war effort looming, he would get a chance to follow once more in the footsteps of his father, George Sr, and of his friend and mentor, Douglas Clark.

The war lasted exactly six years and one day, and killed over 70 million people.

TO THE BOYS.

As many of my friends know well, I am usually a man of few words, but I welcome the opportunity of extending a New Year's Message to the boys of Huddersfield.

Nothing gives me greater pleasure than to meet that clean, healthy type of lad which Huddersfield is so fortunate to possess in good numbers; and if these few lines help any lad towards the development of CHARACTER, I shall be more gratified than if the good old football club to which I have the honour to belong wins every remaining match this season!

Perhaps I may be forgiven, boys, for being more particularly interested in your sporting proclivities. So I would say to you: Play your games hard, but play them clean. Be sportsmen under all circumstances, and never forget that

> "It is excellent
> To have a giant's strength;
> But it it tyrannous
> To use it like a giant."

I want you to take your defeats and disappointments - both on the sports field and in every phase of your lives - like real good "sports." Don't shout about your grievances and troubles - we all have our share of them. Remember the words of that writer who said: If I am called upon to suffer, let me be like the well-bred beast who goes away and suffers in silence.

Work hard; play hard; keep smiling even if the odds do seem unfair. Don't "grouse"; take your "lickings" like men - and you will find that there is a far greater joy in living than you could possibly have realised otherwise.

A Happy New Year to every one of you!

DOUGLAS CLARK.

Elizabeth James & Imperial War Museum

Duggy served his community during this hard time, once again as their reliable coal merchant and the cheerful god-like figure that would brighten the mood of all who saw him out on his rounds. When he delivered to the local schools, the children would dash out of class when they saw him and his horse coming on to the grounds. They would stare at him in joy and awe as he put on a show of strength for them, tossing sacks of coal around the playground like they were duck-feather pillows.

He continued with this profession for the rest of his days, employing many young Fartown players to help them financially and with their strength and fitness – including a final tally of *three* Pepperell brothers.

He became a keen golfer and was a member at Outlane and Huddersfield golf clubs. Jennie played too. They did everything together.

He was on the committee of Huddersfield Rugby League Football Club, and always there as a mentor to the young talent.

He would join his good friend Lord Lonsdale at the Grasmere Festival each year as a guest of honour.

He and Jennie stayed at the same address for the rest of their lives together, but would spend much of their summers living in a small caravan back near their families in Ellenborough, Maryport. Later in life, they replaced the caravan with a more luxurious wooden chalet, complete with verandah, at the nearby coastal village of Allonby.

The Cumberland community were glad to finally see more of their most beloved export back home. One Sunday afternoon, he and Jennie called in at their favourite fish and chip shop, and waited patiently to be served behind a drunken man who had spent his lunchtime in the local pub. When the gentleman was politely asked to wait whilst the next round of cod was in the fryer, he became rude and abusive to the ladies behind the fish counter and in the presence of Jennie. When profanities began to emanate from the mouth of the man, Duggy stepped in and insisted he desist from his rude aggression. When the man continued, Duggy picked him up as if he was a small child and hung him on the coat hook on the back of the entrance door by the scruff of his coat and left him squirming there whilst he and Jennie were served haddock and chips. He told the buffoon that he would release him once he had calmed down and promised there would be no more bad language in front of the ladies. Duggy threatened to leave with him still hung there, but realising no one else would be strong enough to get him down, he soon relented. As Duggy and Jennie exited the shop, the gentleman was apologising to the staff.

After such a busy life, Duggy enjoyed spending time with his family and childhood friends. They would play golf on the beautiful coastal links courses. He still kept himself immensely fit and would be seen running along the shore and swimming in the sea at Solway Coast. That made it all the more surprising and tragic when he died suddenly at their Birkby home on 1 February 1951. He was just 59 years of age. He suffered coronary thrombosis – a type of heart disease.

Huddersfield Rugby League: A Lasting Legacy

Who knows, maybe the doctors who had told him he would live to an elderly age if he didn't do anything too physically strenuous for the rest of his life following his war injuries were correct; but what he accomplished in the 20 years following that verdict are what made for such a truly *Extraordinary Life.* Douglas Clark was laid to rest at the cemetery in Maryport. His low and humble headstone is inscribed with the final lines from Julius Caesar:

> *His life was gentle and elements so mixed in him that*
> *Nature might stand up*
> *And say to all the world,*
> *'This was a man'.*

— William Shakespeare

EPILOGUE

HALLS OF FAME

THE ASHES continued to be held biannually (with the exception of the wartime years) until 2003, when the format of the tours was changed to formally incorporate other countries, such as New Zealand, in 'tri-nations' and round-robin-style tournaments. In truth, the Ashes had become uncompetitive, as Australia and their top young athletes fell in love with rugby league, which had become their national sport. Back in England, Association Football went from strength to strength and eclipsed rugby in terms of fanbase, finances and marketability. After the Lions' 1970 triumph in Australia, they were comfortably ahead in terms of series wins, by 12 to seven. But they would not win another and the 'Kangaroos' blitzed 13 straight series over a 30-year period – many 3-0 whitewashes – to go ahead by 20 victorious tours to 19.

As this book is released, the 40th Ashes series should be taking place, as England host the first instalment of the oldest and most intense rivalry in sport – hoping to win for the first time in 50 years and create a 112-year stalemate.[1]

The Team of All Talents (1911–1920), also known as The Team that Never Kicks, pioneered what we now know as rugby league. Harold Wagstaff and Douglas Clark led a team that

---

1   As I wrote this on 16 March 2020, the tour was in doubt owing to the ongoing Covid-19 pandemic.

set new standards and forever differentiated the sport from its rival code, rugby union. They played fast, flowing rugby that supplemented their silverware with a unique pride the players shared with their supporters, knowing that they were also by far the most entertaining team, too.

They won 15 major trophies: three Northern Union league championships, three Challenge Cup finals, six Yorkshire League titles and three Yorkshire Cup finals. And all that with a four-year hiatus to contribute to the winning of World War One.

Fartown are now known as the Huddersfield Giants and play in the modern-day Super League, which is an international success and contains teams not only from the north of England but also from France and Canada. Both London and Wales have had representation and even New York City has a fledgling franchise with aspirations of a future place in the global competition.

The Rugby League Hall of Fame – held at The George Hotel, Huddersfield, where the sport was founded – was commissioned in 1988 and, as of 2019, had just 28 inductees. Fartown legends Albert Rosenfeld, Harold Wagstaff and Douglas Clark are among them.

That immortal trio are joined by Ben Gronow in the Huddersfield Giants' own Hall of Fame and all have their framed photographs on display at the John Smith's Stadium – where a bust of Douglas was also commissioned in 2010.

Douglas Clark rugby league career statistics:
Huddersfield:
Debut: 25 September 1909; Hull KR (away)

Season	Appearances	Tries	Major Trophies
1909-10	26	4	1
1910-11	38	5	-
1911-12	38	12	2
1912-13	35	20	3
1913-14	36	7	2
1914-15	31	6	4
1919	4	-	1
1919-20	32	12	3
1920-21	27	3	-
1921-22	31	6	1
1922-23	34	8	-
1923-24	39	7	-
1924-25	35	7	-
1925-26	32	1	-
1926-27	17	-	1
1927-28	26	1	-
1928-29	4	-	2
Totals	485	99	20

Final match: 23 February 1929; Castleford (away). The tally of
485 appearances is a record that still stands to this day.

Representing Cumberland (31 caps; 5 tries):

Year	Home	Score	Away	Try
1910	Yorkshire	28 - 11	Cumberland	√
1910	Cumberland	8 - 13	Lancashire	
1911	Lancashire	7 - 28	Cumberland	
1911	Cumberland	16 - 13	Yorkshire	√
1912	Cumberland	11 - 0	Lancashire	
1912	Yorkshire	19 - 5	Cumberland	
1913	Lancashire	24 - 3	Cumberland	
1913	Cumberland	8 - 3	Yorkshire	√
1919	Cumberland	5 - 3	Lancashire	
1920	Cumberland	6 - 27	Yorkshire	
1921	Yorkshire	30 - 12	Cumberland	
1922	Cumberland	12 - 25	Australia	√
1922	Cumberland	7 - 18	Lancashire	
1922	Lancashire	9 - 4	Cumberland	
1922	Lancashire	46 - 9	Cumberland	
1923	Cumberland	5 - 24	Lancashire	
1923	Yorkshire	51 - 12	Cumberland	
1924	Cumberland	20 - 0	Yorkshire	√
1924	Lancashire	8 - 0	Cumberland	
1925	Cumberland	5 - 6	Lancashire	
1925	Yorkshire	13 - 31	Cumberland	
1927	Cumberland	3 - 18	New Zealand	
1927	Lancashire	12 - 5	Cumberland	
1927	Cumberland	27 - 2	Lancashire	
1927	Glamorgan & Monmouth	12 - 18	Cumberland	
1927	Yorkshire	5 - 11	Cumberland	
1928	Cumberland	15 - 5	Glamorgan & Monmouth	
1928	Lancashire	10 - 5	Cumberland	
1929	Cumberland	8 - 5	Australia	
1929	Glamorgan & Monmouth	14 - 6	Cumberland	
1930	Yorkshire	9 - 3	Cumberland	

Representing England (6 caps; 5 tries):

Year	Home	Score	Away	Try
1912	England	31 - 5	Wales	√√
1913	England	40 - 16	Wales	
1914	England	16 - 12	Wales	
1921	England	35 - 9	Wales	√
1921	England	11 - 0	O Nats	√
1925	England	19 - 5	Wales	√

Great Britain Test match career (11 caps; 3 tries):

Year	Home	Score	Away	Try
1911	Great Britain	11 - 11	Australia	
1912	Great Britain	8 - 33	Australia	√
1914	Australia	5 - 23	Great Britain	√
1914	Australia	12 - 7	Great Britain	
1914	Australia	6 - 14	Great Britain	
1920	Australia	8 - 4	Great Britain	
1920	Australia	21 - 8	Great Britain	
1920	Australia	13 - 23	Great Britain	
1920	New Zealand	7 - 31	Great Britain	
1920	New Zealand	3 - 19	Great Britain	
1920	New Zealand	10 - 11	Great Britain	√

If it is at all possible, Douglas Clark's wrestling career is even more legendary and was even more pioneering than his stellar rugby league one.

He won dozens of Cumberland & Westmorland tournaments, including the holy grail – the Grasmere 'All-Weights' championship – on five occasions: 1922, 1924, 1927, 1928 and 1934. The fifth tournament win, at the ripe old age of 43, meant that he was awarded the Canon Rawnsley Cup as his own. He also won the world heavyweight championship in 1925, 1926 and 1930.

He had achieved everything in the sport, and coinciding perfectly with the end of his rugby career came the advent of professional wrestling in Britain, in what would quickly become known as 'All-In Wrestling'.

Douglas Clark became Great Britain's first pro wrestling superstar, the first-ever holder of the 'T. Herbert Kaye World Championship' belt. He was the first undisputed 'All-In' British heavyweight champion and vacated that title on retirement having never lost to a British professional wrestler in several hundred contests. He was also the long-time holder of the British Empire heavyweight crown. He travelled around the world to spread the business far and wide, inspiring future generations, and leaving a legendary legacy.

There have been many since who have tried to get to the top of the industry with Union Jack-emblazoned attire and a 'John Bull in Trunks' persona. A couple, in particular, have succeeded, in the form of Halifax's Shirley Crabtree and Lancashire-born Davey Boy Smith.

Despite it being a golden era, Douglas Clark was recently named as the 1930s' 'Wrestler of the Decade' by Wrestling Heritage.

In every aspect of Duggy's life, he certainly went *All-In*.

Much like the rest of the world, George de Relwyskow Jr would never be the same after World War Two. Not only had his legendary father died during the conflict, but he walked with a limp and had scarring around his scalp. He had sustained the injuries in a landmine explosion after he had parachuted behind enemy lines. But even his wife was in the dark about how and why he had been in such mortal danger – he had only signed up as a physical training instructor, hadn't he? His wrestling career was over, but as the 1950s began and he lost his mentor Douglas Clark too, he knew that he had a role to play if the beloved sport of his late father and good friend was to have a revival. He started a small wrestling promotion in the north of England.

Professional wrestling was in disarray as promoters attempted to get their shows back on the road. Many sporting arenas and even local councils had banned the shows, due to its reputation of violence.

Almost the whole generation from the initial 'All-In' decade of the 1930s were now retired or well past their primes. Bert Assirati, however, had gone from strength to strength – literally. His anger and bitterness at being so regularly overlooked for the title opportunities and main-event slots had led to him having a no-nonsense attitude towards the promoters and the new wave of talent – which were no longer necessarily wrestlers from a legitimate fighting background, as the sport moved more towards entertainment.

Bert was recognised as the British heavyweight champion in the late 1940s, and even had a short spell as world champion. He then embarked on a three-year world tour from 1952–1955. But even abroad, promoters and wrestlers alike found him difficult to work with. Stiff and punishing, he would not help their stars to look good in the contests, or would demand a king's ransom to do so. The wrestlers hated working with him as he would torture them in the ring, just to ensure they knew that he was the alpha male and the dominant force. His times in India and Pakistan are legendary, as up to 100,000-strong crowds would squeeze into venues to see him. At just 5ft 6in tall, he would legitimately beat up and bully other heavyweights, most of them significantly bigger than he – even winning a match against 7ft 7in giant German Kurt 'Gargantua' Zehe.

The promoters needed Bert more than he needed them, and the only way he could be controlled was with enormous sums of money. He had become an elusive attraction around the world, with people desperate to take their once-in-a-lifetime opportunity to see him. He would also perform – for the right price – strongman and gymnastic exhibitions, leaving huge audiences astounded by his feats of power and balance.

By the time he returned to Britain, the wrestling landscape had changed completely. The British Wrestling Federation (BWF) had been set up as a governing body to bring some order to the sport. A post-war era was required and with most of the 1930s protagonists out of the picture, it was seen that the violent 'All-In' product, which promoted itself as a bloodthirsty, no-holds-barred spectacle, was not reflective of the current mood of the country.

Atholl Oakeley had passionately tried to reignite what he felt was *his* sport, particularly in London and the surrounding areas, but the BWF refused to give his productions their support and he was being squeezed out as they reissued the rule book, calling them the 'Mountevans rules'. Whilst almost identical, they were written with a focus on what was allowed, rather than the 'All-In' approach of stating that everything was allowed but for a few minor indiscretions. There was to be less bloodshed and a product closer to that of family entertainment was to be produced. Suddenly, there was more emphasis on the colourful characters and the physical appearance of the stars rather than any legitimate fighting background or ability. This further incensed the already-frustrated Bert.

George de Relwyskow Jr was one of four promoters from around the country to merge as Joint Promotions, who would enforce Mountevans rules and the more family-friendly ethos of the BWF. Everyone else in the business would be a struggling independent promoter – and with that, Atholl Oakeley was forced into retirement. More promoters signed up to Joint, who quickly monopolised the whole country. The deal was simple: all the talent got shared around the regions so that each got a product of a similar standard and with the same rates of pay, to stop one territory hoarding all the best wrestlers.

The brand new television channel ITV launched in 1955 and were looking to fill their schedule with fresh, new content – and Joint Promotions had the product for them.

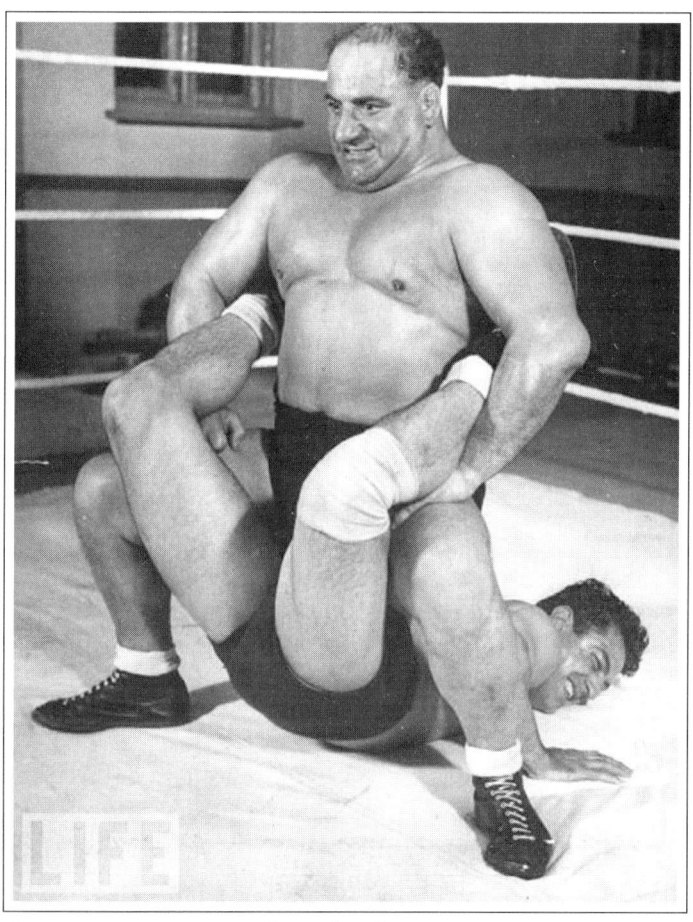

Veteran Bert Assirati enjoyed punishing his opponents

Professional wrestling would now air live on prime-time national TV.

Three young brothers from Halifax were part of this new wrestling scene. All with blond hair, two were average sized but one – ironically named Shirley – was a huge man standing 6ft 6in tall and with a world-record 64-inch chest – something that would later see him in the *Guinness Book of World Records*. He had begun weight-training and bodybuilding in the late 1940s and was spotted as a potential professional wrestler in its new ilk due to his good looks, physique and great strength. His two athletic brothers, Max and Brian, had gone along into the business with him and all three were on the circuit in the mid-1950s.

'Blond Adonis' Shirley Crabtree had gained momentum and popularity by the end of the decade and was being considered as the future face of the industry. He appeared eerily similar to how Douglas Clark had looked a quarter of a century earlier – fair-haired and muscular, wearing a navy blue singlet with the Union Jack embroidered on the chest.

But no other champion could hold serious credibility with the fans whilst Bert Assirati was still on the scene. He was recognised as the British heavyweight champion by the BWF, but Joint – and their new talent roster – did not want to work with him. His reputation for torturing his opponents was getting worse. The less credible he found them as a genuine and legitimate skilled man of the mat, the more he punished them for entering *his* domain: *his* world.

When the BWF received news of Bert having sustained a serious injury, and with Assirati now in his fifties, they took the opportunity to strip him of the title, in the hope he would finally disappear.

A tournament was held for the vacant title and a victorious Shirley Crabtree became the British heavyweight champion. He soon added a European title and was on his way to becoming a star. But Bert Assirati didn't disappear into the sunset as planned, and once his injury had healed he returned and laid down challenge after challenge in an harassment campaign of the giant Crabtree – completely against all promotional instructions or in keeping with any storyline. He saw Shirley as the perfect example of what the modern wrestling scene had become.

Bert even turned up at live events to confront Shirley in front of the fascinated crowd and would have to be led away by security and other wrestlers. Despite the public's desperation for the match to be made, neither the BWF, Joint nor Crabtree wanted it to happen – they knew Bert would not allow Shirley to impress and instead would probably maim and embarrass him.

In 1963, Bert finally gave up his reign of terror and announced his retirement. But he had significantly damaged the brand and the up-and-coming reputation of Shirley – who by now had lost both his British and European belts and had dropped down the Joint hierarchy.

By 1966, the Crabtree brothers left Joint Promotions and the wrestling business, using the money they had earned to open 'Big Daddy's' nightclub in Halifax. The place was a hit and they used their popularity and contacts in the area to get the best acts to perform on their stages of a weekend. Soon, they were combining the two careers as they began promoting small, independent wrestling shows around West Yorkshire, and again, they were a hit. Max, especially, seemed to have a natural flair for the promotional side of the business.

It was while looking for new talent to fill up a local wrestling show that Shirley found a 30-year-old fellow former rugby league player he recognised from playing against him in their younger days. He found a behemoth of giant strength, who had recently began training in the art of professional wrestling. He found Featherstone's Malcolm Kirk.

Both Shirley and Mal would soon find themselves working for George de Relwyskow Jr and their professional relationship would last 20 eventful years – but end in tragic fashion.

Douglas Clark has a permanent exhibition on display at the Imperial War Museum North, in Manchester, which holds a significant collection of the priceless sporting and war memorabilia he left behind – including his war diaries, dozens upon dozens of medals and trophies and some of the antique sporting apparel he wore, as well as a plethora of photographs, letters and documents.

His widow, Jennie, also donated a trophy from his huge collection to their beloved Outlane Golf Club in 1966, and the annual 'Douglas Clark Cup' is still one of the most fiercely competed events in their calendar.

Devoted Jennie lived out the rest of her days with a shrine to Duggy in the corner of their living room in Storths Road, Birkby. It contained some of the photos and memorabilia that has ended up on display in his current shrine, which is open to the public in Manchester. Many of the photographs had Duggy's writing and Shakespeare quotes scribbled on the back. Jennie survived him by 35 years, passing away in 1986 at the age of 89.

ACKNOWLEDGEMENTS AND BIBLIOGRAPHY

('Thank you' to the individuals and organisations in **bold** text)

13:58
7 December 2019
Imperial War Museum research room
London

I WAS stood outside the small door to the research room, awaiting my 2pm appointment, which was to last three hours. I'd arrived in plenty of time but needed help finding the room, which is hidden away in a corner on the second floor. Once I had been chaperoned to the locked door (the research room closes for lunch, with morning and afternoon appointments available), I went for a look around the fascinating exhibits of the **Imperial War Museum**, London. I'd been there before but the displays were still as fascinating; still as haunting.

Eager to make full use of the slot I had booked to read, photograph and, if necessary, painstakingly copy out the war diaries of **Douglas Clark** word for word, I had come back to the same tucked-away door with a couple of minutes to spare. It was still locked but this time, when I peered through the glass, I could see that a lady was sat at the front desk. She noticed me, looked down at her watch through the tiny spectacles perched on the end of her nose and gestured to me with two fingers

Testimonial booklet written in the 1920s

(the 'peace' sign rather than any insulting profanity, signifying I still had to wait two minutes). Soon after, she rose to her feet, walked towards me and unlocked the door. I introduced myself. Despite this being my second book, this day was the first time I had afforded myself the privilege of calling myself 'an author' – which still feels strange and surreal.

My groundwork for the project had started in earnest that same spring. Very basic internet exploration and the discovery of a testimonial booklet written about Clark in the 1920s had given me the skeleton of what I knew was a truly amazing story. But I needed to put some meat on those bones.

I'd like to give special mention to the team at **Wrestling Heritage**, particularly '**Hack**' and **Ron** – who had clearly gone above and beyond the call of duty in researching Duggy's 1936 and 1937 Australian wrestling tours for an online article on the subject. The whole team were always on hand to answer my questions via their Wrestle-Talk forum. They also told me about the **British Newspaper Archive** website and its Australian equivalent, **Trove**. I went on to use these sites extensively.

I bought and read Lyn MacDonald's *Passchendaele, The Roots of Rugby League* by Trevor Delaney, the wonderfully entertaining autobiography of **Sir Atholl Oakeley**, *Blue Blood on the Mat,* and a recently published biography of Harold Wagstaff: *A Northern Union Man,* by Graham Williams and **Robert Gate**, who had also compiled Douglas Clark's rugby careers statistics for *Huddersfield Rugby League: A Lasting Legacy* – a scheme financed by the Heritage Lottery Fund. That project took years of dedicated research by volunteers and local contributors to put on events and produce publications in honour and appreciation of the historic connection between the town and the sport it founded. The proudest and longest lasting achievements of the group are two epic textbooks: Standing on the Shoulders of Giants and Huddersfield in World War One. Those books were fundamental to my research. They both contained similar but extensive detail on Douglas Clark's life at war, including some of the key extracts from his war diaries. One of the main contributors to the books and to the project as a whole was **David Gronow** – grandson of Ben. David dedicated much of his life to producing literature and unearthing thousands of items of memorabilia and photographs from his grandfather's golden era. He was a popular figure around the Huddersfield sporting world and his legacy lives on in those books – as well as others that he produced. He tragically died of a heart attack in August 2014, whilst watching Yorkshire play a county cricket match at Headingley, shortly before the publication of the books. Many of the photographs used in this book were donated to the heritage project by David, and they subsequently gave me permission to use them too.

David, too, had visited the IWM research rooms and transcribed the war diaries – I knew this as he is acknowledged in the books as having done so on their behalf. As brilliant as the excerpts published in them were, I felt a responsibility to my own project to read and transcribe the whole thing myself, so that I could include more of the first-hand account in my dedicated biography of Duggy. So I booked my appointment, return train fare to London and a day off from a hectic home life – my baby son **Bruno** being just one month old.

Many of the artefacts in possession of IWM are in storage, and some are on display in Manchester. The London-based research room is just for studying the documents they hold in their archives. I had no idea what other 'documents' IWM may hold in regards to Douglas Clark – so I specified just the diary to be made available for me to transcribe.

The lady showed me to the desk that had been reserved for me. I was expecting to see an ancient-looking browny-green leather notebook, but instead there simply sat a standard blue cardboard document folder with both my name and

Duggy's scribbled on the front. I thanked her for her help and sat down. I opened the folder suspiciously. Had they got my request wrong? What could be in here? I was very pleasantly surprised to find a hoard of photographs, letters and other documents clearly from Duggy's personal archive that had been passed on to his family and subsequently to the IWM. Included in the thick wad of papers was a paper-clipped stack of 42 A4 pages, which turned out to be a photocopied version of the war diary. Duggy's century-old handwriting was aesthetically beautiful but almost illegible. The photocopying had taken away another layer of definition and I knew there was no chance of me copying out the text in three hours, and a photograph of the photocopy was just pointless. I was disappointed that I wasn't going to see and handle the original, and that I wasn't going to get back on the train to Huddersfield from London with what I had come for – unlike Duggy had 90 years earlier.

My disappointment was short-lived. There was so much more in the file than I had expected; it was a little treasure chest of Duggy's memories. I accepted that I would only have the previously published diary excerpts and would spend my research appointment time taking photographs and making notes from all the other pieces in the folder.

By 4.30pm, I was worked up. I had filtered through everything, taken photos and notes. I had cropped and edited the photos I had taken and put them in a specific order in the research folder on my iPad (all stuff I could have done on the train or back at home). I must admit to some procrastination in there too, as I nosily peered around at the other desks and the diverse people that were there doing their own research. Were they authors too? Maybe they were students (*extremely* mature students, if they were). On balance of probability, I deemed it most likely they were searching for mention of their brave mothers, fathers and grandparents amongst the books and documents that they were searching through and taking notes from.

With 20 minutes of my appointment remaining, I carefully put all the papers back into the file and took it to the front desk to sign out. There had been a shift-change. A new lady was behind the counter. She seemed surprised I was leaving early. *'Bloody hell,'* I thought, *'I bet no one leaves before their time is up, so precious are the resources being made available to them.'*

'Yes, I've done all I can, thank you'. I told her.

'Oh, so you don't want to see what is in those?' she asked, looking over my shoulder. I turned around to see a trolley full of six large cardboard boxes, each with 'DOUGLAS CLARK' written on them in black marker pen. The first lady hadn't told me that the blue folder contained just the bits of the collection the gentleman who I had booked the appointment through had thought would be most useful to me, and that all the rest of the collection was sat just ten yards away from me the whole time.

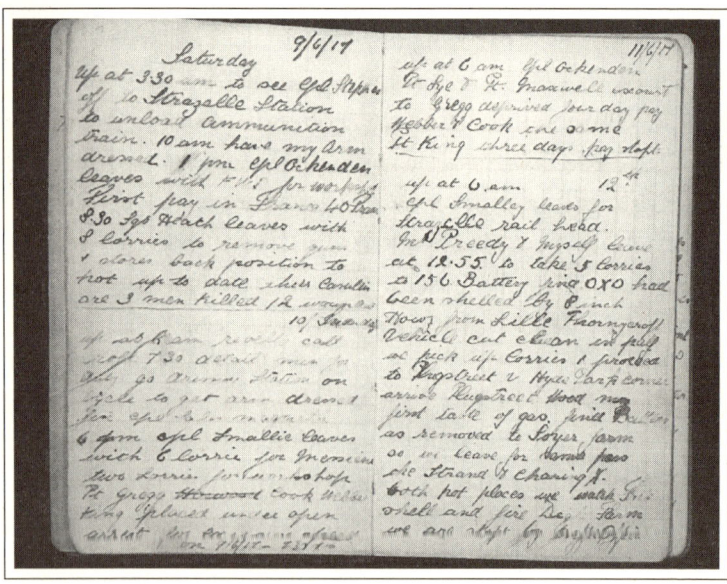

Example handwritten page from Douglas Clark's war diary
Imperial War Museum

I told her I desperately wanted to see what was in those boxes. We both looked at the clock.

'We close at 5pm, sharp,' she told me, sternly. I raced to the trolley and one by one carried them to my desk and scanned through the contents. There were some amazing photographs – many of the ones you have seen in this book – that I had almost missed out on. There were letters and telegrams, contracts and agreements, match programmes and newspaper cuttings, all crucial to my research. I had almost walked away from it all.

I put the final box on the desk and opened it at 16.58. The lady stood over me, showing me her wrist and imaginary watch. I raced through it hoping I actually didn't see anything of value, but I had to know what was in there. As I lifted the final piece of paper, I knew there was something underneath, as I wasn't yet at the bottom. There it sat: the weathered, flaking leather. The war diary. There was no point in me – famously clumsy – even bothering to touch it. I sat the papers carefully back on it and put the lid on the box.

'Thank you,' I said to the lady, with a smile and a nod, and I left.

On the train home, I e-mailed **Elizabeth James**.

Some months earlier, I had contacted *Cumbria Life* magazine and asked them if they could put out an appeal to their readers for information about Douglas Clark. They put out an advertisement with my e-mail address on it, and the lovely people of Cumbria – known as Cumberland up until 1974 – answered my call. **Dr Colin Murray**, **Barry Davidson** and **Chris Bland** all sent items to me through the post that were very useful. Even more humbling was when descendants of Duggy began to contact me. **Joe** and **Audrey Fagan**, **Frank Clark** and **Alan Clark** offered much useful information and photographs. But my breakthrough really came when a gentleman by the name of **Mike Bacon** replied to say that his wife **Janet** (née Gate) was the niece of Jennie Clark (née Gate). Furthermore, Janet's sister Elizabeth James was generally regarded as the family historian on the subject of their 'Uncle Douglas', so he passed on my details to his sister-in-law, and she duly got in touch.

Elizabeth was very close to her Auntie Jennie and had subsequently inherited the mountain of memorabilia that made up the story of Duggy's extraordinary life. It was indeed Elizabeth who had donated many of the priceless parts of the collection to the War Museum – but she still held much more. She invited me to her home to view the stack of heirlooms. I had already made my appointment at IWM, and so we settled on a date ten days later for me to visit her in Gloucestershire.

I e-mailed Elizabeth on the train back from London just to update her on my rather mixed day of success and disappointment. I had failed to get a full version of the war diaries, but did have some photographs and letters that I knew added some immense value to my work. She replied, unsurprised that I had found Duggy's handwriting illegible, and said that she had some handwritten pieces by him that she would endeavour to copy out before my visit.

One week before Christmas, I made the three-hour drive down to Elizabeth's address. I was warmly welcomed by the lovely lady, who put on a lunch of soup and sandwiches, followed by mince pies.

She had arranged her collection atop a large table. There were dozens of folders containing hundreds of newspaper clippings, as well as letters, notebooks and dozens of photographs. Hours went by in an instant as I scanned through every item, taking copies of what I needed.

I could have listened to Elizabeth tell her anecdotes of 'Uncle Douglas' all day long. She had been nine years old when he had died and she remembered many moments in his company well. She laughed as she told me how he and Jennie would come by their house straight from the golf course. This giant of a man wearing traditional checked 'Plus-Fours' and a tweed flat-cap would squeeze into their home and warmly greet everyone. When he got to her diminutive father Richard (brother of Jennie), he would say, 'Take 'hod, Dick,' and smother his brother-in-law in a playful Cumberland & Westmorland grapple.

She spoke warmly of Stanley Pepperell, who remained a close and loyal friend to his mentor's widow. Elizabeth accompanied an elderly Jennie to his funeral in 1985.

Finally, she gave me a folder that was for me to take away. There was an envelope in it that contained some anecdotes of Duggy from another niece of his, **Joyce Dempsey** – including the one about him hanging the drunken loudmouth on the back of the chip shop door. But best of all, it contained all of Duggy's autobiographical works that he had handwritten later in his life. Elizabeth had copied all of it out in her (extremely legible) handwriting. Duggy had written page after page about the major parts of his adolescence and sporting life up to and including the famous 1914 tour of Australia. Presumably, his premature death was what made the writing stop there. I had stumbled across yet another treasure trove.

In between discussing all things Duggy, Elizabeth was also genuinely desperate to hear about my baby, Bruno. Her eyes lit up when I showed her pictures of him. As I prepared to leave, delighted with my loot and full to the brim with sandwiches, mince pies, tea and coffee, she asked if I would drop her off at the post office on my way out of the lovely rural village in which she lives. I was delighted to be able to do her a favour. As we said our goodbyes, she gave me an envelope and told me it was for Bruno. There was a £20 note inside.

On the subject of Bruno, I would also like to thank my wonderful wife, **Nicky**, who may have done an extra night feed or two (or three, or four …) whilst supporting me and allowing me to burrow away with my writing.

This book is based on real events and real people. The timeline of events, the facts and the sporting results are as accurate as possible. Some scenes have been dramatised to tell the story in the most entertaining way possible. However, in my quest for accuracy, research into the Robinson wrestling family proved very frustrating. I came across no fewer than nine variations of Christian names beginning with the letter 'J' covering the three generations mentioned. There were references to them hailing from Newcastle, Cockermouth and Keswick – but also that the Geordie clan did originate from Cumbria. At times, I believed there must have been two separate Robinson wrestling dynasties from that same era. The problem I had was that Duggy had written about a bitter rivalry in 1915 with wily veteran 'Jack', but I could not find any other reference to a Jack Robinson from that era – although the 1913 Grasmere champion was John Robinson – who was described eerily similar in age and size to that of 'Jack'. I made an assumption that this was one and the same person.

Another young 'Jack' Robinson came back from South Africa in 1948 ready to challenge Bert Assirati for the British title. I am in no doubt this was the youngest Joseph who would later become 'Tiger Joe'. Maybe they had an ancestor called Jack they were honouring by using this ring name/ nickname.

With research avenues dry and some of the ones I had contradictory, I was forced to make assumptions. And so in the story, the family tree is thus: the Cumberland & Westmorland legend was John, but he was commonly known as 'Jack'. John was from Cumberland but moved to Newcastle. He had a son, Joseph, who also became a Grasmere champion and transferred his skills to the 'All-In' style upon its advent in 1930. Joseph had a son he named after himself and they moved to South Africa. Joseph junior would become the star wrestler, stuntman and actor, Tiger Joe Robinson.

One area of research I was compelled to keep going back to was that of the father and son, the two George de Relwyskows. Their wrestling careers were impressive and fascinating, but their sacrifice and contribution individually to both world wars I found simply breathtaking. The true extent of their remarkable efforts in the conflicts, in which they served as hand-to-hand combat instructors and trained others in arts such as 'silent killing', only came to light after each of their deaths. In the case of George Jr, that would be 40 years later, as his widow sorted through his private papers following his funeral. Alongside mentoring secret-agents-to-be in unarmed combat, he had gone on to graduate as an MI6 secret agent himself, and had infiltrated enemy lines numerous times.

Lynn Philip Hodgson's wonderful *Inside Camp X* piqued my interest. Mr Hodgson was kind enough to personally pass on more information to me about George Jr than he had included in his book.

News of my project had made its way around the local sporting landscape as I had contacted more and more people for information, and on the Saturday morning before Christmas my mobile phone rang. A gentleman introduced himself as **David Thorpe**, and somewhere in the recess of my cluttered brain, I recognised the name. He told me that he had been part of the Huddersfield heritage project and, sure enough, his name was on the front cover of *Standing on the Shoulders of Giants.* He had heard about my work and said he held all of the research files on Douglas Clark that were made during production of the two aforementioned books. He was keen to pass on the information and we arranged to meet for a coffee in the new year, when he would talk me through the contents of the files and allow me to take whatever I felt I required.

Bruno's first Christmas came and went in a blur of sleepless nights and cheese boards, and soon the pre-arranged fresh winter morning arrived and myself and David met at the cafe above the 'big' Sainsbury's. He is a very friendly man and was keen to help me, and clearly passionate about local rugby league history. He scanned through all of the documents in his files. Some of them I already had versions of, and some I did not. Some were more useful than others. Then he casually leafed over one particular plastic wallet that was almost bursting at the seams, so many leaves of A4 were crammed into it. 'That is his typed-up war diaries,' he said. Wow. My eyes must have lit up as he stalled and turned back to that particular plastic wallet. It was the final piece of the puzzle, and there had been a copy gathering dust in Huddersfield all along. It transpires that when his friend and colleague, David Gronow, had made the same journey to London that I had, he managed to painstakingly copy out the entire diary, and then type it all up.

Over our coffee, Mr Thorpe also told me about a book only published in 2018, called *The Greatest Sacrifice: Fallen Heroes of the Northern Union,* written by **Chris Roberts** and his wife, Jane. I bought and read the book and it was a huge help, particularly on the tragic death of Fred Longstaff. I sent David a text thanking him for the recommendation and to my surprise he replied with the contact details of Chris, the co-author, in case I needed further clarity on any of the information.

Chris accepted my invitation to become the latest addition to my growing panel of proofreaders. Being a writer himself and having extensive knowledge of the Northern Union era of rugby league and also of World War One, it seemed a great opportunity to get his expert thoughts. On the 'panel', he joined my brother **Martin** and my friend **Matthew Isherwood** – and all three duly obliged with the level of suggestions, corrections and expertise I was looking for.

Martin works in the movie industry and is a better writer than I ever will be. He is also a professional wrestling enthusiast, with a great knowledge of the inner workings of the industry.

Matthew is a fellow Featherstonian. He is well read, a massive rugby league fan, has a Master's Degree in Modern History and did his dissertation on the formation of the Northern Union, so I thought him another perfect man to have on board. When he told his father about the project and its origins, Matt, who lives in New York, quickly found himself bombarded with long text messages. It transpires that his dad – a local councillor – was good friends with Malcolm Kirk and couldn't wait to tell his favourite hilarious anecdotes of Featherstone's 'King Kong'.

When I initially began research on the potential Mal Kirk project, I read *Who's the Daddy: The Life and Times of Shirley Crabtree*, by Ryan Danes. Subsequently, when I later stumbled across the name Bert Assirati as one of Douglas Clark's most bitter rivals in the early 1930s, I recognised the 'Islington Hercules'. Through Bert and Shirley, there was a direct lineage from Duggy to Mal. And right at the heart of all of it was the mesmerising life stories of the two George de Relwyskows. But all of that is for another book, sometime in the future.

Finally, I hope you, the reader, enjoyed this amazing story as much as I enjoyed researching and writing it. Despite only discovering the majority of Duggy's own writing after I had completed my first draft, I was able to retrospectively use his words as the narrative to parts one and two, merely joining up the dots by reading related books and articles.

However, it appears Douglas Clark never wrote anything privately about his life in professional wrestling. I adored writing part three. Piecing together what Sir Atholl Oakeley had written in his autobiography with the timeline of events prepared by the Wrestling Heritage guys, alongside the hundreds of newspaper clippings available to me, was fascinating. I truly believe that the freedom and enjoyment I found in writing this reflects

Duggy's own feelings about this section of his life. 'All-In' wrestling allowed him to show his charisma and his charm to the world; to be a leader, a pioneer, a showman and a storyteller alongside his fellow athletes.

And who was I to tell the story any differently than I sincerely believe Douglas had told it himself?